UNCERTAINTY QUANTIFICATION AND MODEL CALIBRATION

Edited by **Jan Peter Hessling**

Uncertainty Quantification and Model Calibration
http://dx.doi.org/10.5772/65579
Edited by Jan Peter Hessling

Contributors

Zhiping Qiu, Lei Wang, Yuning Zheng, Fouzi Harrou, Chunlin Ji, Xiao Guo, Hesheng Tang, Dawei Li, Songtao Xue, Shuxing Yang, Fenfen Xiong, Fenggang Wang, A. Gustavo Gonzalez, Xiaowang Zhou, Stephen M. Foiles, Agustín G. Asuero, Julia Martín, David Daffos Ruiz De Adana, Alberto Romero Gracia, Jan Peter Hessling

Published by InTech
Janeza Trdine 9, 51000 Rijeka, Croatia

Publishing Process Manager Maja Bozicevic
Technical Editor SPi Global
Cover InTech Design team

First published July, 2017
Printed in Croatia
Legal deposit, Croatia: National and University Library in Zagreb

Additional hard copies can be obtained from orders@intechopen.com

Uncertainty Quantification and Model Calibration, Edited by Jan Peter Hessling
p. cm.
Print ISBN 978-953-51-3279-0
Online ISBN 978-953-51-3280-6

For EU product safety concerns:
IN TECH d.o.o., Prolaz Marije Krucifikse Kozulić 3, 51000 Rijeka, Croatia,
info@intechopen.com or visit our website at intechopen.com.

Meet the editor

Jan Peter Hessling earned his PhD degree in theoretical physics from Chalmers University of Technology, Gothenburg, Sweden, 1996, and his MSc degree in physics from the University of Massachusetts, USA, 1991. Since then, he has been devoted to novel mathematical concepts, recently focusing on modeling uncertainty and dynamic analysis. Peter is the original proposer of Deterministic Sampling for uncertainty quantification and model calibration and Dynamic Metrology for analysis of dynamic measurements utilizing custom digital filtering. Peter has authored 3 book chapters for InTech and about 20 journal articles as leading author, current Google h-index=10. Since 2016, his concepts are further developed in the privately held company Kapernicus AB, dedicated to applied mathematical R&D, with services offered worldwide.

Contents

Preface

"Wisest is [s-]he who knows [s-]he does not know."

- Jostein Gaarder, Sophie's World

This book disseminates and illustrates a selection of aspects and applications of modern methods for uncertainty quantification (UQ), by independent authors active in different fields of science and technology. It is not meant to be exhaustive or representative, even though each contribution is self-contained and complete within the task addressed. Instead, the presented studies summarize research efforts from all over the world, often addressing real, important but also critical issues of our modern society, like risk assessment. The targeted audience consists of anyone interested in credible computations, with at least rudimentary training in scientific modeling and mathematical statistics. The texts are primarily meant to motivate further reading. Being overviews, many details are left out. The reader is therefore advised to make extended use of the list of references presented in the end of each chapter.

Uncertainty quantification distinguishes what is believed known from what is not, to maximize our wisdom, in concurrence with the quotation above. Truthfully, respecting limits of our knowledge will render prediction intervals of maximum credibility, for best possible agreement with subsequent observations. The ultimate goal for quantifying uncertainty of calculations is almost exclusively to make optimal decisions about what not yet has occurred, on the basis of available knowledge and experience. Its utilization may be obvious, as when selecting only the most viable designs or prototypes in product development for expensive experimental testing. Critical aspects of uncertainty quantification are sometimes disguised. In weather forecasting, improper uncertainties of wind speeds, temperature and other hazards, due to imperfect treatment of observation data in the data assimilation, even might become life-threatening. A valid number of uncertainty or statistical coverage of possible outcomes can be far more important than just the best estimate from a deterministic analysis—irrespective of its quality. One example is calculated core temperatures in nuclear power plants. There is thus a multitude of possible effects, risks, applications and highly complex contexts, in need of uncertainty quantification.

This book therefore starts with a *Prelude,* consisting of one hopefully mind-setting introduction (Chapter 1). It provides an overall perspective and tries to explain why anyone should bother about uncertainty of models, simulations and calculations. Typically required knowledge and versatile references are weaved into a description of the general procedure, briefly mentioning common pitfalls and some expected difficulties of uncertainty quantification. That sets an appropriate framework for studying the specific contributions that follow, also for uninitiated readers.

Wisdom must be acquired before it can be utilized. There are thus two directions of uncertainty propagation. *Uncertainty quantification* (UQ) labels the utilization of our wisdom. Known but uncertain mathematical models predict an uncertain result, usually a scalar quantity like temperature or a high-dimensional field such as fluid flow velocity. *Model calibration* (MC) is the process of acquiring wisdom in terms of a mathematical model with uncertainty, from experimental calibration data. The development of uncertainty quantification approaches splits into methods and applications. From a scientific point of view, applications validate the utility and the appropriateness of the methods used. Methodological perspectives are therefore predominantly given before applications. Chapters 2–5, with focus on UQ, discuss polynomial chaos (Chapter 2) and interval methods (Chapter 3), before the applications of seismic damage assessment (Chapter 4) and molecular dynamics (Chapter 5). Chapters 6–9, mainly devoted to MC, start with methods of Bayesian estimation (Chapter 6) and regression analysis (Chapter 7) and finish with multivariable fault detection of critical processes (Chapter 8) and analytical chemistry (Chapter 9).

Determination of simplified surrogate models provides a special case of model calibration. Surrogates are matched to calculated results obtained with the full model, instead of measured data. Due to its complexity, model calibration is often circumvented by assessing uncertainties of parameters independently of what the model would return and any experimental data set. That is the prevailing approach for approaches like polynomial chaos or when the model has been derived from physical principles. If so, model calibration is substituted with prior knowledge obtained by other means. Such a perspective is consistent with the discussed Bayesian approach.

Current practice of uncertainty quantification is rapidly evolving but still entails numerous unresolved issues, of both theoretical and practical character. We hope you will find the subject as challenging and interesting as all of us currently active in this intriguing field of science do. Let this book inspire.

Jan Peter Hessling
Kapernicus AB—Science
Gothenburg, Sweden

Section 1

Prelude

Chapter 1

Introductory Chapter: Challenges of Uncertainty Quantification

Jan Peter Hessling

Additional information is available at the end of the chapter

http://dx.doi.org/10.5772/intechopen.69517

1. Preamble

Uncertainty is beyond awareness our indisputable decision-maker. A meeting announced to start at 12:00 may implicitly be understood to start in the time interval 12:00–12:01. Hence, we should have arrived at 12:01, at the latest. Alternatively, the interval could be 12:00–12:05. The communicated uncertainty of the start of the meeting is clearly *ambiguous*: accustomed to analog clocks discretized in 5-minute intervals, the latter is plausible, but used to digital clocks the former makes more sense. A meeting scheduled at 12, however, means something quite different to most of us. In that case, it can start as late as 12:30. The invisible practice in everyday life is to communicate uncertainty through a vaguely perceived *precision*, suggesting random variability. It is more often than not confused with *accuracy*, or systematic deviation (see **Figure 1**).

Results repeated within ±1% variation tell nothing about the range of possible errors or uncertainty. An entirely deterministic algorithm has perfect precision. This is normally the situation

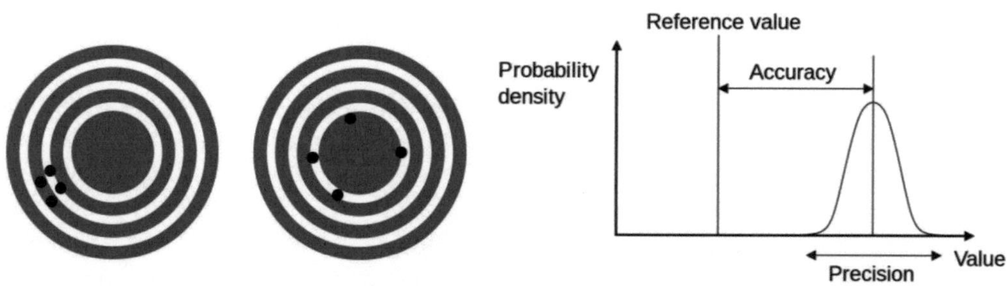

Figure 1. Illustrations [1] of precision (left) and accuracy (middle) of four *samples* (•), and corresponding schematic probability density for the *population* of all possible outcomes (right), often utilized in uncertainty quantification.

of scientific modeling, before uncertainties are considered. The precision usually thought of as random variability for any given set up is often re-interpreted as the total variability between known different situations. That is a dubious strategy to assign numbers of uncertainty. Without extensive consideration, it is generally impossible to assess whether or not the considered history is *representative* for the current problem. For instance, errors in modeling of fluid flow velocities and electromagnetic fields at nearly singular points in space or time, such as sharp corners, or deficiencies in describing collective phenomena like resonances, are usually far too complex to be understood by studying examples only. An extensive analysis based on a large or even infinite set of hypothetical variations is required. The widely practiced intuitive assessment of uncertainty exemplified above, based on experience and communicated with precision, jeopardizes decision-making: uncertainties of this kind are subjective and encourage different interpretations. Invalid uncertainty assessment is also a major cause of false rejection of modeling as a general tool, depriving us all means for making educated guesses through scientific model prediction of important matters, like future weather conditions and risk of major nuclear power accidents.

1.1. The goal

Uncertainty quantification targets objective association of quantitative traceable numbers representing uncertainty to modeling, simulation, and calculation results. By applying a well-documented and widely accepted method with known performance, for the last 20–30 years of so, such a methodology has been established and widely recognized for measurement models, to the extent a quantitative assessment of uncertainty now almost always is required for measurement apparatus. It is not yet so for scientific modeling, as the advanced computations in modern science and technology generally are far more difficult to analyze than measurement models. The uncertainty should predict the range of possible modeling errors, but without exaggeration. If so, modeling results and observations are *consistent*, which means no more than they are not contradictory. Expressed in terms of conventional mathematical statistics developed by Fisher [2] and Popper [3], the hypothesis that the model accurately reproduces observations cannot be *falsified*. These perspectives, outlined in the early 20th century while studying, e.g., crop growth in agriculture and demography, still hold well for modern uncertainty quantification addressing complex applications, such as nuclear power generation, fatigue testing, etc. Mathematical statistics is indeed the genesis of most uncertainty quantification approaches and techniques utilized today.

The mere evaluation of uncertainty is, however, not automatically of any value. Unwarranted assumptions of uncertainties entering the evaluation are deceiving. Respecting what is not known is usually far more important than accurately describing what is known. Lack of knowledge tends to increase the uncertainty and often leads to *ambiguity*, an important ingredient in qualitative science. In quantitative science addressed here though, any lack of well-defined information is normally defied by bold simplifying assumptions, simply because current methodologies require complete knowledge. Closing the gap of ambiguity in this way reflects *willful ignorance* [4]. Therefore, it is important to consider alternative hypotheses of uncertainty. For instance, parameter correlations are very rarely known, but nevertheless have a major influence on the evaluated uncertainty. In this respect, it is important to view the model with all of its parameters as one *composite* unit. The hypothesis touched upon above, stating that the model reproduces observations, implies that propagated parameter errors combine *coherently*, according to the behavior of the deterministic model equations. Correlations are thus essential components of uncertainty, as they may attenuate or amplify contributions from different uncertain parameters by means of destructive or constructive interference. If such effects are not taken into account, uncertainty quantification may evolve into con artistry.

1.2. The preparation

In many respects and for good reasons, methods of uncertainty quantification (UQ) [5] are in their infancy. The need of viable and credible UQ methods is rapidly increasing, with higher utilization of advanced computations. The excess computational power at disposal for UQ is unfortunately not increasing nearly as rapidly as the total resources. The reason is simple. Most computational models are discretized in space and time, truncated, or simplified by neglecting minor but complicated contributions. Such approximations cannot be traced to lack of knowledge or ability, but are often required to enable computation. As soon as the resources increase, eliminating these model reductions as much as possible is most logical and desirable. Weather forecasting [6] illustrates the principle. Proper propagation of disturbances requires comparable resolution in space and time. Reducing the unit cell of analysis from 10 km × 10 km down to 5 km × 5 km to render more detailed forecasts increases the computational load no less than $2^4 = 16$ times. Even so, the unit cell will still be larger than desired. Additional resources will therefore mainly be spent on improvements of the deterministic model formulation in the future, leaving a relatively small fraction to be spent on improved UQ. However, with model samples that can be evaluated independently in different computer kernels, the challenge of improved UQ by additional sampling translates into an economical issue. Then it does not compete with the advancement of computer architecture required to solve the dependent deterministic equations.

UQ combines several advanced mathematical disciplines and can be applied to a plethora of disparate applications not only in technology and science, but also in econometrics and for risk assessment. This makes the subject exceedingly difficult to master, but also hard to understand and learn by studying examples. *Physical modeling* usually provides the basis for setting up the underlying deterministic model. Major simplifications as well as coarse assumptions are common. For instance, Navier-Stokes equations of fluid flow may require both physical and mathematical idealizations like continuous media and differentiability, as well as neglect of higher-order turbulence contributions. Already at this first stage, contributions to uncertainty are building up. *Finite element methods* (FEMs) discretize physical fields in space and time caused by fixed (solids) or moving (fluids) matter. *Signal processing* techniques such as temporal sampling, digital filtering, and state space formulations for Kalman filtering and model prediction control convert infinite-dimensional continuous physical differential models to finite systems of difference equations, suitable for computers. *Numerical methods* then provide the means for solving these equations, with maximum efficiency and minimum error. Preferably with known error estimates, which may be re-phrased in terms of uncertainty in the proceeding UQ. Knowledge of *computer science* is needed for efficient programming and maintaining numerical precision throughout the calculation, but also for managing large complex software modules. The studied system may also exhibit critical properties. The chaotic nature of weather forecast models is one example. More than 50 years ago, Lorenz assessed an absolute upper prediction horizon of about two weeks [6]. Explained by "the butterfly effect" [6, p. 206], this limit is still believed to be accurate: Even the slightest possible change in initial conditions may render a monumental change in the forecast after some time, which clearly is a major complication for credible UQ. Understanding these preparatory stages is crucial, as they accommodate many sources of uncertainty.

1.3. Overview

Uncertainty quantification can now be addressed. Statistics of all kinds of uncertain quantities are then propagated in two possible directions, as explained in **Figure 2** (adapted from Ref. [7]).

Fundamentally, statistics of *populations* rather than finite samples drawn from them are propagated, which avoids *sampling variance*, the principal complication addressed in mathematical statistics with *statistical inference* [2]. There are thus two generic types of uncertainty[1] to some extent corresponding to accuracy and precision, respectively:

- Epistemic uncertainty, i.e., unknown and unpredictable systematic but repeatable errors due to lack of knowledge and imperfect simplifications.

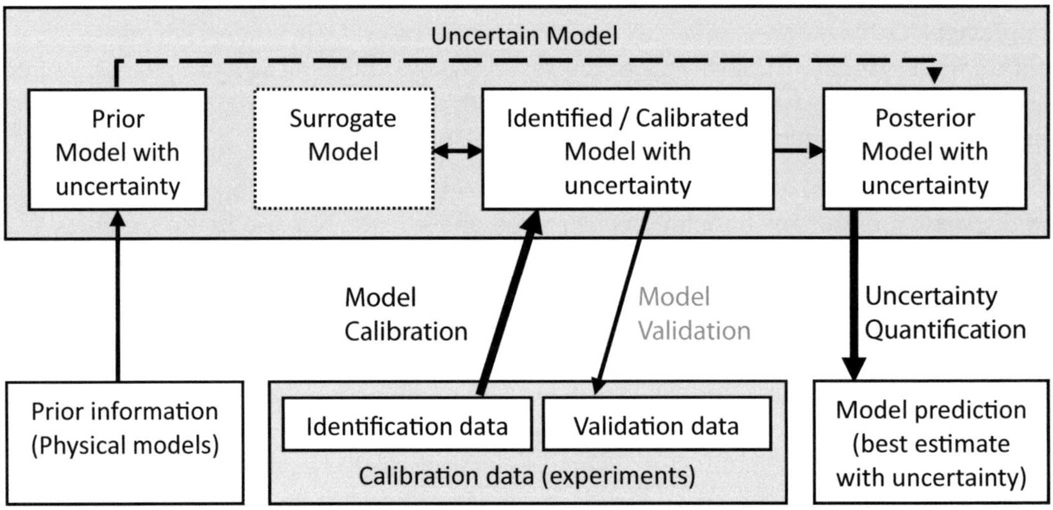

Figure 2. Uncertainty quantification (UQ) and model calibration, or inverse UQ. Identifying or matching the model against identification data often requires simplified surrogate models. The model should be checked or validated before it is utilized for prediction comprising a best estimate and its uncertainty.

[1]Errors are *realized* uncertainty. The uncertainty predicts the range of possible errors. Such errors are unknown, otherwise we would eliminate them. Their analysis requires a concept like uncertainty.

- Aleatoric uncertainty, i.e., non-repeatable errors of a statistical nature. Typically, the variable outcome of finite random draws (sampling variance).

Applications of UQ are typically concerned with epistemic uncertainty due to imperfect modeling, calculation and signal processing, finite discretization (FEM) as well as inaccurate boundary and initial conditions, etc. Mathematical statistics, on the other hand, focuses on aleatoric uncertainty due to finite statistical sampling. In the latter case, modeling has an entirely different character. The quantities of interest are usually not a result of a complex model implemented in a large computer program but rather directly observable, like mean and variance of some measure of performance, frequency, length, or response time. In that case, the uncertainty due to the variability of small observation sets presumably dominates over model errors.

1.4. Some common tools

Bayesian approaches [8] make the difference between epistemic and aleatoric uncertainties almost invisible. Generalizing observed frequencies of observation to also include other kinds of knowledge requires a shift of perspective from experimental testing, to the observer and his/her degree of belief. Since our belief rarely is complete or totally absent, this still has the appearance of probability, but is conceptually different. Nevertheless, belief is the enabler for unifying epistemic and aleatoric uncertainty consistently within the same framework of UQ. Our belief often refers to a model's track record, or how it has performed in different situations over a long period of time. That may be difficult to assess quantitatively, but could in principle be made with multimodel calibration. Only independent data sets/model results must be included, as dependencies will underestimate the uncertainty severely. Worth emphasizing is also that any piece of *prior information* available before the uncertainty is quantified must reflect some kind of knowledge or experience. Any reduction of uncertainty due to a guessed prior is purely hypothetical and deceptive.

Random sampling reduces the difference between the practices of UQ and mathematical statistics even further by introducing sampling variance of finite random ensembles, making it a primary target to control in both fields. The basic motivation for random sampling is its simplicity, while a severe drawback is the added sampling variance. Much larger ensembles than the computational power allows for may be required. The obvious work-around is to substitute the full model with a much less demanding approximate surrogate model, which allows for excessive sampling. The surrogate is often *affine*, i.e., linear in uncertain parameters and obtained with traditional *linear regression*. Aleatoric sampling errors are then exchanged with presumably smaller epistemic ones. Alternatively, the sampling variance may be reduced by imposing deterministic components in the random sampling methodology, like stratified sampling, perhaps combined with latin-hypercube [9] or orthogonal sampling exclusion rules. It is indeed possible to extend these amendments of determinism into entirely deterministic sampling, as in the *unscented* Kalman filter [10]. The sampling variance is then completely(!) exchanged with sampling errors due to imperfections of the reproducible sampling rule [11]. Just knowing the modeling error is entirely reproducible is of great value when differential changes are of primary interest, as in product development.

Model calibration or inverse UQ is an inverse problem usually requiring an implicit solution. The high complexity of the full model normally prohibits ubiquitous trial-and-error search and steepest descent methods like the Newton-Raphson method [12], to minimize the model prediction error. Just as for excessive random sampling, surrogate models are often utilized. In this case though, the iterative character of many inverse solutions requires even higher computational efficiency. The maximum likelihood method is perhaps the most common approach to inverse propagation of uncertainty. Virtually all methods require complete statistical information. That is a major issue since available information normally is incomplete. Just like Bayesian estimation can be invalidated by faulty prior distributions, inappropriate assumptions of unknown calibration data statistics may invest far too much credibility in the calibrated model, making it likely to fail any validation test. What is particularly detrimental is the ubiquitous assumptions of uncorrelated calibration errors. Allowance of incomplete statistical information in model calibration is therefore one of the most urgent tasks to address in future development of model calibration, to remedy overconfident faulty model predictions.

Author details

Jan Peter Hessling

Address all correspondence to: peter@kapernicus.com

Kapernicus AB, Hallingsjo, Sweden

References

[1] Images retrieved from Wikimedia Commons, the Free Media Repository [Internet]. Available from: https://commons.wikimedia.org [Accessed: 27-04-2017]

[2] Fisher RA. Statistical Methods, Experimental Design, and Scientific Inference. Oxford: Oxford University Press; 1990

[3] Popper Karl. The Logic of Scientific Discovery. London and New York: Routledge Classics; 2002

[4] Weisberg HI. Willful Ignorance: The Mismeasure of Uncertainty. Hoboken, NJ: John Wiley & Sons; 2014

[5] Smith RC. Uncertainty Quantification: Theory, Implementation, and Applications. Vol. 12. SIAM - Society for Industrial and Applied Mathematics; 2013

[6] Kalnay E. Atmospheric Modeling, Data Assimilation and Predictability. Cambridge: Cambridge University Press; 2003

[7] Hessling JP. Identification of complex models. SIAM/ASA Journal on Uncertainty Quantification. 2014;**2**(1):717-744

[8] Sivia D, Skilling J. Data Analysis: A Bayesian Tutorial. Oxford: Oxford University Press; 2006

[9] Helton JC, Davis FJ. Latin hypercube sampling and the propagation of uncertainty in analyses of complex systems. Reliability Engineering and System Safety. 2003;**81**(1): 23-69

[10] Julier SJ, Uhlmann JK. Unscented filtering and nonlinear estimation. Proceedings of the IEEE. 2004;**92**(3):401-422

[11] Hessling JP. Deterministic sampling for propagating model covariance. SIAM/ASA Journal on Uncertainty Quantification. 2013;**1**(1):297-318

[12] Ypma TJ. Historical development of the Newton–Raphson method. SIAM Review. 1995;**37**(4): 531-551

Section 2

Uncertainty Quantification

Chapter 2

Polynomial Chaos Expansion for Probabilistic Uncertainty Propagation

Shuxing Yang, Fenfen Xiong and Fenggang Wang

Additional information is available at the end of the chapter

http://dx.doi.org/10.5772/intechopen.68484

Abstract

Uncertainty propagation (UP) methods are of great importance to design optimization under uncertainty. As a well-known and rigorous probabilistic UP approach, the polynomial chaos expansion (PCE) technique has been widely studied and applied. However, there is a lack of comprehensive overviews and studies of the latest advances of the PCE methods, and there is still a large gap between the academic research and engineering application for PCE due to its high computational cost. In this chapter, latest advances of the PCE theory and method are elaborated, in which the newly developed data-driven PCE method that does not depend on the complete information of input probabilistic distribution as the common PCE approaches is introduced and improved. Meanwhile, the least angle regression technique and the trust region scenario are, respectively, extended to reduce the computational cost of data-driven PCE to accommodate it to practical engineering design applications. In addition, comprehensive comparisons are made to explore the relative merits of the most commonly used PCE approaches in the literature to help designers to choose more suitable PCE techniques in probabilistic design optimization.

Keywords: uncertainty propagation, probabilistic design, polynomial chaos expansion, data-driven, sparse, trust region

1. Introduction

Uncertainties are ubiquitous in engineering problems, which can roughly be categorized as aleatory and epistemic uncertainty [1, 2]. The former represents natural or physical randomness that cannot be controlled or reduced by designers or experimentalists, while the latter refers to reducible uncertainty resulting from a lack of data or knowledge. In systems design, all sources of uncertainties need to be propagated to assess the uncertainty of system quantities of interest, i.e., uncertainty propagation (UP). As is well known, UP is of great importance to design under uncertainty, which greatly determines the efficiency of the design. Since generally sufficient data are available for aleatory uncertainties, probabilistic methods are commonly employed for computing response distribution statistics based on the probability distribution specifications of input [3, 4]. Conversely, for epistemic uncertainties, data are generally sparse, making the use of probability distribution assertions questionable and typically leading to nonprobabilistic approaches, such as the fuzzy, evidence, and interval theories [5–7]. This chapter mainly focuses on propagating the aleatory uncertainties to assess the uncertainty of system quantities of interest using probabilistic methods, which is shown in **Figure 1**.

A wide variety of probabilistic UP approaches for the analysis of aleatory uncertainties have been developed [8], among which the polynomial chaos expansion (PCE) technique is a rigorous approach due to its strong mathematical basis and ability to produce functional representations of stochastic quantities. With PCE, the function with random inputs can be represented as a stochastic metamodel, based on which lower-order statistical moments as well as reliability of the function output can be derived efficiently to facilitate the implementation of design optimization under uncertainty scenarios such as robust design [9] and reliability-based design [10]. The original PCE method is an intrusive approach in the sense that it requires extensive modifications in existing deterministic codes of the analysis model, which is generally limited to research where the specialist has full control of all model equations as well as detailed knowledge of the software. Alternatively, nonintrusive approaches have been developed without modifying the original analysis model, gaining increasing attention, thus is the focus of this chapter. As a well-known PCE approach, the generalized PCE (gPCE) method based on the Askey scheme [11, 12] has been widely applied to UP for its higher accuracy and better convergence [13, 14] compared to the classic Wiener PCE [15]. Generally, the random input does not necessarily follow the five types of probabilistic distributions (i.e., normal, uniform, exponential, beta, and gamma) in the Askey scheme. In this case, the transformation should be made to transfer each random input variable to one of the five distributions. It would induce substantially lower convergence rate, which makes the

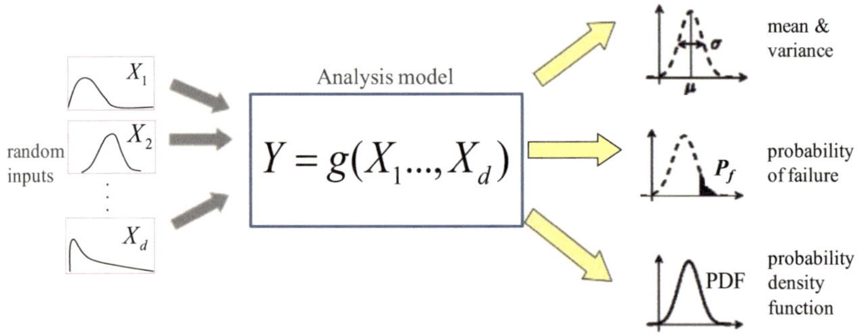

Figure 1. Illustration of uncertainty propagation.

nonoptimal application of Askey polynomial chaos computationally inefficient [8]. Therefore, the Gram-Schmidt PCE (GS-PCE) [16] and multielement PCE (ME-PCE) [17] methods have been developed to accommodate arbitrary distributions through constructing their own orthogonal polynomials rather than referring to the Askey scheme.

All the PCE methods discussed above are constructed based on the assumption that the exact knowledge of the involved joint multivariate probability density function (PDF) of all random input variables exists. Generally, by assumption of independence of the random variables, the joint PDF is factorized into univariate PDFs of each random variable in introducing PCE in the literature. However, the random input could exist as some raw data with a complicated cumulative histogram, such as bi-modal or multi-modal type, for which it is often difficult to obtain the analytical expression of its PDF accurately. Under these scenarios, all the above PCE approaches become ineffective since they all have to assume the PDFs to be complete. To address this issue, the data-driven PCE (DD-PCE) method has been proposed [18], in which its accuracy and convergence with diverse statistical distributions and raw data are tested and well demonstrated. With this PCE method, the one-dimensional orthogonal polynomial basis is constructed directly based on a set of data of the random input variables by matching certain order of their statistic moments, rather than the complete distributions as in the existing PCE methods, including gPCE, GS-PCE, and ME-PCE.

At present, great research achievements about PCE have been made in the literature, which have also been applied to practical engineering problems to save the computational cost in UP. However, there is still a large gap between the academic study and engineering application for the PCE theory due to the following reasons: (1) the complete information of input PDF often is not known in engineering, which cannot be solved by most PCE methods presented in the literature; (2) the computational cost of existing PCE approaches is still very high, which cannot be afforded in practical problems, especially when applied to design optimization; and (3) there is a lack of comprehensive exploration of the relative merits of all the PCE approaches to help designers to choose more suitable PCE techniques in design under uncertainty.

2. Data-driven polynomial chaos expansion method

Most PCE methods presented in the literature are constructed based on the assumption that the exact knowledge of the involved PDF of each random input variable exists. However, the PDF of a random parameter could exist as some raw data or numerically as a complicated cumulative histogram, such as bimodal or multimodal type, which is often difficult to obtain the analytical expression of its PDF accurately. To address this issue, the data-driven PCE method (DD-PCE for short in this chapter) has been proposed. DD-PCE follows the similar general procedure as that of the well-known gPCE method. For gPCE, the one-dimensional orthogonal polynomial basis simply comes from the Askey scheme in **Table 1** and is a function of standard random variables. While for DD-PCE, the one-dimensional orthogonal polynomial basis is constructed directly based on the data of random input by matching certain order of statistic moments of the random inputs and is a function of the original random variables.

Distribution types	PDFs	Polynomials	Weights	Intervals
Normal	$\frac{1}{\sqrt{2\pi}}e^{-x^2/2}$	Hermite $H_n(x)$	$e^{-x^2/2}$	$[-\infty, +\infty]$
Uniform	1/2	Legendre $P_n(x)$	1	$[-1, 1]$
Beta	$\frac{(1-x)^\alpha(1+x)^\beta}{2^{\alpha+\beta+1}B(\alpha+1,\beta+1)}$	Jacobi $P_n^{(\alpha,\beta)}(x)$	$(1-x)^\alpha(1+x)^\beta$	$[-1, 1]$
Exponential	e^{-x}	Laguerre $L_n(x)$	e^{-x}	$[0, +\infty]$
Gamma	$\frac{x^\alpha e^{-x}}{\Gamma(\alpha+1)}$	General Laguerre $L_n^{(\alpha,\beta)}$	$x^\alpha e^{-x}$	$[0, +\infty]$

Table 1. Random variable types and the corresponding orthogonal polynomials.

2.1. Procedure of data-driven PCE method

Step 1. Represent the output y as a PCE model of order p.

$$y \approx \sum_{i=0}^{P} b_i \Phi_i(\boldsymbol{X}) = \sum_{i=0}^{P} b_i \prod_{j=1}^{d} P_j^{(\alpha_j^i)}(X_j) \tag{1}$$

where P+1 $(1+P=(d+p)!/(d!p!))$ is the number of PCE coefficients b_i that is the same as gPCE; $\Phi_i(\boldsymbol{X})$ is the d-dimensional orthogonal polynomial produced by the full tensor product of one-dimensional orthogonal polynomials $P_j^{(\alpha_j^i)}(X_j)$; and α_j^i represents the order of $P_j^{(\alpha_j^i)}(X_j)$ and clearly satisfies $0 \leq \sum_{j=1}^{d} \alpha_j^i \leq p$.

$P_j^{(\alpha_j^i)}(X_j)$ corresponding to the jth dimensional random input variable x_j in Eq. (1) is defined as below, in which the index α_j^i is replaced by k_j for simplicity below:

$$P_j^{(k_j)}(X_j) = \sum_{s=0}^{k_j} p_{s,j}^{(k_j)} * (X_j)^s, \ j = 1, 2, \ldots, d \tag{2}$$

where $p_{s,j}^{(k_j)}$ is the unknown polynomial coefficient to be solved.

Step 2. Solve the unknown polynomial coefficient $p_{s,j}^{(k_j)}$ to construct the one-dimensional orthogonal polynomial basis.

Since the construction of $P_j^{(\alpha_j^i)}(X_j)$ on each dimension is the same, the subscript j denoting the dimension number is omitted thereafter for simplicity. Based on the property of orthogonality, one clearly has

$$\int_{x\in\Omega} P^{(k)}(X) P^{(l)}(X) d\Gamma(X) = \delta_{kl}, \forall k, l = 0, 1, \ldots, p \tag{3}$$

where δ_{kl} is the Kronecker delta, Ω is the original stochastic span, and $\Gamma(X)$ represents the cumulative distribution function of the random variable X.

It is assumed that all the coefficients $p_s^{(k)}$ in Eq. (2) are not equal to 0, and then $P^{(0)} = p_0^{(0)}$. For simplicity, the coefficient of the highest degree term in each $P^{(k)}$ is set as $p_k^{(k)} = 1, \forall k$. According to Eq. (3), one has

$$\int_{x\in\Omega} p_0^{(0)} \left[\sum_{s=0}^{k} p_s^{(k)} X^s \right] d\Gamma(X) = 0 \tag{4}$$

In the same way as above, one has

$$\begin{gathered} \int_{x\in\Omega} \left[\sum_{s=0}^{1} p_s^{(1)} X^s \right] \left[\sum_{s=0}^{k} p_s^{(k)} X^s \right] d\Gamma(X) = 0 \\ \vdots \qquad\qquad\qquad \vdots \\ \int_{x\in\Omega} \left[\sum_{s=0}^{k-1} p_s^{(k-1)} X^s \right] \left[\sum_{s=0}^{k} p_s^{(k)} X^s \right] d\Gamma(X) = 0 \end{gathered} \tag{5}$$

There are totally k equations in Eqs. (4) and (5). Through substituting Eq. (4) into the first equation in Eq. (5), and then substituting Eq. (4) and the first equation in Eq. (5) to the second equation in Eq. (5), and so on, one set of new equations can be derived:

$$\begin{gathered} \int_{x\in\Omega} \sum_{s=0}^{k} p_s^{(k)} X^s d\Gamma(X) = 0 \\ \int_{x\in\Omega} \sum_{s=0}^{k} p_s^{(k)} X^{s+1} d\Gamma(X) = 0 \\ \vdots \\ \int_{x\in\Omega} \sum_{s=0}^{k} p_s^{(k)} X^{s+k-1} d\Gamma(X) = 0 \end{gathered} \tag{6}$$

It is observed that $\int_{\xi\in\Omega} X^k d\Gamma(X)$ is actually the kth order statistic moment of x, i.e., $\int_{x\in\Omega} X^k d\Gamma(X) = \mu_k$. Therefore, Eq. (6) can be rewritten as

$$\begin{bmatrix} \mu_0 & \mu_1 & \cdots & \mu_k \\ \mu_1 & \mu_2 & \cdots & \mu_{k+1} \\ \vdots & \vdots & \vdots & \vdots \\ \mu_{k-1} & \mu_k & \cdots & \mu_{2k-1} \\ 0 & 0 & \cdots & 1 \end{bmatrix} \begin{bmatrix} p_0^{(k)} \\ p_1^{(k)} \\ \vdots \\ p_{k-1}^{(k)} \\ p_k^{(k)} \end{bmatrix} = \begin{bmatrix} 0 \\ 0 \\ \vdots \\ 0 \\ 1 \end{bmatrix} \tag{7}$$

where $\mu_i (i = 0, 1, \ldots, 2k-1)$ is the ith order statistic moment of x, which can be easily calculated from the given input data statistically or the PDFs of random inputs by integral. Of course, when the number of given data is not large enough, errors would be induced in the moment calculation.

Clearly, to obtain a k-order one-dimensional orthogonal polynomial basis, 0 to $(2k - 1)$-order statistic moments of x should be matched, which can be calculated based on the PDF or statistically based on the data set. Of course, when the number of data is not large enough, errors would be induced in the moment calculation. The polynomial coefficients for the one-dimensional orthogonal polynomial basis can be obtained by solving Eq. (7) with the Cramer's Rule.

Step 3. Calculate the PCE coefficients b_i by the least square regression technique.

Step 4. Once the PCE coefficients are obtained, a stochastic metamodel (i.e., PCE model) that is much cheaper than the original model is provided. Evaluate on the PCE model by Monte Carlo simulation (MCS) to obtain the probabilistic characteristics of y. Since the PCE model is cheap, a large amount of sample points can be used. For the statistic moments, the analytical expressions can also be conveniently derived based on the PCE coefficients:

$$\begin{cases} E[y] = E\left[\sum_{i=0}^{P} b_i\psi_i(\boldsymbol{X})\right] = b_0 \\ \sigma^2[y] = E[y^2] - E^2[y] = \sum_{i=0}^{P} b_i^2 E[\psi_i^2(\boldsymbol{X})] - E^2[y] \\ Skew[y] = E\left[\left(\frac{y-E[y]}{\sigma[y]}\right)^3\right] = \frac{E[y^3] - 3E[y]\sigma^2[y] - E^3[y]}{\sigma^3[y]} \\ Kur[y] = \frac{E[(y-E[y])^4]}{\sigma^4[y]} = \frac{E[y^4] - 4E[y]E[y^3] + 6E^2[y]\sigma^2[y] + 3E^4[y]}{\sigma^4[y]} \end{cases} \tag{8}$$

2.2. Extension of Galerkin projection to DD-PCE

In the existing work about DD-PCE, only the regression method is employed to calculate the PCE coefficients. To the experience of the authors, the matrix during regression may become ill-conditioned during regression for higher-dimensional problems since the sample points required for regression that is often set as two times of the number of PCE coefficients $P + 1$ [19] is increased greatly causing a large-scale matrix during regression. To solve higher-dimensional problems, the Galerkin projection method in conjunction with the sparse grid technique has been widely used in gPCE due to its high accuracy, robustness, and convergence [20], which has also been observed and demonstrated during our earlier studies on PCE in recent years. In this section, the Galerkin projection method for PCE coefficients calculation is extended to the DD-PCE approach to address higher-dimensional UP problems. **Figure 2** shows the general procedure of the improved DD-PCE method.

With the projection method, the Galerkin projection is conducted on each side of Eq. (1):

$$\langle y\Phi_j(\boldsymbol{X})\rangle = \left\langle \sum_{i=0}^{P} b_i\Phi_i(\boldsymbol{X})\Phi_j(\boldsymbol{X}) \right\rangle, (j = 0, 1, \cdots, P) \tag{9}$$

where $\langle \bullet \rangle$ represents the operation of inner product as below

$$\langle g, f\rangle = \int gf dH(\boldsymbol{X}) \tag{10}$$

where H($\boldsymbol{X}$) is the joint cumulative distribution function of random input variables $\boldsymbol{X}$.

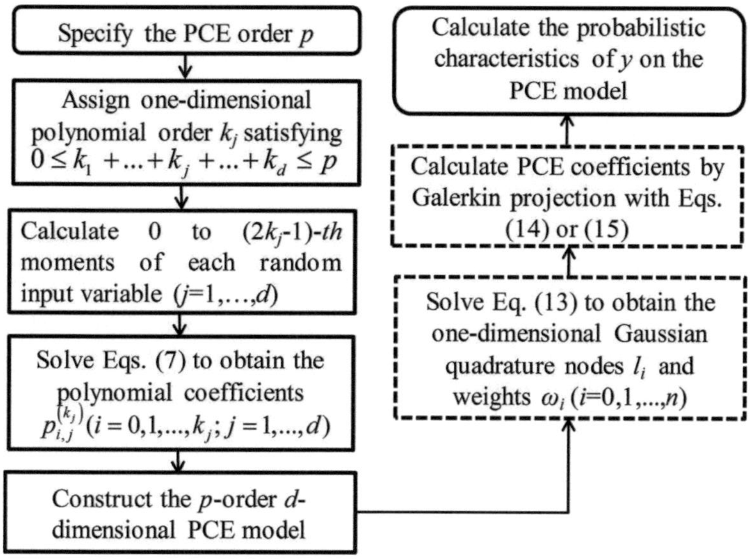

Figure 2. Procedure of the improved DD-PCE.

Based on the orthogonality property of orthogonal polynomials, the PCE coefficient can be calculated as

$$b_i = E[y\Phi_i(\boldsymbol{X})]/E[\Phi_i(\boldsymbol{X})\Phi_i(\boldsymbol{X})], (i = 0, 1, \cdots, P) \tag{11}$$

Similar to gPCE, the key point is the computation of the numerator in Eq. (11), which can be expressed as

$$E[y\Phi_i(\boldsymbol{X})] = \int_{\xi \in \Omega} y\Phi_i(\boldsymbol{X}) dH(\boldsymbol{X}) \tag{12}$$

The Gaussian quadrature technique, such as full factorial numerical integration (FFNI) and spare grid numerical integration, has been widely used to calculate the numerator in the existing gPCE approaches, with which the one-dimensional Gaussian quadrature nodes and weighs are directly derived by multiplying some scaling factors on the nodes and weights from the existing Gaussian quadrature formulae and then the tensor product is employed to obtain the multidimensional nodes. For some common type of probability distributions, for example, normal, uniform, and exponential distributions, their PDFs have the similar formulations as the weighting functions of the Gaussian-Hermite, Gaussian-Legendre, and Gaussian-Laguerre quadrature formula. Therefore, l_i and w_i can be conveniently obtained based on the tabulated nodes and weights of Gaussian quadrature formula [21], which are shown in **Table 2**, where l_i^{G-H} and ω_i^{G-H}, l_i^{G-La} and ω_i^{G-La}, l_i^{G-Le} and ω_i^{G-Le}, respectively, represent the quadrature nodes and weights of Gaussian-Hermite, Gaussian-Laguerre, and Gaussian-Legendre quadrature formula; λ is the parameter of exponential distribution; and μ_1 and μ_0 denote the lower and upper bounds of uniform distribution.

Normal		Exponential		Uniform	
l_i	ω_i	l_i	ω_i	l_i	ω_i
$\sqrt{2}\,\sigma l_i^{G-H} + \mu$	$\frac{\omega_i^{G-H}}{\sqrt{\pi}}$	$\frac{l_i^{G-La}}{\lambda}$	ω_i^{G-La}	$\frac{\mu_1-\mu_0}{2} l_i^{G-Le} + \frac{\mu_1+\mu_0}{2}$	$\frac{\omega_i^{G-Le}}{2}$

Table 2. l_i and ω_i calculated based on Gaussian quadrature.

However, the distributions of random inputs may not follow the Askey scheme, or are even nontrivial, or even exist in some raw data with a cumulative histogram of complicated shapes. Thus, such way to derive these nodes and weighs is not applicable in this case. In this work, a simple method is proposed based on the moment-matching equations below to obtain the one-dimensional quadrature nodes and weights.

$$\begin{aligned} &\omega_0 + \omega_1 + \cdots + \omega_n = \int_{x\in\Omega} 1 d\Gamma(x) \\ &\omega_0 l_0 + \omega_1 l_1 + \cdots + \omega_n l_n = \int_{x\in\Omega} x d\Gamma(x) \\ &\vdots \\ &\omega_0 (l_0)^n + \omega_1 (l_1)^n + \cdots + \omega_n (l_n)^n = \int_{x\in\Omega} x^r d\Gamma(x) \end{aligned} \tag{13}$$

where l_i and ω_i ($i = 0, 1, \ldots, n$) are respectively the ith one-dimensional Gaussian quadrature nodes and weights, which theoretically can be obtained by solving Eq. (13).

However, Eq. (13) are multivariate nonlinear equations, which are difficult to solve when the number of equations is large ($n + 1 > 7$). It is noted that the one-dimensional polynomial basis $P^{(k)}$ corresponding to each dimension constructed above is orthogonal. Therefore, its zeros are just the Gaussian quadrature nodes l_i, which can be easily obtained by solving $P^{(k)} = 0$. Through substituting l_i into Eq. (13), the $n + 1$ weights ω_i can be conveniently calculated. To calculate Eq. (13) of PCE order p, generally at least $p + 1$ one-dimensional nodes should be generated to ensure the accuracy, i.e., $n \geq p$, which means that 0 to at least pth statistic moments of the random variable $\boldsymbol{X}$ should be matched. In this work, n is set as $n = p$.

In the same way, the nodes and weights in other dimensions are obtained conveniently. Then, the numerator can be calculated by the full factorial numerical integration (FFNI) method [8] for lower-dimensional problems ($d < 4$) as

$$E[y\,\Phi_i(\boldsymbol{X})] = \mathrm{E}[Z(\boldsymbol{X})] \approx \sum_{i_1=1}^{m_1} \omega_{i_1} \cdots \sum_{i_j=1}^{m_j} \omega_{i_j} \cdots \sum_{i_d=1}^{m_d} \omega_{i_d} Z(l_{i_1}, \cdots, l_{i_j}, \cdots, l_{i_d}) = \sum_{j=1}^{N} W_j Z(L_j) \tag{14}$$

where l_{i_j} and ω_{i_j}, respectively, represent the one-dimensional nodes and weights of the jth random input variable, which can be obtained using the way introduced above; L_i and W_i ($i = 1, \ldots, N$) are the d-dimensional nodes and weights, respectively.

Generally, m is set as $m \geq p + 1$ (p is the order of the PCE model). If the number of nodes N for calculating $\mathrm{E}[y\Phi_i(\boldsymbol{X})]$ is too small, which is not matched with the PCE order, large error would be induced. Therefore, the conclusion that the higher the PCE order, the more accurate the UP results is based on the fact that $E[y\Phi_i(X)]$ has been calculated accurately enough. Clearly, the number of nodes N is increased exponentially with the increase of dimension d, causing curse of dimensionality. Therefore, FFNI is only suitable for lower-dimensional problems ($d < 4$).

For higher-dimensional problems ($d \geq 4$), the sparse grid numerical integration method [22] can be used to calculate $E[y\Phi_i(X)]$ to reduce the computational cost:

$$E[y\Phi_i(\boldsymbol{X})] = E[Z(\boldsymbol{X})] \approx \sum_{q-d+1 \leq |i| \leq q} (-1)^{q-|i|} \binom{d-1}{q-|i|} (\omega_{i_1} \ldots \omega_{i_j} \ldots \omega_{i_d})\, Z(l_{i_1}, \cdots, l_{i_j}, \cdots, l_{i_d}) \tag{15}$$

where $|i| = i_1 +, \ldots, + i_d$ and $i_1, \ldots, i_d$ are the accuracy index corresponding to each dimension.

For the FFNI-based method, if m nodes are selected on each dimension ($m_1 = \ldots = m_d = m$), $2m - 1$ accuracy level can be obtained. For the sparse grid-based method, $2k + 1$ accuracy level can be obtained with the accuracy level $k = q - d$. For example, if $k = 2$ and $d = 8$, for the sparse grid-based method, 17 nodes are required yielding 5th ($2 \times 2 + 1$)-order accuracy level. For the FFNI-based method, to obtain the same accuracy level 5 ($2 \times 3 - 1$), m should be $m = 3$ requiring 3^8 nodes. Clearly, to obtain the same accuracy level, the number of nodes of the sparse grid-based method is much smaller than that of the FFNI-based method if d is relatively large.

In this chapter, we focus on extending the Galerkin projection to the DD-PCE method to address higher-dimensional UP problems and then exploring the relative merits of these PCE approaches. For the case with only small data sets, both DD-PCE and the existing distribution-based method (gPCE) may produce large errors for UP, and the estimation of PDF for the existing PCE methods is problem dependent and very subjective. It is difficult to make a comparison effectively between DD-PCE and the existing PCE methods. Therefore, during the comparison, it is assumed that there are enough data of the random input to ensure the accuracy of the moments.

2.3. Comparative study of various PCE methods

In this section, the enhanced DD-PCE method, the recognized gPCE method, and the GS-PCE method that can address arbitrary random distributions are applied to uncertainty propagation to calculate the first four statistic moments (mean μ, standard deviation σ, skewness β_1, kurtosis β_2) and probability of failure (P_f), of which the results are compared to help designers to choose the most suitable PCE method for UP. To comprehensively compare the three PCE approaches, four cases are respectively tested on four mathematical functions with varying nonlinearity and dimension shown in **Table 3** and *N, U, Exp, Wbl, Rayl,* and *Logn* denote normal, uniform, exponential, Weibull, Rayleigh, and lognormal distribution, respectively. P_f is defined as P_f = probability ($y \leq 0$).

The PCE order is set as $p = 5$ for all the functions for comparison, which means that 0–9th statistic moments of the random inputs should be matched to construct the one-dimensional orthogonal polynomials for the DD-PCE approach. For the first and second functions, FFNI-based Galerkin projection is used to calculate the PCE coefficients, while for the latter two,

Function 1: $y = x_1+x_2+x_3$

Case 1: x_1 ~$U(1,2)$, x_2 ~$N(1,0.2)$, x_3 ~ $Exp(0.5)$

Case 2: x_1 ~$Wbl(2,6)$, x_2 ~$Rayl(3)$, x_3 ~ $Logn(0,0.25)$

Case 3: x_1~BD, x_2~ BD, x_3~$N(0,0.2)$

Case 4: 500 and 10^7 sample points x_1~BM, x_2~ BM, x_3~$N(-0.8,0.2)$

Function 2: $y = \sin(x_1) - \cos^2(x_2) + x_3\sin(x_1) + 0.9$

Case 1: x_1 ~$N(0.5,0.2)$, x_2 ~$U(0,1.5)$, x_3 ~ $Exp(0.1)$

Case 2: x_1 ~$Wbl(2,3)$, x_2 ~$Rayl(0.2)$, x_3 ~ $Logn(0,0.25)$

Case 3: x_1~ BD, x_2~ BD, x_3~$U(0,1)$

Case 4: 500 and 10^7 sample points x_1~BM, x_2~ BM, x_3~$U(0.4,2)$

Function 3: $y = e^{-x1}\cos(x_2) + x_3e^{-x4x5} - e^{-x6}$

Case 1: x_1 ~$N(1,0.2)$, x_2 ~$U(-1,1)$, x_3 ~ $N(1,0.2)$, x_4 ~ $U(-1,1)$, x_5 ~ $N(0,0.2)$, x_6 ~ $U(0,2)$

Case 2: x_1 ~$Wbl(1,5)$, x_2 ~$Rayl(0.5)$, x_3 ~ $Logn(0.5,0.25)$,x_4 ~ $Rayl$ (0.3), x_5 ~ $Wbl(1,5)$, x_6 ~ $Rayl(1)$

Case 3: x_1~ BD, x_2~ BD, x_3~ $N(2,0.2)$, x_4 ~ $U(-1,0)$, x_5 ~ $N(1,0.2)$, x_6 ~ $U(-1,4)$

Case 4: 500&10^7sample points x_1~BM, x_2~$Rayl$ (0.3), x_3~BM ,x_4 ~$Rayl$ (0.3), x_5 ~BM, x_6 ~$Rayl$ (1)

Function 4: $y = x_1^2x_2^2 - x_3^2x_4^2 + x_5^2x_6^2 - x_7^2x_8^2 + x_9^2x_{10}^2$

Case 1: x_1 ~ $N(1,0.2)$, x_2 ~ $U(0,2)$, x_3 ~ $N(0,0.2)$, x_4 ~ $U(0,2)$, x_5 ~ $N(1,0.2)$, x_6 ~ $U(0,2)$, x_7 ~ $N(0,0.2)$, x_8 ~ $U(0,2)$, x_9 ~ $N(1,0.2)$, x_{10} ~ $U(0,2)$

Case 2: x_1 ~$Wbl(1,5)$, x_2 ~$Rayl(1)$, x_3 ~$Wbl(1,5)$, x_4 ~$Rayl(0.3)$, x_5 ~$Wbl(1,5)$, x_6 ~$Rayl(1)$, x_7 ~$Wbl(1,5)$, x_8 ~$Rayl(0.3)$, x_9 ~Wbl (1,5), x_{10} ~$Rayl(1)$

Case 3: x_1 ~ $N(1,0.2)$, x_2 ~ $N(1,0.2)$, x_3 ~ BD, x_4 ~ BD, x_5 ~ $N(1,0.2)$, x_6 ~ $N(1,0.2)$, x_7 ~ BD, x_8 ~ BD, x_9 ~ $N(1,0.2)$, x_{10} ~ $N(1,0.2)$

Case 4: 500 and 10^7 sample points x_1 ~ $N(1.5,0.2)$, x_2 ~ $N(1,0.2)$, x_3 ~ BM, x_4 ~ BM, x_5 ~ $N(1,0.2)$, x_6 ~ $N(1,0.2)$, x_7 ~ $N(0,0.2)$, x_8 ~ $N(0,0.2)$, x_9 ~ $N(1,0.2)$, x_{10} ~ $N(1,0.2)$

Table 3. Test functions and random input information of four cases.

the sparse grid-based method with accuracy level $k = 4$ is used since the dimension is higher. The results of MCS with 10^7 runs are used to benchmark the effectiveness of the three methods.

In Case 1, all the random input distributions are known and belong to the Askey scheme. The test results are shown in **Tables 4–7**, where the bold numbers with underline are the relatively best results and e represents the relative errors of the first four moments (μ, σ, β_1, β_2) with respect to MCS. P_f estimated by MCS is presented with 95% confidence interval. The results marked with * are from the sparse grid-based method. From these tables, it is found that with the same number of function calls (denoted as Ns), DD-PCE, gPCE, and GS-PCE produce almost the same results of the statistic moments, which are very similar to those of MCS (with the largest error as 2.6927%). The estimation of P_f for all the methods is within the 95% confidence interval with respect to MCS, indicating the high accuracy of UP. Although the orthogonal polynomial basis for DD-PCE is constructed by matching only 0–9th statistic moments of the random input variable instead of the complete PDFs for gPCE and GS-PCE, the results are accurate enough in this case. Moreover, the application of sparse grid technique to DD-PCE can greatly reduce the function calls for higher-dimensional problems (see **Tables 5** and **6**), while

Methods	MCS	DD-PCE	*g*PCE	GS-PCE
e_μ (%)	–	0.0050	**0**	0.0100
e_σ (%)	–	0.0164	(0.0164)	0.0164
e_{β_1} (%)	–	0.1367	0.1367	**0.1094**
e_{β_2} (%)	–	0.4877	0.3032	**0.2199**
$P_f\,(1e^{-3})$	[8.5185,8.6328]	8.5472	8.5901	8.5688
N_s	10^7	125	125	125

Table 4. Results of function 1 (Case 1).

Methods	MCS	DD-PCE	*g*PCE	GS-PCE
e_μ (%)	–	0.0115	**0**	0.0231
e_σ (%)	–	0.0516	**0**	0.0258
e_{β_1} (%)	–	**0**	0.4202	5.4852
e_{β_2} (%)	–	0.1725	**0.0814**	0.0958
$P_f\,(1e^{-3})$	[3.1403,3.2101]	3.1713	3.2017	3.1936
N_s	10^7	125	125	125

Table 5. Results of function 2 (Case 1).

Methods	MCS	DD-PCE*	*g*PCE*	GS-PCE*
e_μ (%)	–	**0**	0.0112	0.0225
e_σ (%)	–	0.0288	0.0288	(0.0288
e_{β_1} (%)	–	2.2284	2.6927	**1.7642**
e_{β_2} (%)	–	0.6040	0.6074	**0.5028**
$P_f\,(1e^{-3})$	[4.8454,4.9318]	4.8993	4.8669	4.9074
N_s	10^7	1820	1820	1820

Table 6. Results of function 3 (Case 1).

Methods	MCS	DD-PCE*	*g*PCE*	GS-PCE*
e_μ (%)	–	0.0123	0.0296	**0.0074**
e_σ (%)	–	**0.0402**	0.0723	0.0522
e_{β_1} (%)	–	0.1018	**0.0890**	0.1399
e_{β_2} (%)	–	0.1050	**0**	0.1326
$P_f\,(1e^{-3})$	[4.2476,4.3286]	4.2627	4.2881	4.2562
N_s	10^7	10,626	10,626	10,626

Table 7. Results of function 4 (Case 1).

exhibiting good accuracy. Especially for the fourth function, with FFNI, the computational cost is very large ($N_s = 976{,}562$).

In Case 2, all the random input distributions are known but do not belong to the Askey scheme. In this case, the Rosenblatt transformation is employed for the gPCE method first. However, DD-PCE and GS-PCE can be directly used. The results are shown in **Tables 8–11**. It is observed that overall DD-PCE and GS-PCE perform better than gPCE, yielding results that are close to those of MCS. The reason is that the transformation in gPCE would induce error. Specifically, in **Tables 9** and **10**, the gPCE method causes relatively large errors due to the transformation. In addition, note the numbers with shadow, they are clearly larger than those

Methods	MCS	DD-PCE	gPCE	GS-PCE
e_μ (%)	–	0.0196	**0.0087**	0.0175
e_σ (%)	–	0.0298	**0.0099**	0.0199
e_{β_1} (%)	–	0.2573	0.2059	**0.2059**
e_{β_2} (%)	–	0.2170	0.2263	**0.0899**
$P_f\,(1e^{-4})$	[1.9818,2.1602]	2.0360	2.1490	2.0480
N_s	10^7	125	125	125

Table 8. Results of function 1 (Case 2).

Methods	MCS	DD-PCE	gPCE	GS-PCE
e_μ (%)	–	0.0243	0.0182	**0.0061**
e_σ (%)	–	0.0467	0.2101	**0**
e_{β_1} (%)	–	**1.8877**	8.0227	2.5956
e_{β_2} (%)	–	0.0307	1.1659	**0.0279**
$P_f\,(1e^{-4})$	[9.0052,9.3808]	9.0130	7.9720	9.0250
N_s	10^7	125	125	125

Table 9. Results of function 2 (Case2).

Methods	MCS	DD-PCE*	gPCE*	GS-PCE*
e_μ (%)	–	**0**	0.0084	**0**
e_σ (%)	–	**0.0443**	0.0887	**0.0443**
e_{β_1} (%)	–	**0.3471**	0.6480	0.4397
e_{β_2} (%)	–	**0.0419**	0.1927	0.1368
$P_f\,(1e^{-3})$	[1.0859,1.1271]	1.0963	1.2291	1.1188
N_s	10^7	1820	1820	1820

Table 10. Results of function 3 (Case2).

Methods	MCS	DD-PCE*	gPCE*	GS-PCE*
e_μ (%)	–	0.0240	**0.0180**	0.0320
e_σ (%)	–	**0.0111**	0.0722	0.0250
e_{β_1} (%)	–	0.2170	**0.1979**	0.2362
e_{β_2} (%)	–	**0.4229**	1.9117	0.4582
P_f (1e^{-3})	[4.4019,4.4843]	4.4635	4.6942	4.4200
N_s	10^7	10,626	10,626	10,626

Table 11. Results of function 4 (Case 2).

of DD-PCE and GS-PCE, and P_f is outside the range of the 95% confidence interval of MCS. The interpretation is that since the first function is linear, the impact of transformation employed in gPCE on the accuracy of UP is small; while, for the second and third functions, they are more complicated and nonlinear (including trigonometric and exponential terms), the error induced by the transformation employed in gPCE is amplified more. The fourth function is a nonlinear polynomial one, which is easier to be handled than functions 2 and 3 in doing UP. Therefore, the results are generally accurate except P_f that is still outside the range of the 95% confidence interval of MCS. Moreover, the application of sparse grid greatly reduces N_s, exhibiting good potential applications for higher-dimensional problems.

In Case 3, the PDFs of some variables is bounded (BD) as below,

$$f(x) = \begin{cases} 2x, 0 < x < 1 \\ 0, \text{otherwise} \end{cases} \tag{16}$$

and the rest of the variables follow typical distributions. In this case, the Rosenblatt transformation is also employed for the gPCE method first.

From the results in **Tables 12–15**, it is found that generally large errors are induced by gPCE, especially the numbers with shadow in the tables. Since the first two variables follow the distribution bounded in an interval, the error induced by the transformation is large and all values of P_f are outside the confidence intervals for gPCE. While, the results of DD-PCE and GS-PCE are generally accurate and comparable, which are still very close to those of MCS. It should be noted that although the error of gPCE is the largest, all P_f by the three methods are

Methods	MCS	DD-PCE	gPCE	GS-PCE
e_μ (%)	–	**0**	0.0150	**0**
e_σ (%)	–	0.0195	24.1063	**0**
e_{β_1} (%)	–	0.1359	36.9565	**0.1132**
e_{β_2} (%)	–	**0.0545**	12.3239	**0.0545**
P_f (1e^{-3})	[4.9841,5.0717]	5.0038	5.2620	5.0333
N_s	10^7	125	125	125

Table 12. Results of function 1 (Case 3).

Methods	MCS	DD-PCE	gPCE	GS-PCE
e_μ (%)	–	**0.0083**	0.0914	**0.0083**
e_σ (%)	–	**0.0213**	19.7662	**0.0213**
e_{β_1} (%)	–	0.4186	123.2093	**0.3256**
e_{β_2} (%)	–	0.0555	12.7841	**0.0476**
$P_f\,(1^{e-3})$	[1.4429,1.4903]	1.4449	1.7890	1.4452
N_s	10^7	125	125	125

Table 13. Results of function 2 (Case 3).

Methods	MCS	DD-PCE*	gPCE*	GS-PCE*
e_μ (%)	–	**0.0359**	0.7473	0.0598
e_σ (%)	–	**0.3983**	(4.2798	0.3693
e_{β_1} (%)	–	0.1221	22.5570	0.2036
e_{β_2} (%)	–	0.6186	77.1134	0.6321
$P_f\,(1e^{-3})$	[3.1972,3.2676]	***2.6222***	***8.9269***	***2.6071***
N_s	10^7	1820	1820	1820

Table 14. Results of function 3 (Case 3).

Methods	MCS	DD-PCE*	gPCE*	GS-PCE*
e_μ (%)	–	**0.0039**	6.4980	0.0194
e_σ (%)	–	0.0409	8.2618	**0.0164**
e_{β_1} (%)	–	0.1187	50.3681	**0.0475**
e_{β_2} (%)	–	**0.1720**	11.8984	0.1949
$P_f\,(1e^{-3})$	[8.6089,8.7237]	8.6559	0.8227	8.6728
N_s	10^7	10,626	10,626	10,626

Table 15. Results of function 4 (Case 3).

outside the confidence intervals for function 3 (italic numbers) since this function is the most nonlinear and complicated. Hence, we increase the PCE order p and accuracy level k of the sparse grid to $p = 6$ and $k = 5$, and the results of P_f for DD-PCE, gPCE, and GS-PCE are 3.1263, 3.1446, and 3.1350, exhibiting evident improvement. Clearly with the same Ns, DD-PCE and GS-PCE are much more accurate than gPCE when nontrivial distribution is involved. These results further demonstrates the effectiveness and advantage of the enhanced DD-PCE for UP.

In Case 4, the distributions of the random input variables are unknown and only some data exist. Although, based on the data, the analytical PDF can be obtained through some experience systems, such as Johnson or Pearson system [8], if the distribution of the data is very complicated, such as with a complicated cumulative histogram of bi- or multimodes, it is often very difficult to obtain the analytical PDF accurately. As is well-known that the Pearson system based on the first four statistic moments of the random variable would produce large errors for bimode (BM) or multimode PDFs. Evidently, the existing PCE approaches, including gPCE and GS-PCE, may produce large errors since they all depend on the exact PDFs of the random inputs in this case. However, DD-PCE can still work since it is a data-driven approach. To explore the effectiveness and advantage of DD-PCE over the other two approaches, it is assumed that the input data for some random input variables have a complicated bimode (BM) histogram shown in **Figure 3** and the data for the rest from the typical distributions. Therefore, for the convenience and effectiveness of test, all the input data are generated based on the PDFs, of which the PDF of BM distribution is shown in Eq. (17). It should be pointed out that the PDFs actually are unknown and only some data exist in practice.

$$f_{\mathrm{PDF}} = \frac{0.647}{0.1\sqrt{2\pi}} \exp\left(-\frac{x^2}{2\times 0.1^2}\right) + \frac{0.353}{0.2\sqrt{2\pi}} \exp\left(-\frac{(x-1)^2}{2\times 0.2^2}\right), x\in[-\infty, +\infty] \tag{17}$$

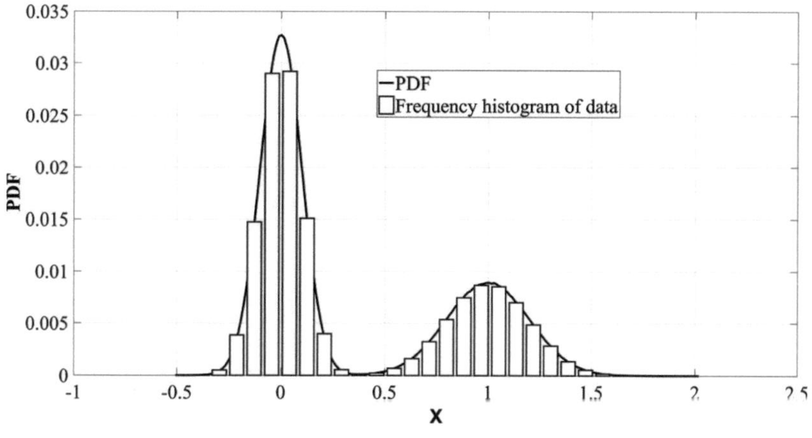

Figure 3. PDF plot of the bimodal distribution.

We tested small (500) and large (10^7) numbers of input data to investigate the impact of number of data on the accuracy of UP. The results are shown in **Tables 16–19,** from which it is noticed that the results of DD-PCE are generally very close to those of MCS when the number of sample points of the random input variables is large (10^7). When only 500 sample points are used, the errors are much larger. It means that the accuracy of DD-PCE is improved with the increase of the number of sample points. The reason is very simple that with the increase of the number of sample points, the statistic moments of random input variables calculated are more accurate, which would undoubtedly increase the accuracy of UP. The observation exhibits great agreements to what has been reported in work of Oladyshkin and Nowak. Similar to Case 3, the estimated P_f is outside the confidence intervals for function 3 since this function is the most nonlinear and the random distribution is more irregular, which can be improved by

Methods	MCS	DD-PCE (10^7)	DD-PCE (500)
e_μ (%)	–	0.0066	1.4873
e_σ (%)	–	0.0196	0.0688
e_{β_1} (%)	–	0.0150	0.0451
e_{β_2} (%)	–	0.0052	3.2327
$P_f\,(1e^{-3})$	[1.4772,1.5252]	1.5069	0
N_s	10^7	125	125

Table 16. Results of function 1 (Case 4).

Methods	MCS	DD-PCE(10^7)	DD-PCE(500)
e_μ (%)	–	0.0132	0.4350
e_σ (%)	–	0.0109	0.1957
e_{β_1} (%)	–	0.1159	13.4783
e_{β_2} (%)	–	0.0131	0.8956
$P_f\,(1e^{-3})$	[6.4478,6.5474]	6.4703	8.000
N_s	10^7	125	125

Table 17. Results of function 2 (Case 4).

Methods	MCS	DD-PCE(10^7)	DD-PCE(500)
e_μ (%)	–	0.0327	0.6047
e_σ (%)	–	2.7503	5.3717
e_{β_1} (%)	–	3.8373	9.5932
e_{β_2} (%)	–	0.5563	1.3573
$P_f\,(1e^{-3})$	[7.7830,7.8924]	6.6667	6.0000
N_s	10^7	1820	1820

Table 18. Results of function 3 (Case 4).

Methods	MCS	DD-PCE(10^7)	DD-PCE(500)
e_μ (%)	–	0.0024	0.1925
e_σ (%)	–	0.0241	3.5156
e_{β_1} (%)	–	0.4149	214.4537
e_{β_2} (%)	–	0.0170	11.9346
$P_f\,(1e^{-3})$	[9.2650,9.3842]	9.2937	0
N_s	10^7	10626	10626

Table 19. Results of function 4 (Case 4).

http://dx.doi.org/10.5772/intechopen.68484

increasing N_s. This means that the generally the more nonlinear the function and the more irregular the random input distribution, the more difficult it is to achieve accurate UP results. These results further demonstrate the effectiveness and advantage of the enhanced DD-PCE method for UP.

To study the convergence property of the enhanced DD-PCE method, the errors (e) of moments and P_f with different PCE orders obtained by the proposed one as well as gPCE and GS-PCE are shown in **Figures 4–7**, taking Function 2, for example. Clearly, similar to the existing two methods, with the increase of the PCE order, the errors decrease significantly, exhibiting an approximate exponential convergence rate. Meanwhile, it is observed that the speed of convergence in Case 1 (Askey scheme) is the fastest. Generally, the more irregular the input distribution and the more nonlinear the function, the slower is the convergence process. In addition, it is also

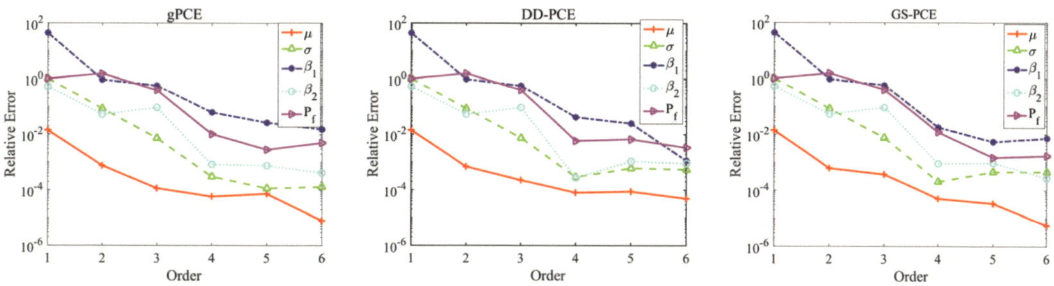

Figure 4. Errors with respect to different PCE orders (Case 1).

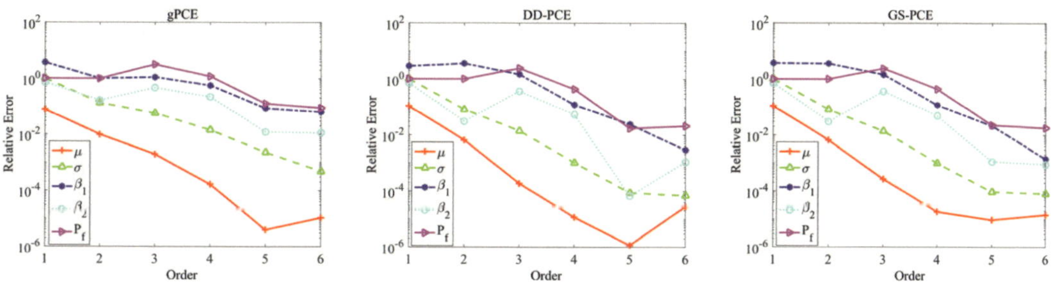

Figure 5. Errors with respect to different PCE orders (Case 2).

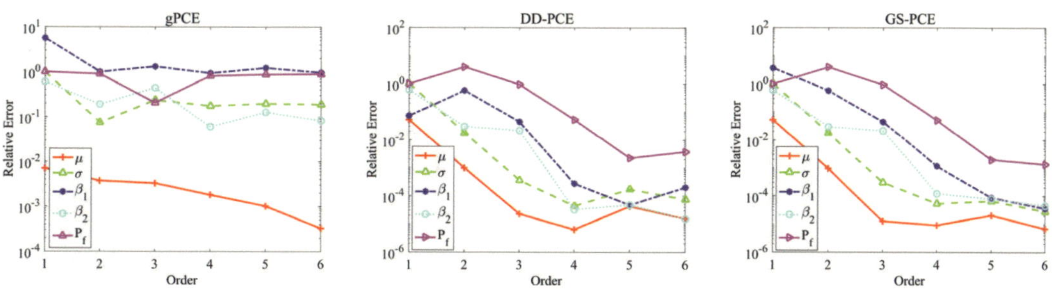

Figure 6. Errors with respect to different PCE orders (Case 3).

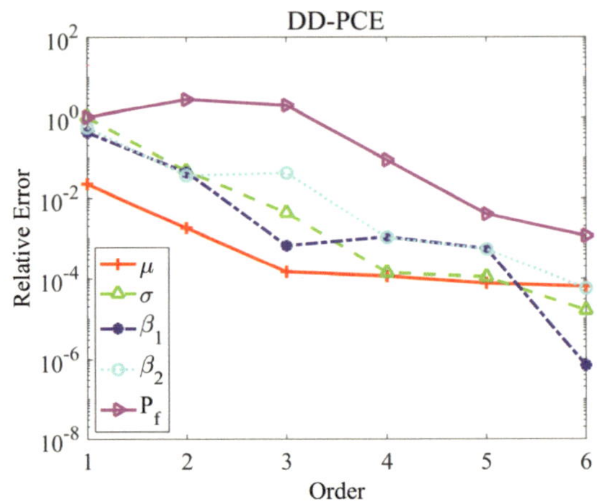

Figure 7. Errors with respect to different PCE orders (Case 4).

noticed that for Case 3, since x_1 and x_2 follow the nontrivial distribution, the convergence rate is very slow for gPCE (see left in **Figure 6**) due to the error induced by the transformation.

2.4. Summary

Overall, the three approaches produce comparably good results when the random inputs follow the Askey scheme. However, gPCE is the most mature and convenient to be implemented since there is no need to construct the orthogonal polynomials. When the PDFs of random inputs are unknown but do not follow the Askey scheme, large errors would be induced by the transformation for gPCE and the rest two PCE methods are comparable in accuracy and implementation complexity. It should also be pointed out that for DD-PCE, when constructing one-dimensional polynomials, the statistic moments (often 0–10 order) should be calculated first. If large gap exists between the high-order and low-order moments, the matrix singularity would happen in solving the linear equations (Eq. (7)). Therefore, in this case, GS-PCE is preferable especially when the function is highly nonlinear. When the PDF is unknown and cannot be obtained accurately, such as when random inputs exist as some raw data with a complicated cumulative histogram, only the DD-PCE method can still perform well since it is a data-driven method instead of the probabilistic-distribution-driven, while large errors would be produced if GS-PCE and gPCE are employed. However, more efforts should be made to solve the numerical problems in the DD-PCE method to make it more robust and applicable in constructing the one-dimensional orthogonal polynomials.

3. A sparse data-driven PCE method

The size of the truncated polynomial terms in the full PCE model is increased with the increase of the dimension of random inputs d and the order of PCE model p (see Eq. (1)), resulting in a significant growth of the computational cost. Therefore, attempts are made in this section on the full DD-PCE method introduced in Section 2 to reduce the computational cost. Accordingly, a sparse PCE approximation, which only contains a small number of polynomial terms compared to a classical full representation, is eventually provided by using the least angle regression (LAR) theory [23] and the sequential sampling method. The original LAR method is used for variables selection, aiming to find the most important variables with respect to a function response. In this work, LAR is extended to select some polynomial terms $\Phi_i(\boldsymbol{x})$ from the full PCE model that have the greatest impact on the model response $y \approx M(\boldsymbol{x}) = \sum_{i=0}^{P} b_i\Phi_i(\boldsymbol{x})$ in a similar way.

Although the computational cost and accuracy are dependent on the PCE order, how to determine a suitable order that compromises between accuracy and efficiency is not within the scope of this chapter. In common situations, PCE of order p = 2 or 3 can produce results with good agreement to MCS for the output PDF estimation [24]. For more rigorous approaches of adaptively determining the order of the PCE model rather than specifying it in advance, readers can refer to references [25, 26].

3.1. Procedure of data-driven PCE method

A step-by-step description of the proposed method is given in detail as below with a side-by-side flowchart in **Figure 8**.

Step 1. Given the information of the random inputs (raw data or probabilistic distributions), specify the PCE order p, and then construct the full DD-PCE model without computing the PCE coefficients.

Step 2. Generate the initial input sample points $\boldsymbol{X} = [\boldsymbol{x}_1,\ldots,\boldsymbol{x}_m,\ldots,\boldsymbol{x}_N]^T$ according to the distributions of the random inputs or select the sample points from the given raw data, where $\boldsymbol{x}_m = [x_{m1}, \ldots, x_{md}]$. Meanwhile, calculate the corresponding real function responses $\boldsymbol{y} = [y_1,\ldots,y_m,\ldots,y_N]^T$.

$\boldsymbol{X}$ is standardized to have mean 0 and unit length, and that the response $\boldsymbol{y}$ has mean 0.

$$\frac{1}{N}\sum_{m=1}^{N} x_{\mathrm{mn}} = 0, \quad \sqrt{\sum_{m=1}^{N} x_{\mathrm{mn}}^2} = 1 \quad (n = 1, \ldots, d), \quad \frac{1}{N}\sum_{m=1}^{N} y_m = 0 \tag{18}$$

Then one has all the standardized data as

$$\overline{\boldsymbol{X}} = \begin{bmatrix} \overline{x}_{11}, \overline{x}_{12}, \ldots, \overline{x}_{1d} \\ \overline{x}_{21}, \overline{x}_{22}, \ldots, \overline{x}_{2d} \\ \cdots \quad \cdots \\ \overline{x}_{N1}, \overline{x}_{N2}, \ldots, \overline{x}_{Nd} \end{bmatrix}, \overline{\boldsymbol{y}} = (\overline{y}_1, \ldots, \overline{y}_N)^T \tag{19}$$

Step 3. Set the iteration number as K = 0 and compute the values of all polynomial terms $\Phi_i(\boldsymbol{x})$ (i = 0, 1, …, P) of the full PCE model in Eq. (1) by, respectively, substituting each input sample point $\boldsymbol{x}_m$ into them. Then one obtains the information matrix as

$$\Phi = \begin{bmatrix} \Phi_0(\boldsymbol{x}_1) & \Phi_1(\boldsymbol{x}_1), \ldots, & \Phi_P(\boldsymbol{x}_1) \\ \vdots \cdots & & \vdots \\ \Phi_0(\boldsymbol{x}_N) & \Phi_1(\boldsymbol{x}_N), \ldots, & \Phi_P(\boldsymbol{x}_N) \end{bmatrix} \tag{20}$$

Step 4. The LAR algorithm is employed to automatically detect some number (often $K + 1$) of significant orthogonal polynomial terms from the first $K + 1$ terms $\Phi_i(\boldsymbol{x})$ ($i = 0, 1, \ldots, K$) in Eq. (1), which will be retained to construct a sparse candidate PCE model that has a smaller scale than the full PCE model. For the introduction of the original LAR algorithm, readers can refer to reference [23] for more details.

Step 5. To save the computational cost, the leave-one-out cross-validation method [27] is employed to evaluate the accuracy of the candidate sparse PCE model constructed above, which is represented as the leave-one-out error analytically as below:

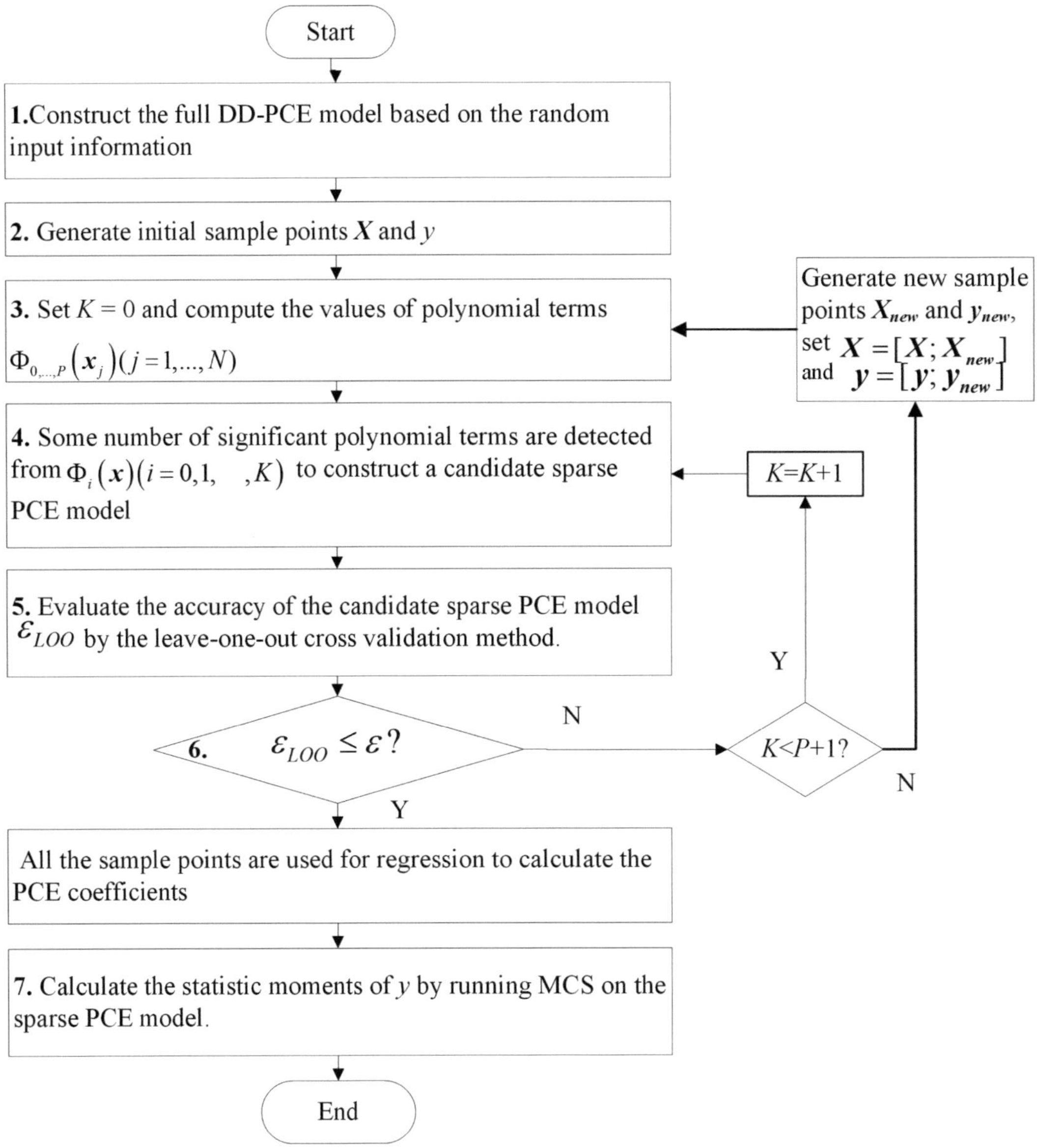

Figure 8. The flowchart of the sparse DD-PCE method.

$$Err_{\text{LOO}} = \frac{1}{N}\sum_{j=1}^{N}\left(\frac{g(\mathbf{x}_j) - \hat{g}_{\boldsymbol{I}}^{(-j)}(\mathbf{x}_j)}{1 - h_j}\right)^2 \tag{21}$$

where $g(\boldsymbol{x}_j)$ is the response value from the original model at the sample point $\boldsymbol{x}_j$; $\hat{g}_{\boldsymbol{I}}^{(-j)}$ represents the candidate sparse PCE model comprised of all the selected polynomial terms, of which the indices are stored in $\boldsymbol{I}$; the PCE coefficients of $\hat{g}_{\boldsymbol{I}}^{(-j)}$ are computed through using the ordinary least-square regression method based on the leave-one-out approach, i.e., the sample points for regression are $\boldsymbol{X}^{(-j)} = [x_1,\ldots,x_{j-1}, x_{j+1},\ldots,x_N]^T$ and $\boldsymbol{y}^{(-j)} = [y_1,\ldots,y_{j-1}, y_{j+1},\ldots,y_N]^T$.

Once the PCE coefficients are calculated, the predicted value by the candidate sparse PCE model at the sample point $\boldsymbol{x}_j$ is calculated as $\hat{g}_{\boldsymbol{I}}^{(-j)}(\mathbf{x}_j)$; h_j is the jth diagonal element of the matrix $\boldsymbol{\Phi}_A(\boldsymbol{\Phi}^T{}_A\boldsymbol{\Phi}_A)^{-1}\boldsymbol{\Phi}^T{}_A$, where $\boldsymbol{\Phi}_A$ is a $N \times k$ matrix comprised of all the selected column vectors $\boldsymbol{\Phi}_i = [\Phi_i(x_1), \ldots, \Phi_i(x_N)]^T$ $(i \in I)$ and k is the number of selected polynomial terms.

To evaluate the accuracy more effectively, the relative error is employed based on Err_{LOO} as

$$\varepsilon_{\text{LOO}} = Err_{\text{LOO}}/\hat{V}(\mathbf{y}) \tag{22}$$

where $\hat{V}(\mathbf{y})$ denotes the empirical variance of the response sample points $\boldsymbol{y}$, which is calculated by

$$\hat{V}(\mathbf{y}) = \frac{1}{N-1}\sum_{j=1}^{N}(y_j - \overline{y})^2, \overline{y} = \frac{1}{N}\sum_{j=1}^{N} y_j \tag{23}$$

Step 6. Check the stop criterion:

If the accuracy ε_{LOO} satisfies the target threshold ε, i.e., $\varepsilon_{\text{Loo}} \leq \varepsilon$, the procedure will be stopped, the PCE model obtained by LAR in Step 4 will be considered as the final one, and all the sample points will be used for regression to calculate the PCE coefficients of the current sparse PCE model;

If $\varepsilon_{\text{Loo}} > \varepsilon$ and $K < P$, set $K = K + 1$ and go to Step 4 to find another candidate sparse PCE model by LAR;

If $\varepsilon_{\text{Loo}} > \varepsilon$ and $K = P$, generate some new sample points $\boldsymbol{X}_{\text{new}}$ with the sequential sampling technique and calculate the corresponding responses $\boldsymbol{y}_{\text{new}}$, and add the new sample points into the old ones as $\boldsymbol{X} = [\boldsymbol{X}; \boldsymbol{X}_{\text{new}}]$ and $\boldsymbol{y} = [\boldsymbol{y}; \boldsymbol{y}_{\text{new}}]$, then go to Step 3 to find another candidate sparse PCE model.

In this work, if the PDF of random input is known, a large number of sample points are generated as the database according to the PDF beforehand; if the PDF of random input is unknown, the raw data are considered as the database. Each sample point in the database has its own index. The initial sample points are selected from the database through randomly and uniformly generating their indices. Then these sample points will be removed from the database and the rest will be indexed again. Similarly, by randomly and uniformly generating the indices, the sequential sample points will be selected from the reduced database. By using this sampling strategy, the sample points are distributed uniformly as far as possible, which is helpful to improve the accuracy of the PCE coefficient calculation.

Step 7. Based on the final sparse PCE model, the probabilistic properties of y can be obtained by running MCS or analytically.

3.2. Comparative study

In this section, the proposed sparse DD-PCE method (shortened as sDD-PCE hereafter) is applied to three mathematical examples to calculate the mean and variance of the output responses. The full DD-PCE (shortened as fDD-PCE hereafter) method that adopts a full PCE structure and one-stage sampling with the size of one times the number of PCE coefficients is also applied to UP, of which the results are compared to those of sDD-PCE to demonstrate its effectiveness and advantage.

The test examples of varying dimensions including their input information are shown in **Table 20**, in which the symbols $\mathcal{N}, \mathcal{U}$ and $\mathcal{E}$ respectively, denote normal, uniform, and exponential distribution. To fully explore the applicability of sDD-PCE, three different cases of the random input information that almost cover all the situations in practice (Case 1: raw data; Case 2: common distribution; Case 3: nontrivial distribution) are considered. The nontrivial bimodal distribution (denoted as $\mathcal{BD}$) used in Section 2.3 (Eq. (16)) is considered.

Another type of nontrivial distribution considered here is invented by conducting square operation on the sample points from some common distributions (see Case 3 in Function 2). The target accuracy ε of sDD-PCE is set as 10^{-5}. Meanwhile, to ensure the effectiveness of comparison between sDD-PCE and fDD-PCE, the order of the PCE model p is set as the same

Function 1: $f_1 = X_1X_2$

Case 1: 10^5 raw data

Case 2: $X_1 \sim \mathcal{N}(1,0.2^2)$, $X_2 \sim \mathcal{U}(0.4,1.6)$

Case 3: X_1 and $X_2 \sim \mathcal{BD}$

Function 2: $f_2 = -X_1^2X_2^2 - 2X_3^4 + 3X_4^2 - 0.5X_5 + 4.5$

Case 1: 10^5 raw data

Case 2: $X_1 \sim \mathcal{N}(1,0.2^2)$, $X_2 \sim \mathcal{U}(0.4,1.6)$, $X_3 \sim \mathcal{E}(0.1)$, $X_4 \sim \mathcal{U}(-0.5,1)$, $X_5 \sim \mathcal{U}(0.5,1)$.

Case 3: $X_1 \sim \mathcal{BD}$, $X_2 \sim \mathcal{U}$ (0.4,1.6).^2, $X_3 \sim \mathcal{U}$ (0.5,1) .^2, $X_4 \sim \mathcal{U}(-0.5,1)$, $X_5 \sim \mathcal{U}(0.5,1)$.

Function 3: $f_3 = -20\exp\left(-0.2\sqrt{\frac{1}{10}\sum_{i=1}^{10}x_i^2}\right) - \exp\left(\frac{1}{10}\sum_{i=1}^{10}\cos(2\pi x_i)\right)$

Case 1: 10^5 raw data

Case 2: $X_1 \sim \mathcal{N}(1,0.2^2)$, $X_2 \sim \mathcal{U}(0.4,1.6)$, $X_3 \sim \mathcal{U}(-1.5,15)$, $X_4 \sim \mathcal{U}(-1,2)$, $X_5 \sim \mathcal{U}(-15,1)$, $X_6 \sim \mathcal{N}(2,0.2^2)$, $X_7 \sim \mathcal{U}(-3,3)$, $X_8 \sim \mathcal{U}(-15,1.5)$, $X_9 \sim \mathcal{U}(-2,15)$, $X_{10} \sim \mathcal{U}(-2,15)$.

Case 3: X_1 and $X_2 \sim \mathcal{BD}$, $X_3 \sim \mathcal{U}(-1.5,15)$, $X_4 \sim \mathcal{U}(-1,2)$, $X_5 \sim \mathcal{U}(-15,1)$, $X_6 \sim \mathcal{N}(2,0.2^2)$, $X_7 \sim \mathcal{U}(-3,3)$, $X_8 \sim \mathcal{U}(-15,1.5)$, $X_9 \sim \mathcal{U}(-2,15)$, $X_{10} \sim \mathcal{U}(-2,15)$.

Table 20. Test functions.

(p = 3, 4, 5) for both methods. MCS with 10^8 runs is conducted to benchmark the accuracy of both methods. In Case 1, the probabilistic distributions of all the random input variables are unknown and only a number of raw data (10^5) exist, which cannot be solved by the traditional PCE methods, such as gPCE. Clearly, the more the raw data, the more reliable the results will be. Considering that the main objective of this paper is to investigate the effectiveness and capability of sDD-PCE in reducing the computational cost, it is assumed that a large number of raw data (10^5) exist of the random inputs.

The results are listed in **Tables 21–23**, in which e_m and e_v respectively, denote the errors (%) of mean and variance relative to the results of MCS, N denotes the number of total sample points (function evaluations) used for PCE coefficients estimation during regression, and Na represents that the result cannot be obtained.

From the results some noteworthy observations are made. First, generally with high PCE order (p = 5), the results of sDD-PCE are accurate. Second, for low-dimensional problem (d = 2, Function 1), the efficiency and accuracy of sDD-PCE and fDD-PCE are almost comparable. Specially, for lower orders p = 3 and 4, sDD-PCE is even less efficient. The interpretation is that

	*f*DD-PCE			sDD-PCE		
e_m	0.321	0.099	0.044	0.330	0.201	0.181
e_v	0.232	0.813	0.173	0.203	0.099	0.068
p	3	4	5	3	4	5
N	10	15	21	20	30	20

Table 21. Results of function 1 (Case 1).

	*f*DD-PCE			sDD-PCE		
e_m	6.162	Na	Na	8.803	7.263	2.402
e_v	10.182	Na	Na	16.670	5.026	8.882
p	3	4	5	3	4	5
N	56	126	252	20	20	30

Table 22. Results of function 2 (Case 1).

	*f*DD-PCE			sDD-PCE		
e_m	Na	Na	Na	0.045	0.739	0.239
e_v	Na	Na	Na	18.134	12.882	2.479
p	3	4	5	3	4	5
N	286	1001	3003	30	30	30

Table 23. Results of function 3 (Case 1).

in addition to the regression process, the sample points are also required during the construction of the sparse PCE model for sDD-PCE, while for fDD-PCE, the sample points are only used during regression. Moreover, for em with $p = 3$ (lower order) of Function 1, fDD-PCE is even more accurate with higher efficiency (see underlined numbers). The reason may be that for low-dimensional problems with low-order PCE models, the size of the total polynomial terms is already small and the sparse structure of sDD-PCE is of little help in reducing the number of sample points since additional sample points are required during the selection of important polynomial terms. Therefore, fDD-PCE may produce more accurate results than sDD-PCE since it maintains more information. This will be verified later. Third, with the increase of dimension (from $d = 2, 5$ to $d = 10$), $\mathbf{N}$ is increased significantly with the increase of p for fDD-PCE, causing matrix ill-conditioned problem. So some results ($p = 4$ and 5) even cannot be obtained by fDD-PCE. Specially, for Function 3, the dimension is high ($d = 10$), fDD-PCE cannot produce results for any order p. However, for sDD-PCE, no remarkable increase in $\mathbf{N}$ is noticed since it adopts a sparse PCE model that can adaptively remove the insignificant polynomial terms, while its accuracy is generally improved clearly exhibiting small error relative to MCS. When $p = 5$, only 13 polynomial terms are selected from 3003 total terms for Function 3; while for Function 1, 4 are selected from 21 total terms. Therefore, the larger the dimension, the more obvious the advantage of sDD-PCE over fDD-PCE in efficiency.

In Case 2, the PDFs of all the random inputs are known and assumed to follow common distributions. This is a general case that can be solved by the traditional probabilistic distribution-based PCE methods. The results are shown in **Tables 24–26**. Generally with high PCE order ($p = 5$), the results of sDD-PCE are accurate, demonstrating its effectiveness in dealing with random inputs with known PDFs. Meanwhile, for low-dimensional problem (Function 1), generally sDD-PCE is more accurate with the similar N as fDD-PCE. However, for lower order ($p = 2$) of Function 1, fDD-PCE is even more accurate than sDD-PCE, but with

	*f*DD-PCE			sDD-PCE		
e_m	**0.083**	0.044	0.060	0.710	0.010	0.100
e_v	**0.468**	0.758	0.211	0.975	0.061	0.061
p	3	4	5	3	4	5
N	10	15	21	30	15	20

Table 24. Results of function 1 (Case 2).

	*f*DD-PCE			sDD-PCE		
e_m	24.401	Na	Na	1.244	0.490	0.216
e_v	39.578	Na	Na	4.380	3.271	2.837
p	3	4	5	3	4	5
N	56	126	252	20	20	30

Table 25. Results of function 2 (Case 2).

	fDD-PCE			sDD-PCE		
e_m	Na	Na	Na	3.461	4.432	0.317
e_v	Na	Na	Na	20.155	6.217	4.223
p	3	4	5	3	4	5
N	286	1001	3003	30	30	30

Table 26. Results of function 3 (Case 2).

much smaller N. This observation is consistent with what has been noticed in Case 1 and the reason is that additional sample points are required to selecting important polynomial terms. With the increase of dimension, N is increased significantly with the increase of p for fDD-PCE. However, for sDD-PCE, remarkable improvement in the accuracy is noticed without a remarkable increase in N. These results show great agreements to what has been noticed in Case 1.

In Case 3, the PDFs of all the random inputs are known; however, some of them follow nontrivial distributions. In this case, the traditional gPCE method cannot work well since large errors would be induced in transforming such nontrivial distributions to certain ones in the Askey scheme. The results are shown in **Tables 27–29**, which exhibit great agreements to what has been observed in Case 1 and Case 2. The proposed sDD-PCE method can significantly reduce the number of sample points while with high accuracy. The higher the dimension, the more advantageous the adaptive sparse structure of sDD-PCE can be. In this case, only 11 polynomial terms are selected from 3003 total terms for $d = 10$ with sDD-PCE. Moreover, sDD-PCE can produce accurate and efficient results for nontrivial distributed random inputs.

To verify the guess that for low-dimensional problems with low-order PCE models, fDD-PCE may produce more accurate results than sDD-PCE since it maintains more information.

	fDD-PCE			sDD-PCE		
e_m	1.210	0.854	0.302	1.366	1.044	0.161
e_v	2.321	0.748	0.815	0.805	0.161	0.000
p	3	4	5	3	4	5
N	10	15	21	10	10	10

Table 27. Results of function 1 (Case 3).

	fDD-PCE			sDD-PCE		
e_m	3.324	Na	Na	5.718	1.383	0.680
e_v	7.855	Na	Na	7.634	7.322	2.290
p	3	4	5	3	4	5
N	56	126	252	20	30	30

Table 28. Results of function 2 (Case 3).

	fDD-PCE			sDD-PCE		
e_m	Na	Na	Na	4.114	2.212	0.112
e_v	Na	Na	Na	48.894	15.817	3.101
p	3	4	5	3	4	5
N	286	1001	3003	30	30	30

Table 29. Results of function 3 (Case 3).

Another test is conducted for Function 1 with lower order $p = 2$ with all the three cases, of which the results are shown in **Table 30**. Just as expected, fDD-PCE is clearly more accurate than sDD-PCE while generally with less sample points. For Function 1 with $p = 2$, the total number of polynomial terms is 6, which is very small. With sDD-PCE, only the last polynomial term is removed, while more points are required in removing the insignificant polynomials. So the sparse scheme does not have obvious impact under this circumstance. Therefore, it is concluded that the developed sDD-PCE method is particularly applicable to high-dimensional problems, especially those requiring a high order PCE model.

	Case 1		Case 2		Case 3	
	fDD	sDD	fDD	sDD	fDD	sDD
e_m	0.2801	0.146	0.0366	0.244	0.414	0.807
e_v	0.6344	0.367	0.3577	0.431	0.552	0.477
N	6	7	6	10	6	18

Table 30. Results of function 1 ($p = 2$).

3.3. Summary

The developed sDD-PCE can reduce the number of polynomial terms in the PCE model, thus reducing the computational cost. Generally, the larger the random input dimension, the more obvious the advantage of the developed sDD-PCE over fDD-PCE in efficiency. The sDD-PCE method is much more efficient than fDD-PCE in solving high-dimensional problems, especially those requiring a high order PCE model.

4. Sparse DD-PCE-based robust optimization using trust region

In Section 3, to reduce the computational cost of DD-PCE, a sparse DD-PCE method has been developed by removing some insignificant polynomial terms from the full PCE model, thus decreasing the number of samples for regression in computing PCE coefficients. However, when the sparse DD-PCE is applied to robust optimization, it is conventionally a triple-loop process (see **Figure 9**): the inner one tries to identify the insignificant polynomial terms of the

PCE model (the dash box); the middle is UP; the outer is the search for optima, which clearly is still very time-consuming for problems with expensive simulation models.

As has been mentioned in Section 3, during each optimization iteration, although the sample points required for regression during UP of sDD-PCE are greatly reduced, certain additional number of sample points are required to identify the insignificant polynomial terms by the inner loop. If at some iteration design points, almost the same sparse polynomial terms are retained, the inner loop can clearly be avoided, thus saving the computational cost. To address this issue, the trust region technique widely used in nonlinear optimization is extended in this section. During optimizing, a trust region is dynamically defined. If the updated design point lies in the current trust region, it is considered that the insignificant terms of its PCE model remain unchanged compared to those of the last design point, i.e., the inner loop is eliminated at the updated design point. Meanwhile, to further save the computational cost, the sample points lying in the overlapping area of two adjacent sampling regions are reused for the PCE coefficient regression for the updated design point. The proposed robust optimization procedure employing sparse DD-PCE in conjunction with the trust region scenario is applied to several examples of robust optimization, of which the results are compared to those obtained by the robust optimization without the trust region method, to demonstrate its effectiveness and advantage.

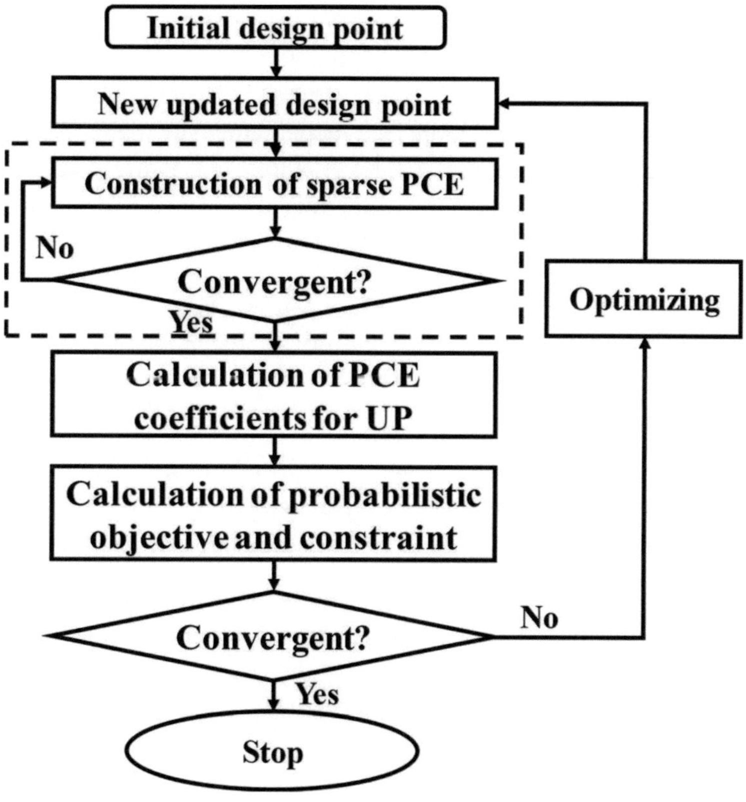

Figure 9. The triple-loop formulation of sDD-PCE-based robust optimization.

4.1. The trust region scenario

The trust region method is a traditional approach that has been widely used in nonlinear numerical optimization [28]. The basic idea of the trust region method is that in the trust region of the current iteration design point, the second-order Taylor expansion is used to approximate the original objective function. If the accuracy of the current second-order Taylor expansion is satisfied, the size of the trust region is increased to speed up the convergence, and if not it is reduced to improve the accuracy of approximation. To reduce the computational cost of design optimization, the idea of the trust region technique has been extended and applied to reliability-based wing design optimization [29], multifidelity wing aero-structural optimization [30], and multifidelity surrogate-based wing optimization [31], which has been widely believed as an efficient strategy in design optimization. For example, when the trust region technique is applied to meta-model-based design optimization, during optimization, the sample points are sequentially generated in the trust region and the radius of the trust region is dynamically adjusted based on the accuracy of the meta-model in the local region.

4.2. Robust design using sparse data-driven PCE and trust region

The scenario of trust region is extended here to reduce the computational cost of sDD-PCE-based robust optimization. The basic idea is that the radius of a trust region is determined by the distance between two successive design points and the variation of the corresponding objective function values. If the updated design point $\mu_{\mathbf{x}}^{k+1}$ lies in the current trust region, it is considered that the insignificant terms of its PCE model remain unchanged compared to those of the last design point $\mu_{\mathbf{X}}^{k}$, i.e., the inner loop is eliminated at the updated design point. Meanwhile, the sample points lying in the overlapping area of two adjacent sampling regions are reused for the PCE coefficient regression for the updated design point to further save the computational cost. Generally, for a practical engineering optimization problem, there is only one performance function that is computationally expensive. Therefore, only one PCE model is required to be constructed and the UP for the rest of the functions can be conveniently implemented by MCS. In this study, it is assumed that the PCE model is only constructed for the objective function and the general steps of the proposed method is as below.

Step 0: Set the iteration number as k = 1 and the initial staring design point $\mu_{\mathbf{x}}^{0}$, do robust optimization with sDD-PCE without trust region and obtain a new design variable $\mu_{\mathbf{x}}^{k}$, where the Latin Hypercube sample points are generated around $\mu_{\mathbf{x}}^{0}$ to calculate the PCE coefficients.

Step 1: After the kth optimization iteration, define/update the trust region at the current obtained new design point $\mu_{\mathbf{x}}^{k}$ as a rectangle with each length as

$$r_1 = max\left\{\zeta_1\left|\mu_{\mathbf{x}}^{k}\right|_2, \zeta_2\right\}, r_2 = max\left\{\zeta_1\left|Y^k\right|, \zeta_2\right\} \tag{24}$$

where $|\mu_{\mathbf{x}}^{k}|_2 = \sqrt{\sum_{i=1}^{d}(\mu_{\mathbf{x}_i}^{k})^2}$ and $|Y^k|$ is the absolute value of corresponding objective function at $\mu_{\mathbf{x}}^{k}$, i.e., $|Y^k| = abs\left(Y(\mu_{\mathbf{x}}^{k})\right)$; ζ_1 and ζ_2 are user-defined parameters, which can be constants or functions with respect to the iteration number k.

Step 2: During the $(k + 1)$th optimization iteration, the obtained new design point is $\mu_{\mathbf{x}}^{k+1}$. Before conducting UP, calculate the variation between two successive design points $\mu_{\mathbf{x}}^{k}$ and $\mu_{\mathbf{x}}^{k+1}$ as $\Delta\mathbf{x} = |\mu_{\mathbf{x}}^{k+1} - \mu_{\mathbf{x}}^{k}|_2 = \sqrt{\sum_{i=1}^{d} (\mu_{\mathbf{x}_i}^{k+1} - \mu_{\mathbf{x}_i}^{k})^2}$ and the variation of the objective function $\Delta Y = |Y^{k+1}(\mu_{\mathbf{x}}^{k+1}) - Y^{k}(\mu_{\mathbf{x}}^{k})|$.

Step 3: If $\Delta\mathbf{X} \le r_2$ and $\Delta Y \le r_2$ both are satisfied, $\mu_{\mathbf{x}}^{k+1}$ is considered to be located in the trust region of $\mu_{\mathbf{x}}^{k}$ defined in Eq. (45), and go to Step 4; if either $\Delta\mathbf{X} \le r_1$ or $\Delta Y \le r_2$ cannot be satisfied, $\mu_{\mathbf{x}}^{k+1}$ is considered to be not located in the trust region of $\mu_{\mathbf{x}}^{k}$ defined in Eq. (45), and go to Step 5.

Step 4: The retained polynomial terms $\Phi_i(x)$ at the updated new design point $\mu_{\mathbf{x}}^{k+1}$ are kept as the same as those for the last design point $\mu_{\mathbf{x}}^{k}$, indicating that the inner loop of UP conducted on $\mu_{\mathbf{x}}^{k+1}$ is removed. The Latin Hypercube sample points are generated around $\mu_{\mathbf{x}}^{k+1}$ according to the distribution type and parameters of **X** with the same number of sample points as that used at the last design point $\mu_{\mathbf{x}}^{k}$ to calculate the PCE coefficients. Meanwhile, the sample points located in the overlapping area of the two successive sampling regions are identified and reused for PCE coefficients calculation to improve the accuracy.

Step 5: The inner loop is conducted on the updated design point $\mu_{\mathbf{x}}^{k+1}$ to detect the significant polynomial terms. Similarly, the sample points located in the overlapping area of the two successive sampling regions are also reused at the updated design point $\mu_{\mathbf{x}}^{k+1}$ in detecting the significant polynomial terms and calculating the PCE coefficients to save the computational cost.

Step 6: Set $k = k + 1$, based on the results of UP, search for the next updated new design point $\mu_{\mathbf{x}}^{k+1}$ and go to Step 1.

The above procedure will continue until the convergent criterion is satisfied. **Figure 10** shows the case that the sample points in the previous optimization iteration are reused in the two successive iterations. As is seen that two points are located in the overlapping area of two successive sampling regions, thus are reused in the next iteration for regression to identify the significant polynomials/calculate the PCE coefficients. In this way, the computational cost can be further reduced.

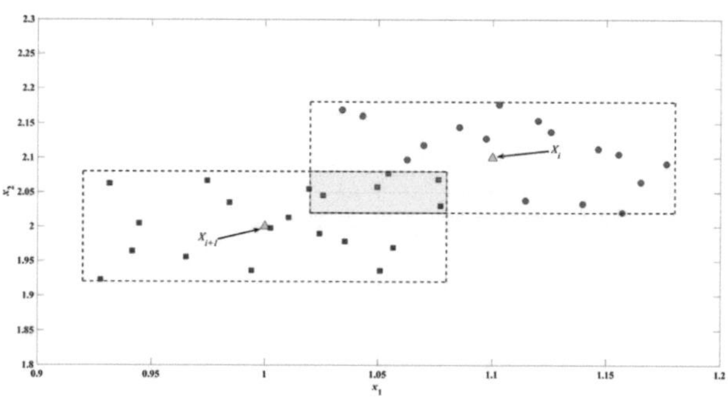

Figure 10. Illustration of the reuse of sample points.

4.3. Comparative studies

The first example is the Ackley Function:

$$f(\mathbf{X}) = -20\exp\left(-0.2\sqrt{\frac{1}{d}\sum_{j=1}^{d}X_j^2}\right) - \exp\left(\frac{1}{d}\sum_{j=1}^{d}\cos\left(2\pi X_j\right)\right) + 22.71282, d = 10 \tag{25}$$

The robust design optimization of this example is:

$$\begin{aligned} &\min F = \mu_f + k\sigma_f \\ &-10 \leq \mu_{X_j} \leq 10, j = 1, 2, \ldots, 10 \end{aligned} \tag{26}$$

All the design variables are considered to follow uniform distribution with variation of ± 0.2 around their mean values and k in Eq. (26) is set as $k = 20$. In this study, the fmincon function in Matlab is used for optimization, and ζ_1 and ζ_2 in Eq. (45) are set as $\zeta_1 = 0.5$ and $\zeta_2 = 0.5$. Meanwhile, the obtained optimal design variables of sDD-PCE-based robust design with and without trust region scenario as well as the deterministic design without considering any uncertainties are respectively substituted into Eq. (26) through MCS (with $1e^6$ runs) to calculate the mean μ_f and standard deviation σ_f of the objective function.

The results are shown in **Table 31**, from which it is found that compared to the robust optimization without the trust region scenario (denoted by without), the obtained performance results (μ_f, σ_f, and F) of the robust optimization with the trust region scenario (denoted by with) are comparable. However, the number of function calls (denoted as Funcall) is clearly reduced. The decrease in computational cost is attributed to the application of trust region scenario and the reusing of sample points. Meanwhile, the optimal designs of the two robust designs are both less sensitive to uncertainties (smaller σ_f) compared to the results of deterministic design (denoted by DD). These results demonstrate the effective and advantage of the proposed method.

The second example is the robust design optimization of an automobile torque arm, shown in **Figure 11**.

In this problem, the four geometrical parameters (a, d_1, d_2, and l) are considered as design variables, and the yielding strength S_y, Young's modulus E, and the applied force Q are deterministic parameters.

$$\begin{aligned} &\min f(a, d_1, d_2, l) = \frac{\pi a d_2^2}{4} + 2\left(l - \frac{d_1}{2} - \frac{d_2}{2}\right)a^2 \\ &s.t.\ g_1(a, d_2, l) = \frac{Q(2l - d_2)d_2}{4IS_y} - 1.0 \leq 0 \\ &g_2(a, d_1, d_2, l) = 1.0 - \frac{\pi^2 E a^4}{3(2l - d_1 - d_2)^2}\frac{d_2 - d_1}{Ql} \leq 0 \\ &5 \leq a \leq 15, 45 \leq d_1 \leq 55, 55 \leq d_2 \leq 65, 110 \leq l \leq 210 \end{aligned} \tag{27}$$

	μ_X^*	μ_f	σ_f	F	Funcall
DD	[0,0,0,0,0,0,0,0,0,0]	1.8839	0.4390	10.6639	–
with	[0.6246,0.7066,0.6687,0.7796,0.5744, 0.6784,0.7470,0.6333,0.6578,0.6904]	4.5014	0.1377	7.2554	12,735
without	[0.6564,0.6935,0.6984,0.7036,0.6691, 0.0299,0.0141,0.6407,0.0205,0.0038]	3.7457	0.2003	7.7517	16,840

Table 31. Results of the Ackley Function.

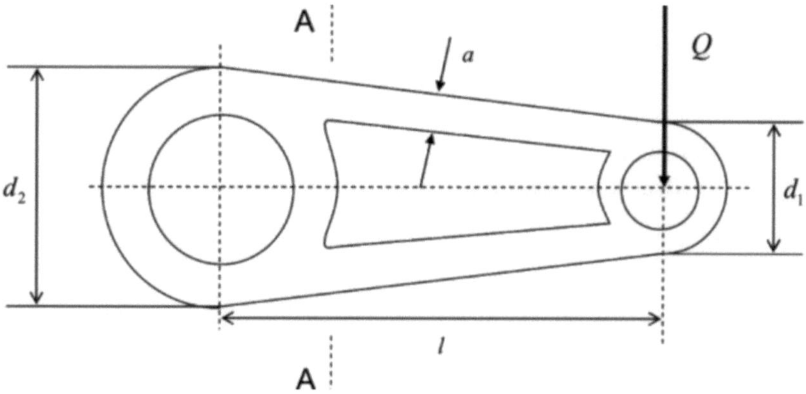

Figure 11. Automobile torque arm.

where the objective function f represents the volume of the arm, the first constraint g_1 denotes the yielding failure at section A-A, the second constraint g_2 denotes the buckling failure at the two connecting rods, and $I = a^2(d_2 - a)^2/2 + a^4/6$.

The distribution parameters of the four design variables and design parameters are shown in **Table 32**.

Random variables	Distribution	Lower bound	Upper bound
a	Uniform	μ_a −0.5 mm	μ_a +0.5 mm
d_1	Uniform	μ_{d1} −0.5 mm	μ_{d1} +0.5 mm
d_2	Uniform	μ_{d2} −0.5 mm	μ_{d2} +0.5 mm
l	Uniform	μ_l −0.5 mm	μ_l +0.5 mm
Parameters		**Values**	
Q	Deterministic	5500 N	
S_y	Deterministic	170 N/mm^2	
E	Deterministic	2.1×10^{10} N/mm^2	

Table 32. Distribution parameters for design variables and design parameters.

The corresponding robust design optimization model is formulated as

$$\begin{aligned} &\min F = \omega_1 \frac{\mu_f}{\mu_f^*} + \omega_2 \frac{\sigma_f}{\sigma_f^*}, \omega_1 = 0.5, \omega_2 = 0.5 \\ &s.t. \;\; G_1(a, d_2, l) = \mu_{g_1} + k\sigma_{g_1} \le 0 \\ &\quad\;\; G_2(a, d_1, d_2, l) = \mu_{g_2} + k\sigma_{g_2} \le 0 \\ &\quad\;\; 5 \le \mu_a \le 15, 45 \le \mu_{d_1} \le 55, 55 \le \mu_{d_2} \le 65, 110 \le \mu_l \le 210 \end{aligned} \tag{28}$$

As has been mentioned above, the PCE model is only constructed for the objective function and the results are shown in **Table 33**. It is noticed that the robust optimization designs with and without the trust region scenario yields comparable results, while the function calls (objective function calls) required by design with trust region is evidently smaller. The deterministic design cannot even obtain a feasible optimal solution with both constraint violated (>0), since it does not consider uncertainties during design. These results further demonstrate the effectiveness and advantage of the proposed method.

4.4. Summary

The employment of the trust region in sDD-PCE-based robust optimization can evidently reduce the computational cost. However, the determination of the trust region in this chapter is still very subjective and a more rigorous method should be explored. In this section as well as Section 3, the scenarios of sparse PCE and trust region are only employed to DD-PCE to save the computational cost. However, the methods proposed here are also applicable to other PCE approaches, such as gPCE and GS-PCE.

In this chapter, the latest advances in PCE theory and approach for probabilistic UP are comprehensively presented in detail. However, it does not limit the application of PCE to nonprobabilistic UP to address epistemic uncertainties. Sudret and Schöbi have proposed a two-level metamodeling approach using nonintrusive sparse PCE to surrogate the exact computational model to facilitate the uncertainty quantification analysis, in which the input variables are modeled by probability-boxes (*p*-boxes), accounting for both aleatory and epistemic uncertainty [32]. The Fuzzy uncertainty propagation in composites has been implemented using Gram-Schmidt polynomial chaos expansion, in which the parameter uncertainties are represented by fuzzy membership functions [5]. A general framework has been proposed for a dynamical uncertain system to deal with both aleatory and epistemic uncertainty using PCE, where the uncertain parameters are described through random variables and/or fuzzy variables [33]. The mix UP approach is proposed, in which the inner loop PDFs are calculated using the PCE, and outer loop bounds can be computed with optimization-based interval

	μ_X^*	μ_f	σ_f	F	G_1	G_2	Funcall
DD	[8.13, 55.00, 55.00, 110.00]	2.6616e^4	1.2171e^3	1	**0.1848**	**5.1509e^4**	82
with	[8.53, 54.10, 58.67, 111.03]	3.1027e^4	1.3355e^3	1.1315	−0.0123	−1.1833e^5	658
without	[8.57, 52.68, 57.50, 110.00]	3.0332e^4	1.3093e^3	1.1077	−4.0000e^{-4}	−1.2913e^2	1283

Table 33. Results of automobile torque arm.

estimation [34]. PCE has also been applied for solving Bayesian inverse problem as "surrogate posterior." However, it has been indicated that the accuracy cannot always be ensured by PCE since a sufficiently accurate PCE for this problem requires a high order, making PCE impractical compared to directly sampling the posterior [35].

Author details

Shuxing Yang*, Fenfen Xiong and Fenggang Wang

*Address all correspondence to: yangshx@bit.edu.cn

School of Aerospace Engineering, Beijing Institute of Technology, Beijing, China

References

[1] Matthies HG. Quantifying uncertainty: Modern computational representation of probability and applications. Extreme Man-Made and Natural Hazards in Dynamics of Structures. Springer Netherlands, 2007;105–135

[2] Kiureghian AD, Ditlevsen O. Aleatory or epistemic? Does it matter? Structural Safety. 2009;**31**(2):105–112

[3] Swiler LP, Romero VJ. A survey of advanced probabilistic uncertainty propagation and sensitivity analysis methods. Proposed for presentation at the 2012 Joint Army Navy NASA Air Force Combustion/Propulsion Joint Subcommittee Meeting; December 3-7, 2012; Monterey, CA

[4] Du X, Chen W. A most probable point-based method for efficient uncertainty analysis. Journal of Design & Manufacturing Automation. 2001;**4**(1):47–66

[5] Mukhopadhyay S, Khodaparast H, Adhikari S. Fuzzy uncertainty propagation in composites using Gram–Schmidt polynomial chaos expansion. Applied Mathematical Modelling. 2016; **40**(7–8):4412–4428

[6] Jiang C, Zheng J, Ni BY, Han X. A probabilistic and interval hybrid reliability analysis method for structures with correlated uncertain parameters. International Journal of Computational Methods. 2015;**12**(4):1540006 (24 pages)

[7] Terejanu G, Singla P, Singh T, Scott PD. Approximate interval method for epistemic uncertainty propagation using polynomial chaos and evidence theory. IEEE American Control Conference; 30 June–2 July 2010; Marriott Waterfront, Baltimore, MD, USA.

[8] Lee SH, Chen W. A comparative study of uncertainty propagation methods for black-box-type problems. Structural & Multidisciplinary Optimization. 2009;**37**(3):239–253

[9] Dodson M, Parks GT. Robust aerodynamic design optimization using polynomial chaos. Journal of Aircraft. 2009;**46**(2):635–646

[10] Coelho R, Bouillard P. Multi-objective reliability-based optimization with stochastic metamodels. Evolutionary Computation. 2011;**19**(4):525–560

[11] Xiu D, Karniadakis GE. The wiener-askey polynomial chaos for stochastic differential equations. SIAM Journal on Scientific Computing. 2002;**24**(2):619–644

[12] Wiener N. The homogeneous chaos. American Journal of Mathematics. 1938;**60**(1):897–936

[13] Fan et al. Parameter uncertainty and temporal dynamics of sensitivity for hydrologic models: A hybrid sequential data assimilation and probabilistic collocation method. Environmental Modelling & Software. 2016;**86**:30–49

[14] Guerine A, Hami AE, Walha L, et al. A polynomial chaos method for the analysis of the dynamic behavior of uncertain gear friction system. European Journal of Mechanics - A/ Solids. 2016;**59**:76-84

[15] Meecham WC, Siegel A. Wiener-Hermite expansion in model turbulence at large Reynolds numbers. Physics of Fluids (1958-1988). 1964;**7**(8):1178–1190. DOI: 10.1063/1.1711359

[16] Witteveen JAS, Bijl H. Modeling arbitrary uncertainties using Gram-Schmidt polynomial chaos. 44th AIAA Aerospace Sciences Meeting and Exhibit; 9–12 January 2006; Reno, Nevada

[17] Wan X, Karniadakis GE. Multi-element generalized polynomial chaos for arbitrary probability measures. SIAM Journal on Scientific Computing. 2006;**28**(3):901–928

[18] Oladyshkin S, Nowak W. Data-driven uncertainty quantification using the arbitrary polynomial chaos expansion. Reliability Engineering & System Safety. 2012;**106**(4):179–190

[19] Hosder S, Walters RW, Balch M. Efficient sampling for non-intrusive polynomial chaos applications with multiple uncertain input variables. 48th AIAA/ASME/ASCE/AHS/ASC Structures, Structural Dynamics and Materials Conference; 23–26 April 2007; Honolulu, Hawall

[20] Eldred MS. Recent advances in non-intrusive polynomial chaos and stochastic collocation methods for uncertainty analysis and design. 50th AIAA/ASME/ASCE/AHS/ASC Structures, Structural Dynamics, and Materials Conference; 4–7 May 2009; Palm Springs, California

[21] Abramowitz M, Stegun I, Mcquarrie D A. Handbook of Mathematical Functions. Dover Publications, New York,1964

[22] Xiong F, Greene S, Chen W, Xiong Y, Yang S A new sparse grid based method for uncertainty propagation. Structural & Multidisciplinary Optimization. 2009;**41**(3):335–349

[23] Efron B, Hastie T, Johnstone I, Tibshirani R. Least angle regression. Mathematics. 2004;**32** (2):407–499

[24] Tatang MA, Pan W, Prinn RG, McRae GJ. An efficient method for parametric uncertainty analysis of numerical geophysical models. Journal of Geophysics Research. 1997;**102** (D18):21925–21932

[25] Hu C, Youn BD. Adaptive-sparse polynomial chaos expansion for reliability analysis and design of complex engineering systems. Structural & Multidisciplinary Optimization. 2011; **43**(3):419–442

[26] Wan X, Karniadakis GE. An adaptive multi-element generalized polynomial chaos method for stochastic differential equations. Journal of Computational Physics. 2005;**209** (2):617–642

[27] Tu J, Cheng YP. An integrated stochastic design framework using cross-validated multivariate metamodeling methods. SAE Technical Paper 2003-01-0876; 2003

[28] Nocedal J, Wright S. Numerical Optimization. Springer Series in Operations Research and Financial Engineering. New York: Springer; 2006

[29] Elham A, Tooren MJLV. Trust region filter-SQP method for multi-fidelity wing aerostructural optimization. Variational Analysis and Aerospace Engineering. 2016;**116**:247–267

[30] Kim S, Ahn J, Kwon JH. Reliability based wing design optimization using trust region framework. 10th AIAA/ISSMO Multidisciplinary Analysis and Optimization Conference; 30 August–1 September 2004; Albany, New York

[31] Robinson TD, Eldred MS, Willcox KE, Haimes R. Surrogate-based optimization using multifidelity models with variable parameterization and corrected space mapping. AIAA Journal. 2008;**46**(11):2814–2822

[32] Schöbi R, Sudret B. Uncertainty propagation of p-boxes using sparse polynomial chaos expansions. 2016, **339**:307–327

[33] Jacquelin E, Friswell MI, Adhikari S, Dessombz O, Sinou J. Polynomial chaos expansion with random and fuzzy variables. Mechanical Systems and Signal Processing. 2016;**75** (15):41–56

[34] Eldred MS, Swiler LP, Tang G. Mixed aleatory-epistemic uncertainty quantification with stochastic expansions and optimization-based interval estimation. Reliability Engineering and System Safety. 2011;**96**(9):1092–1113

[35] Lu F, Morzfeld M, Tu X, Chorin AJ. Limitations of polynomial chaos expansions in the Bayesian solution of inverse problems. Journal of Computational Physics. 2014;**282** (C):138–147

Chapter 3

State-of-the-Art Nonprobabilistic Finite Element Analyses

Wang Lei, Qiu Zhiping and Zheng Yuning

Additional information is available at the end of the chapter

http://dx.doi.org/10.5772/intechopen.68154

Abstract

The finite element analysis of a mechanical system is conventionally performed in the context of deterministic inputs. However, uncertainties associated with material properties, geometric dimensions, subjective experiences, boundary conditions, and external loads are ubiquitous in engineering applications. The most popular techniques to handle these uncertain parameters are the probabilistic methods, in which uncertainties are modeled as random variables or stochastic processes based on a large amount of statistical information on each uncertain parameter. Nevertheless, subjective results could be obtained if insufficient information unavailable and nonprobabilistic methods can be alternatively employed, which has led to elegant procedures for the nonprobabilistic finite element analysis. In this chapter, each nonprobabilistic finite element analysis method can be decomposed as two individual parts, i.e., the core algorithm and preprocessing procedure. In this context, four types of algorithms and two typical preprocessing procedures as well as their effectiveness were described in detail, based on which novel hybrid algorithms can be conceived for the specific problems and the future work in this research field can be fostered.

Keywords: interval finite element method, fuzzy finite element method, arithmetic approach, perturbation approach, sampling approach, optimization approach, subinterval technique, surrogate model

1. Introduction

The traditional finite element analysis (FEA) was performed in the context of deterministic parameters. However, uncertainties associated with material properties, geometric dimensions, and external loads are always unavoidable in engineering. The ability to include uncertainties is of great value for a design engineer. In the last decade, criticism has arisen regarding the general application of the probabilistic concept. Especially when the statistical information on uncertainties is limited [1], the subjective probabilistic analysis result may be obtained by the probabilistic method [2, 3], which proves to be of little value and does not justify the high computational cost [3–5]. Consequently, nonprobabilistic concepts have been introduced.

In this context, interval and fuzzy approaches are gaining more and more momentum for the uncertainty analysis and optimization of numerical models in their descriptions. In the interval approach, uncertainties are considered to be contained within a predefined range and only the lower and upper bounds are necessary for each uncertain parameter. The fuzzy approach further extends this methodology by the α-level technique, where α stands for the extent that a specific value is member of the range of possible input values. From this viewpoint, a fuzzy analysis requires the consecutive solution for a number of interval analysis based on the α-level technique [6]. For this reason, current researches on nonprobabilistic uncertainty propagation mainly focus on the solution and implementation of the interval analysis. In the past decades, the interval and fuzzy concepts in FEA have been studied extensively and some typical solution schemes for the interval FEA (IFEA) and fuzzy FEA (FFEA) were developed. This chapter is to give an overview of state-of-the-art numerical implementations of IFEA and FFEA in applied mechanics.

FFEA aims to obtain a fuzzy description of an FEA result, starting from fuzzy descriptions of all uncertainties. The α-level technique subdivides the membership function range into a number of discrete α-levels. The α-cuts of the input quantities are defined as $x_{i_\alpha} = \{x_i \in X_i, \mu_{\tilde{x}_i}(x_i) \geq \alpha\}$ where $\mu_{\tilde{x}}(x)$ is the membership function. This means that an α-cut is the interval resulting from intersecting the membership function at $\mu_{\tilde{x}_i}(x_i) = \alpha$. The α-level interval describes the grade of membership to the fuzzy set for each element in the domain and enables the representation of a value that is only to a certain degree member of the set. However, the confidence interval defined in statistics is the range of likely values for a population parameter, such as the population mean. The selection of a confidence level for an interval determines the probability that confidence interval produced will contain the true parameter value. The intersection with the membership function of the input uncertainties on each α-level results in an interval and IFEA is formulated, resulting in an interval for the output on the considered α-level. The fuzzy solution is finally assembled from the resulting intervals on each sublevel. The IFEA is based on the interval description of uncertainties and its goal is to capture the range of specific output quantities of interest that corresponds to a given interval description of input uncertainties. For the sake of simplicity, the static analysis of a mechanical system is adopted in this chapter to explain current IFEA schemes. The FEA equation can be expressed in a general form as follows:

$$\mathbf{K}(\mathbf{p})\mathbf{U}(\mathbf{p}) = \mathbf{F}(\mathbf{p}) \tag{1}$$

where **K** and **F** stand for the stiffness matrix and load vector, respectively; **U** represents the static response vector; and **p** is the input parameter vector of the mechanical system. In the IFEA, **p** is quantified as an interval input vector $\mathbf{p}^{\mathrm{I}}$ and shown in **Figure 1**.

where p_i^c is the nominal value, Δp_i is the interval radius. Then, the IFEA equation is accordingly rewritten as follows:

$$\mathbf{K}(\mathbf{p}^{\mathrm{I}})\mathbf{U}(\mathbf{p}^{\mathrm{I}}) = \mathbf{F}(\mathbf{p}^{\mathrm{I}}) \tag{2}$$

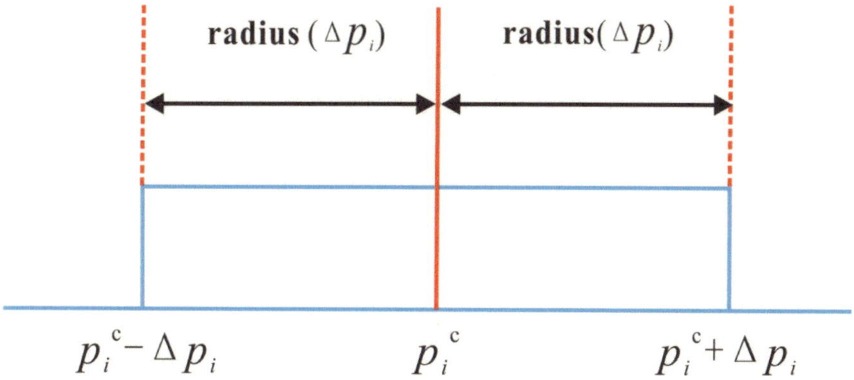

Figure 1. The diagram of interval variable p.

where the superscript "I" hereinafter represents an interval input. The exact solution set of this interval equation can be expressed as:

$$\mathbf{U} = \{\overline{\mathbf{U}} | \mathbf{K}(\overline{\mathbf{p}})\overline{\mathbf{U}} = \mathbf{F}(\overline{\mathbf{p}}), \forall \overline{\mathbf{p}} \in \mathbf{p}^{\mathrm{I}}\} \tag{3}$$

It is noted that interdependencies among entries of the response vector are introduced due to sharing the common input vector and a nonconvex polyhedron is always defined [7], which makes it extremely difficult to obtain the exact solution [5]. However, only individual ranges of some components in the response vector are of interest for real-life problems. Therefore, by neglecting the aforementioned interdependencies, the smallest hypercube approximation denoted as $\mathbf{U}^{\mathrm{I}}$ around the exact solution set is an alternative object for current IFEA. The kth component of $\mathbf{U}^{\mathrm{I}}$ is expressed as follows:

$$U_k^{\mathrm{I}} = \left[U_k^{\mathrm{L}}, U_k^{\mathrm{U}}\right] = \left[\min_{\mathbf{p} \in \mathbf{p}^{\mathrm{I}}} U_k(\mathbf{p}), \max_{\mathbf{p} \in \mathbf{p}^{\mathrm{I}}} U_k(\mathbf{p})\right], \quad k = 1, 2, \ldots, N \tag{4}$$

where superscripts "L" and "U" represent the lower and upper bounds of an interval variable, respectively; N is the total number of response components of interest. Accordingly, the smallest hypercube solution of IFEA equation is expressed as:

$$\mathbf{U}^{\mathrm{I}} = \left[U_1^{\mathrm{I}}, U_2^{\mathrm{I}}, \ldots, U_N^{\mathrm{I}}\right]^{\mathrm{T}} \tag{5}$$

where "T" is a transposition operator.

2. Core algorithms

From published literatures, four types of algorithms for IFEA have been well established. Most of the current schemes are formulated based on these core algorithms.

2.1. Arithmetic approach

The key point of arithmetic approach is to translate the complete deterministic numerical FE procedure to an interval procedure using the arithmetic operations. Each substep of the interval algorithm calculates the range of the intermediate subfunction instead of the deterministic result. Based on this principle, the interval bounds of the output can be obtained. The original solution procedure for IFEA is the interval arithmetic approaches [7–10], in which all basic deterministic algebraic operations are replaced by their interval arithmetic counterparts.

The major advantage of the arithmetic approach is its simplicity. However, the major drawback of this method is its repeated vulnerability to conservatism. It is shown that these methods suffer considerably from the overestimation effect, also referred to as the dependency problem, and for the real-life problems, the resulting overestimation may render the final result totally useless [5]. A simple example is shown as follows. Consider the function

$$f(x) = x^2 - x + 1 \tag{6}$$

applied on the interval $x = [0, 1]$. Applying arithmetic approach, both terms are assumed independently. This leads to the interval solution $f(x) = [0, 2]$. However, the exact range of the function equals $f(x) = \left[\frac{3}{4}, 1\right]$. That is to say, an arithmetic interval operation introduces conservatism in its result if neglecting the correlation that exists between the operands. Besides, the integration of interval arithmetic approaches with software for FEA is also a challenge in real applications.

2.2. Perturbation approach

The perturbation approach has been widely applied in structural response analyses and other applications. Compared to arithmetic approaches, perturbation methods are more popular due to its simplicity and efficiency in IFEA and can be available in the original, improved, and modified versions.

2.2.1. Original version

The first-order Taylor expansions of the interval stiffness matrix and load vector at the nominal (mid-) values of interval parameters were firstly obtained as:

$$\begin{aligned} \mathbf{K}(\mathbf{p}^{\mathrm{I}}) &= \mathbf{K}(\mathbf{p}^{\mathrm{c}}) + \sum_{i=1}^{n} \frac{\partial \mathbf{K}(\mathbf{p}^{\mathrm{c}})}{\partial p_i} \Delta p_i^{\mathrm{I}} = \mathbf{K}^{\mathrm{c}} + \Delta \mathbf{K}^{\mathrm{I}} \\ \mathbf{F}(\mathbf{p}^{\mathrm{I}}) &= \mathbf{F}(\mathbf{p}^{\mathrm{c}}) + \sum_{i=1}^{n} \frac{\partial \mathbf{F}(\mathbf{p}^{\mathrm{c}})}{\partial p_i} \Delta p_i^{\mathrm{I}} = \mathbf{F}^{\mathrm{c}} + \Delta \mathbf{F}^{\mathrm{I}} \end{aligned} \tag{7}$$

where $\mathbf{p}^{\mathrm{c}}$ is the nominal (mid-) value of the interval input vector and $\Delta p_i^{\mathrm{I}} = [-\Delta p_i, \Delta p_i]$ is the interval radius of the *i*th interval parameter, i.e.,

$$\begin{aligned} \mathbf{p}^{c} &= (\mathbf{p}^{U} + \mathbf{p}^{L})/2 = [p_1^c, p_2^c, \ldots, p_n^c]^T \\ \Delta\mathbf{p} &= (\mathbf{p}^{U} - \mathbf{p}^{L})/2 = [\Delta p_1, \Delta p_2, \ldots, \Delta p_n]^T \end{aligned} \tag{8}$$

And the interval radiuses of the stiffness matrix and load vector in Eq. (7) are expressed as follows, respectively.

$$\begin{aligned} \Delta\mathbf{K}^{I} &= \sum_{i=1}^{n} \frac{\partial \mathbf{K}(\mathbf{p}^{c})}{\partial p_i} \Delta p_i^{I} = [-\Delta\mathbf{K}, \Delta\mathbf{K}] \\ \Delta\mathbf{F}^{I} &= \sum_{i=1}^{n} \frac{\partial \mathbf{F}(\mathbf{p}^{c})}{\partial p_i} \Delta p_i^{I} = [-\Delta\mathbf{F}, \Delta\mathbf{F}] \end{aligned} \tag{9}$$

The FEA model for the perturbed system can be rewritten as follows:

$$(\mathbf{K}^{c} + \Delta\mathbf{K}^{I})(\mathbf{U}^{c} + \Delta\mathbf{U}^{I}) = \mathbf{F}^{c} + \Delta\mathbf{F}^{I} \tag{10}$$

By expanding Eq. (10) and neglecting the second-order perturbed term, the following equations can be obtained.

$$\begin{aligned} \mathbf{U}^{c} &= (\mathbf{K}^{c})^{-1}\mathbf{F}^{c} \\ \mathbf{K}^{c}\Delta\mathbf{U}^{I} &= \Delta\mathbf{F}^{I} - \Delta\mathbf{K}^{I}(\mathbf{K}^{c})^{-1}\mathbf{F}^{c} \end{aligned} \tag{11}$$

Substituting Eq. (10) into Eq. (11) yields the interval radius of the response vector as:

$$\Delta\mathbf{U}^{I} = (\mathbf{K}^{c})^{-1}\sum_{i=1}^{n} \frac{\partial \mathbf{F}(\mathbf{p}^{c})}{\partial p_i} \Delta p_i^{I} - (\mathbf{K}^{c})^{-1}\sum_{i=1}^{n} \frac{\partial \mathbf{K}(\mathbf{p}^{c})}{\partial p_i} \Delta p_i^{I} (\mathbf{K}^{c})^{-1}\mathbf{F}^{c} \tag{12}$$

And the radius vector of the response vector is estimated in the original interval perturbation method [11] as follows:

$$\Delta\mathbf{U} = \sum_{i=1}^{n} \left(\left|(\mathbf{K}^{c})^{-1}\right| \left|\frac{\partial \mathbf{F}(\mathbf{p}^{c})}{\partial p_i}\right| + \left|(\mathbf{K}^{c})^{-1}\right| \left|\frac{\partial \mathbf{K}(\mathbf{p}^{c})}{\partial p_i}\right| \left|(\mathbf{K}^{c})^{-1}\right| \left|\mathbf{F}^{c}\right| \right) \Delta p_i \tag{13}$$

The smallest hypercube solution can thus be determined as:

$$\mathbf{U}^{I} = [\mathbf{U}^{c} - \Delta\mathbf{U}, \mathbf{U}^{c} + \Delta\mathbf{U}] \tag{14}$$

The major drawback of this method is that a significant overestimation is introduced by the original interval perturbation method, indicating that it applies to the interval analysis of problems with "small" interval parameters.

2.2.2. *Improved version*

The most typical improved interval perturbation method was proposed in Ref. [12], in which the radius vector of the response vector was calculated as follows:

$$\Delta \mathbf{U} = \sum_{i=1}^{n} \left| (\mathbf{K}^{c})^{-1} \frac{\partial \mathbf{F}(\mathbf{p}^{c})}{\partial p_i} - (\mathbf{K}^{c})^{-1} \frac{\partial \mathbf{K}(\mathbf{p}^{c})}{\partial p_i} (\mathbf{K}^{c})^{-1} \mathbf{F}^{c} \right| \Delta p_i \tag{15}$$

Accordingly, the smallest hypercube solution of IFEA can also be determined by Eq. (14). Although with better accuracy compared to the original one, an interval translation effect, i.e., the translation of the resulting interval w.r.t. the accurate one, is always introduced by the improved interval perturbation method.

2.2.3. *Modified versions*

Compared with the original version of the perturbation approach where only first-order terms are considered, the main aspect of the following two modified interval perturbation methods [13, 14] is that the interval bounds are calculated by retaining part of higher order terms in Neumann series. Therefore, the modified methods can obtain more accurate response bounds. The key expressions are summarized as follows:

$$\begin{aligned} \mathbf{U}^{c} &= (\mathbf{K}^{c})^{-1} \left[\mathbf{I} + \sum_{i=1}^{n} \mathbf{E}_i^{c} \right] \mathbf{F}^{c} \\ \Delta \mathbf{U}^{I} &= \sum_{k=1}^{n} \left\{ (\mathbf{K}^{c})^{-1} \left[\mathbf{I} + \sum_{i=1}^{n} \mathbf{E}_i^{c} \right] \frac{\partial \mathbf{F}(\mathbf{p}^{c})}{\partial p_k} \right\} \Delta p_k^{I} + \sum_{i=1}^{n} (\mathbf{K}^{c})^{-1} \Delta \mathbf{E}_i^{I} \mathbf{F}^{c} \end{aligned} \tag{16}$$

where

$$\begin{aligned} \mathbf{E}_i^{c} &= \left((\mathbf{I} + \Delta p_i \mathbf{K}_i)^{-1} + (\mathbf{I} - \Delta p_i \mathbf{K}_i)^{-1} - 2\mathbf{I} \right) / 2 \\ \Delta \mathbf{E}_i &= \left| (\mathbf{I} + \Delta p_i \mathbf{K}_i)^{-1} - (\mathbf{I} - \Delta p_i \mathbf{K}_i)^{-1} \right| / 2 \end{aligned} \tag{17}$$

and

$$\mathbf{K}_i = \frac{\partial \mathbf{K}(\mathbf{p}^{c})}{\partial p_i} (\mathbf{K}^{c})^{-1} \tag{18}$$

Different estimations of the radius vector of the response vector were, respectively, obtained as follows:

$$\Delta \mathbf{U} = \left| \sum_{k=1}^{n} \left\{ (\mathbf{K}^{c})^{-1} \left[\mathbf{I} + \sum_{i=1}^{n} \mathbf{E}_i^{c} \right] \frac{\partial \mathbf{F}(\mathbf{p}^{c})}{\partial p_k} \right\} \Delta p_k + \sum_{i=1}^{n} (\mathbf{K}^{c})^{-1} \Delta \mathbf{E}_i \mathbf{F}^{c} \right| \tag{19}$$

$$\Delta \mathbf{U} = \sum_{k=1}^{n} \left| (\mathbf{K}^{c})^{-1} \left[\mathbf{I} + \sum_{i=1}^{n} \mathbf{E}_i^{c} \right] \frac{\partial \mathbf{F}(p^{c})}{\partial p_k} \right| \Delta p_k + \sum_{i=1}^{n} \left| (\mathbf{K}^{c})^{-1} \Delta \mathbf{E}_i \mathbf{F}^{c} \right| \tag{20}$$

It should be pointed out that significant unpredicted estimation is always introduced by Eqs. (19) and (20). A more reasonable estimation of the radius vector of the response vector is simultaneously determined herein as follows:

$$\Delta\mathbf{U} = \sum_{k=1}^{n} \left| (\mathbf{K}^c)^{-1} \left[\mathbf{I} + \sum_{i=1}^{n} \mathbf{E}_i^c \right] \frac{\partial \mathbf{F}(\mathbf{p}^c)}{\partial p_k} \right| \Delta p_k + \sum_{i=1}^{n} \left| (\mathbf{K}^c)^{-1} \right| \Delta\mathbf{E}_i \left| \mathbf{F}^c \right| \tag{21}$$

And a slight conservatism is alternatively resulted in by Eq. (21). The smallest hypercube solution for the IFEA is finally determined as Eq. (14). It is worth mentioning that the spectral radius of $(\mathbf{K}^c)^{-1}\Delta\mathbf{K}$ increases with the increase in $\Delta\mathbf{K}^I$. $(\mathbf{K}^c + \Delta\mathbf{K})^{-1}$ can be expanded with a Neumann series if and only if $\|(\mathbf{K}^c)^{-1}\Delta\mathbf{K}\|$ is less than 1 based on the criteria of convergence for a Neumann series. Therefore, these methods applies to the interval analysis of nonlinear problems with "small" interval parameters and the accuracy for those with "large" interval inputs can be improved by the subinterval technique in Section 3.1. Furthermore, the integration of all interval perturbation methods with current FEA software for the system simulation remains a great challenge.

2.3. Sampling approach

2.3.1. Vertex method

The vertex method was originally developed in Ref. [15], which can be viewed as a sampling technique with vertices being input samples of the FEA model. This method has been popular for the implementation of IFEA [16–21] due to its main aspect of simple formulation and the black-box property. If the behavior of the target response w.r.t. uncertain parameters can be guaranteed to be monotonic, the vertex method firstly proposed in Ref. [15] yields the exact solution. It should be pointed out that the concept of monotonicity in this section means monotonic along all principal directions where only one parameter is changing at a time. However, it is very hard—if not impossible —to prove the property of monotonicity in a general way, e.g., in the application of structural dynamics [22]. The number of FEA runs necessary for the vertex method is given as:

$$N = 2^n \tag{22}$$

where n is the number of interval parameters. It is noted that the computational cost for the vertex method exponentially increases w.r.t. the number of interval parameters, which results in a dimensionality curse.

2.3.2. Transformation method

To promote the accuracy of the vertex method for nonmonotonic problems, transformation methods for the epistemic uncertainty propagation were developed. Its original version was firstly proposed in literature [23]. This method is based on the α-level strategy and on each α-level the interval problem is defined. The interval solution strategy then consists of a dedicated sampling strategy in the space spanned by α-cut of fuzzy parameters. This method is available in a general, a reduced, and an extended form, with the most appropriate form to be selected depending on the type of model to be evaluated [23, 24]. If the behavior of the target response w.r.t. uncertain parameters can be guaranteed to be monotonic, the reduced transformation method yields the exact solution. If it shows nonmonotonic behavior, instead, the extended transformation method can be applied, in which more observation points were added in a well-directed way to the search domain after rating the monotonicity of the response w.r.t. different uncertain parameters on the basis of a classification criterion [24].

The computational cost of the transformation method is governed by the number of FEA runs N to be performed. In the case of the general transformation method, this number is given as:

$$N = \sum_{k=1}^{m+1} k^{n} \tag{23}$$

where m is the number of discrete α-levels and n is the number of fuzzy parameters. It is noted that the number of FEA runs grows exponentially w.r.t. the number of fuzzy inputs, which makes the general transformation method computational tedious for high-dimensional problems. The main aspect of the transformation method, its characteristic property of reducing fuzzy arithmetic to multiple crisp-number operations entails that this method can be implemented without major problems into an existing software environment for system simulation. Expensive rewriting of the program codes is not required [25]. Some of the most recent applications can be found in Refs. [25–32]. Besides, a program named as FAMOUS (fuzzy arithmetical modeling of uncertain systems) has been developed [25], which provides an interface to commercial software environments. Primarily developed in Matlab environment, FAMOUS actually works as a standalone application on both Windows and Linux platforms.

2.4. Optimization approach

In essence, calculating the solution set expressed in Eq. (3) is equivalent to performing a global optimization, aimed at the minimization and maximization of the components of the deterministic analysis results $\{\boldsymbol{U}\}$. The lower and upper bounds of the output of a classical FEA model are determined by the optimization approach through a search algorithm within the domain spanned by the interval parameters. If the global minimum and maximum of the analysis result are found by the search algorithm, it returns the smallest hypercube solution around the exact one. The optimization is performed independently on each element of the response vector. Furthermore, as the behavior of the target response w.r.t. uncertain parameters is rather unpredictable, the computational cost of the optimization approach in general is strongly problem-dependent. It is noted that the optimization approach is immune to the excessive conservatism for the interval arithmetic approaches because the optimization strategy approaches the smallest hypercube solution from its inside, which means that it does not guarantee conservatism until the actual bounds are captured. Additionally, the smooth behavior of the target response w.r.t. uncertain parameters facilitates the search for the global extrema over the space spanned by uncertain parameters. The directional search-based algorithm [16, 33, 34], linear programming [35], and genetic algorithm [36] were utilized to formulate the procedure of IFEA or FFEA. More applications can be found in [37–39]. It is worth mentioning that the optimization approach and Monte Carlo simulation can be adopted to verify the accuracy of other schemes for IFEA and FFEA.

3. Preprocessing procedures

Except for the aforementioned core algorithms for IFEA/FFEA, two types of preprocessing procedures are always adopted to improve either the accuracy or efficiency.

3.1. Subinterval technique

For the accuracy improvement, the subinterval technique w.r.t. interval inputs is developed [11, 40] and can be integrated with the interval arithmetic and perturbation approaches. The main aspect of the subinterval technique is the ability to relax requirements of "small" or "narrow" interval inputs for nonlinear responses. However, there remain two challenges as follows:

1. *Convergence validation*. Similar to the prior determination of the sample size of MC in the probabilistic analysis, the subinterval number for each interval parameter should be first determined to guarantee the convergence of the analysis result.
2. *Efficiency sacrifice*. An exponential increase of the computational cost is introduced as increasing the subinterval number to guarantee the convergence of the analysis result. For example, the computational cost increases by m^n times where n is the number of parameters and m is the number of subintervals for each interval parameter. Thus, the most dominant advantage in efficiency for the interval arithmetic and perturbation approaches over other interval algorithms is significantly sacrificed.

3.2. Surrogate model

To enhance the efficiency of IFEA and FFEA, many surrogate models of the real numerical model are always adopted when dealing with engineering design problems often involving large-scale FEA models. The main aspect of the surrogate model is to avoid the large amount of computational time. Apart from the conventional surrogate models always used in the optimization procedure of IFEA and FFEA, e.g. response surface models [41, 42], Kriging models [43–45], radial basis function models [46–48] and sparse grid meta-models [49–51], those for the sampling and optimization approaches including the high dimensional model representation (HDMR) and the component mode synthesis (CMS) are gaining momentum in recent years. CMS was originally introduced in Ref. [52], in which a Ritz-type transformation to each individual component of a structure was adopted. The deformation of each component is approximated using a limited number of component modes. For each of these vectors, only a single degree of freedom (DOF) was retained in the reduced component model, yielding a large reduction in DOF for each component and the entire structure. Thus, the computational cost for the FEA is drastically reduced. From this viewpoint, CMS can also be seen as a special surrogate model of the expensive numerical FEA for the improvement in the computational efficiency. The repeated FEAs required in the context of IFEA can benefit from this computational time reduction obtained by CMS.

4. Hybrid algorithms

Numerous schemes for IFEA and FFEA have been developed based on the core algorithms and preprocessing procedure, which can be classified into the following three cases.

4.1. Subinterval-based hybrid algorithms

Divide the large interval parameter $p_i^{\mathrm{I}}(i = 1, 2, \ldots, n)$ into N_i subintervals and its r_ith subinterval can be expressed as follow:

$$(p_i^{\mathrm{I}})_{r_i} = \left[p_i^{\mathrm{L}} + \frac{2(r_i - 1)\Delta p_i}{N_i}, p_i^{\mathrm{L}} + \frac{2r_i\Delta p_i}{N_i}\right], \quad r_i = 1, 2, \ldots, N_i \tag{24}$$

The number of subintervals for each interval parameter may be different. N_{sub} combinations can be produced by taking a subinterval out of each interval parameter.

$$N_{\mathrm{sub}} = \prod_{i=1}^{n} N_i \tag{25}$$

For each subinterval combination, the IFEA model can be rewritten as:

$$\mathbf{K}(\mathbf{p}_{r_1r_2\ldots r_n}^{\mathrm{I}})\mathbf{U}(\mathbf{p}_{r_1r_2\ldots r_n}^{\mathrm{I}}) = \mathbf{F}(\mathbf{p}_{r_1r_2\ldots r_n}^{\mathrm{I}}), \ r_i = 1, 2, \ldots, N_i; \ i = 1, 2, \ldots, n \tag{26}$$

where $\mathbf{p}_{r_1r_2\ldots r_n}^{\mathrm{I}}$ stands for a subinterval combination and is composed of the r_1th subinterval of the first interval parameter, the r_2th subinterval of the second one and up to the r_nth subinterval of the nth one. In a conclusion, Eq. (26) stands for N_{sub} subinterval IFEA equations. For each subinterval IFEA equation, the response vector can be obtained by using core algorithms in Section 2, e.g., interval arithmetic approaches, perturbation approaches, and vertex method. For two adjacent subinterval vector $\mathbf{p}_{r_1\ldots r_r\ldots r_n}^{\mathrm{I}}$ and $\mathbf{p}_{r_1\ldots r_r+1\ldots r_n}^{\mathrm{I}}$, the following formulae hold true, i.e.,

$$\mathbf{K}(\mathbf{p}_{r_1\ldots r_r\ldots r_n}^{\mathrm{I}}) \cap \mathbf{K}(\mathbf{p}_{r_1\ldots r_r+1\ldots r_n}^{\mathrm{I}}) = \mathbf{K}(p_{r_1}^{\mathrm{I}}, \ldots, p_{r_r}^{\mathrm{U}} = p_{r_r}^{\mathrm{L}}, \ldots, p_n^{\mathrm{I}}) \tag{27}$$

$$\mathbf{F}(\mathbf{p}_{r_1\ldots r_r\ldots r_n}^{\mathrm{I}}) \cap \mathbf{F}(\mathbf{p}_{r_1\ldots r_r+1\ldots r_n}^{\mathrm{I}}) = \mathbf{F}(p_{r_1}^{\mathrm{I}}, \ldots, p_{r_r}^{\mathrm{U}} = p_{r_r}^{\mathrm{L}}, \ldots, p_n^{\mathrm{I}}) \tag{28}$$

where $p_{r_r}^{\mathrm{U}}$ and $p_{r_r}^{\mathrm{L}}$ are the upper bound of $p_{r_r}^{\mathrm{I}}$ and lower bound of $p_{r_r+1}^{\mathrm{L}}$, respectively. Thus, the intersection of $\mathbf{U}(\mathbf{p}_{r_1\ldots r_r\ldots r_n}^{\mathrm{I}})$ and $\mathbf{U}(\mathbf{p}_{r_1\ldots r_r+1\ldots r_n}^{\mathrm{I}})$ does not equal to an empty set, i.e.,

$$\mathbf{U}(\mathbf{p}_{r_1\ldots r_r\ldots r_n}^{\mathrm{I}}) \cap \mathbf{U}(\mathbf{p}_{r_1\ldots r_r+1\ldots r_n}^{\mathrm{I}}) \neq \varnothing \tag{29}$$

It is shown from Eq. (29) that the interval response vectors for each subinterval combination are simply connected. Therefore, the interval response vector can be obtained as follows by using the interval union operation.

$$\mathbf{U}(\mathbf{p}^{\mathrm{I}}) = \bigcup_{\substack{r_i = 1,2,\ldots,N_i \\ i=1,2,\ldots,n}} \mathbf{U}(\mathbf{p}^{\mathrm{I}}_{r_1 r_2 \ldots r_i \ldots r_n}) = \left[\min_{r_i=1,2,\ldots,N_i} \left(\mathbf{U}(\mathbf{p}^{\mathrm{I}}_{r_1 r_2 \ldots r_i \ldots r_n}) \right), \max_{r_i=1,2,\ldots,N_i} \left(\mathbf{U}(\mathbf{p}^{\mathrm{I}}_{r_1 r_2 \ldots r_i \ldots r_n}) \right) \right] \tag{30}$$

The above subinterval method is shown in **Figure 2** with 50 subintervals when considering one uncertain parameter x.

The interval arithmetic approach, subinterval technique and Taylor series expansion were integrated [40]. More applications can be found in [13, 53, 54].

4.2. Surrogate model-based hybrid algorithms

Taylor series expansion was integrated with the interval arithmetic approach in [40] and a method named as Taylor expansion with extrema management was proposed by integrating the higher order Taylor series expansion and the optimization approach [55] to detect possible nonmonotonic influences.

The transformation method was integrated with HDMR in Ref. [25]. And a component mode transformation method was developed [56] by combing the CMS with the transformation method to provide a significant reduction of the computational cost for large mechanical problems with uncertain parameters. Besides, a hybrid method was proposed for the interval frequency response analysis by integrating the optimization and interval arithmetic approach in [57], which was further integrated with CMS in Ref. [22]. An acceptable computational cost and a limited amount of conservatism in the analysis result were achieved by these hybrid algorithms.

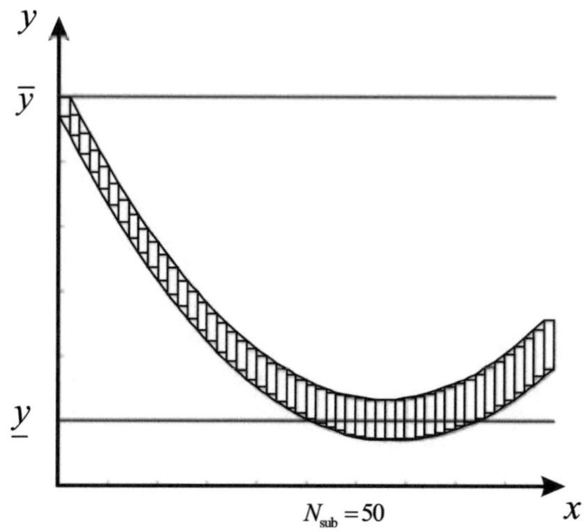

Figure 2. The diagram of subinterval method.

4.3. Hybrid core algorithms

The aforementioned core algorithms can be combined together to achieve a better tradeoff between the accuracy and efficiency, e.g., frameworks [22, 57–60] formulated by the global optimization methods and interval arithmetic ones.

To improve the computational efficiency, any core algorithm in Section 2 can be integrated with reanalysis method [61], which is fundamentally an intrusive FEA. It is noted that the major computational cost of IFEA consists of repeated solutions of the deterministic FEA systems while the main goal of the re-analysis method is to accelerate this conventional FEA solution process. It is shown that the application of the re-analysis method in the context of IFEA can reduce the computational cost by one order of magnitude compared to those based on the conventional FEA strategy [5].

5. Conclusions

This chapter presents the state-of-the-art and recent advances in nonprobabilistic finite element analyses. The main advantages and shortcomings of each nonprobabilistic finite element analysis method are discussed.

The arithmetic approach is the most straightforward strategy for nonprobabilistic finite element analyses. However, this chapter further shows that the interval arithmetic implementation of the finite element procedure is conservative. Therefore, the development of an adequate methodology for solving the uncertain parameter dependency problem is still the main challenge in the domain of arithmetic approach. The perturbation approach has been widely used in structural response analyses and other applications due to its simplicity and efficiency. The accuracy of the original perturbation methods can be improved by retaining part of higher order terms in Neumann series or Taylor series as shown in the improved and modified versions. The sampling approach like vertex method yields the exact solution under the condition that the behavior of the target response w.r.t. uncertain parameters can be guaranteed to be monotonic and has been popular for the implementation of IFEA due to its main aspect of simple formulation and the black-box property. However, when tackling the nonmonotonic problems, the extended transformation methods should be applied by adding more observation points in a well-directed way. The optimization approach is more and more acknowledged as standard procedure in an interval finite element context except for the high computational cost.

Moreover, in this context, two typical preprocessing procedures, e.g., subinterval technique and surrogate model to improve either the accuracy or efficiency are described in detail. Additionally, novel hybrid algorithms, including subinterval-based hybrid algorithms, surrogate model-based hybrid algorithms and hybrid core algorithms can be conceived by combining the aforementioned core algorithms and preprocessing procedures to achieve a better tradeoff between the accuracy and efficiency for the specific problems and the future work in this research field can be fostered.

Author details

Wang Lei, Qiu Zhiping* and Zheng Yuning

*Address all correspondence to: zpqiu@buaa.edu.cn

Institute of Solid Mechanics, School of Aeronautic Science and Engineering, Beihang University, Beijing, China

References

[1] Ben-Haim Y, Elishakoff I. Convex models of uncertainty in applied mechanics. Amsterdam: Elsevier Science Publishers; 1990.

[2] Elishakoff I. Essay on uncertainties in elastic and viscoelastic structures: From A. M. Freudenthal's criticisms to modern convex modeling. Computers & Structures. 1995;**56** (6):871–895. doi:http://dx.doi.org/10.1016/0045-7949(94)00499-S

[3] Elishakoff I. Possible limitations of probabilistic methods in engineering. Applied Mechanics Reviews. 2000;**53**(2):19–36. doi:10.1115/1.3097337

[4] Moens D, Vandepitte D. A survey of non-probabilistic uncertainty treatment in finite element analysis. Computer Methods in Applied Mechanics and Engineering. 2005;**194** (12–16):1527–1555. doi:http://dx.doi.org/10.1016/j.cma.2004.03.019

[5] Moens D, Hanss M. Non-probabilistic finite element analysis for parametric uncertainty treatment in applied mechanics: Recent advances. Finite Elements in Analysis and Design. 2011;**47**(1):4–16. doi:http://dx.doi.org/10.1016/j.finel.2010.07.010

[6] Nguyen HT. A note on the extension principle for fuzzy sets. Journal of Mathematical Analysis and Applications. 1978;**64**(2):369–380. doi:http://dx.doi.org/10.1016/0022-247X (78)90045-8

[7] Moore RE, Kearfott RB, Cloud MJ. Introduction to Interval Analysis. Philadelphia, PA: Society for Industrial and Applied Mathematics; 2009.

[8] Degrauwe D, Lombaert G, De Roeck G. Improving interval analysis in finite element calculations by means of affine arithmetic. Computers & Structures. 2010;**88**(3–4):247–254. doi:http://dx.doi.org/10.1016/j.compstruc.2009.11.003

[9] Behera D, Chakraverty S. Fuzzy finite element analysis of imprecisely defined structures with fuzzy nodal force. Engineering Applications of Artificial Intelligence. 2013;**26** (10):2458–2466. doi:http://dx.doi.org/10.1016/j.engappai.2013.07.021

[10] Serhat Erdogan Y, Gundes Bakir P. Inverse propagation of uncertainties in finite element model updating through use of fuzzy arithmetic. Engineering Applications of Artificial Intelligence. 2013;**26**(1):357–367. doi:10.1016/j.engappai.2012.10.003

[11] Qiu Z, Elishakoff I. Antioptimization of structures with large uncertain-but-non-random parameters via interval analysis. Computer Methods in Applied Mechanics and Engineering. 1998;**152**(3):361–372. doi:http://dx.doi.org/10.1016/S0045-7825(96)01211-X

[12] McWilliam S. Anti-optimisation of uncertain structures using interval analysis. Computers & Structures. 2001;**79**(4):421–430. doi:http://dx.doi.org/10.1016/S0045-7949(00)00143-7

[13] Xia B, Yu D, Liu J. Interval and subinterval perturbation methods for a structural-acoustic system with interval parameters. Journal of Fluids and Structures. 2013;**38**:146–163. doi: http://dx.doi.org/10.1016/j.jfluidstructs.2012.12.003

[14] Wang C, Qiu Z, Wang X, Wu D. Interval finite element analysis and reliability-based optimization of coupled structural-acoustic system with uncertain parameters. Finite Elements in Analysis and Design. 2014;**91**:108–114. doi:http://dx.doi.org/10.1016/j.finel.2014.07.014

[15] Dong W, Shah HC. Vertex method for computing functions of fuzzy variables. Fuzzy Sets and Systems. 1987;**24**(1):65–78. doi:http://dx.doi.org/10.1016/0165-0114(87)90114-X

[16] Rao S, Sawyer JP. Fuzzy finite element approach for analysis of imprecisely defined systems. AIAA Journal. 1995;**33**(12):2364–2370. doi:10.2514/3.12910

[17] Chen L, Rao SS. Fuzzy finite-element approach for the vibration analysis of imprecisely-defined systems. Finite Elements in Analysis and Design. 1997;**27**(1):69–83. doi:http://dx.doi.org/10.1016/S0168-874X(97)00005-X

[18] Akpan UO, Koko TS, Orisamolu IR, Gallant BK. Practical fuzzy finite element analysis of structures. Finite Elements in Analysis and Design. 2001;**38**(2):93–111. doi:http://dx.doi.org/10.1016/S0168-874X(01)00052-X

[19] Qiu Z, Wang X, Chen J. Exact bounds for the static response set of structures with uncertain-but-bounded parameters. International Journal of Solids and Structures. 2006;**43**(21):6574–6593. doi:http://dx.doi.org/10.1016/j.ijsolstr.2006.01.012

[20] Qiu Z, Xia Y, Yang J. The static displacement and the stress analysis of structures with bounded uncertainties using the vertex solution theorem. Computer Methods in Applied Mechanics and Engineering. 2007;**196**(49–52):4965–4984. doi:10.1016/j.cma.2007.06.022

[21] Xu M, Qiu Z, Wang X. Uncertainty propagation in SEA for structural–acoustic coupled systems with non-deterministic parameters. Journal of Sound and Vibration. 2014;**333**(17):3949–3965. doi:http://dx.doi.org/10.1016/j.jsv.2014.03.003

[22] De Gersem H, Moens D, Desmet W, Vandepitte D. Interval and fuzzy dynamic analysis of finite element models with superelements. Computers & Structures. 2007;**85**(5–6):304–319. doi:http://dx.doi.org/10.1016/j.compstruc.2006.10.011

[23] Hanss M. The transformation method for the simulation and analysis of systems with uncertain parameters. Fuzzy Sets and Systems. 2002;**130**(3):277–289. doi:http://dx.doi.org/10.1016/S0165-0114(02)00045-3

[24] Hanss M. The extended transformation method for the simulation and analysis of fuzzy-parameterized models. International Journal of Uncertainty, Fuzziness and Knowledge-Based Systems. 2003;**11**(06):711–727. doi:doi:10.1142/S0218488503002491

[25] Hanss M, Turrin S. A fuzzy-based approach to comprehensive modeling and analysis of systems with epistemic uncertainties. Structural Safety. 2010;**32**(6):433–441. doi:http://dx.doi.org/10.1016/j.strusafe.2010.06.003

[26] Turrin S, Hanss M, Gaul L. Fuzzy arithmetical vibration analysis of a windshield with uncertain parameters. In: Proceedings of the Ninth International Conference on Recent Advances in Structural Dynamics - RASD, Southampton 2006

[27] Hanss M, Becker J, Maess M, Gaul L. Fuzzy arithmetical analysis of smart structures with uncertainties. In: Proceedings of the First International Conference on Uncertainty in Structural Dynamics, Sheffield; 2007

[28] Junge M, Brunner D, Becker J, Maess M, Roseira J, Hanss M. Combination of fuzzy arithmetic and a fast boundary element method for acoustic simulation with uncertainties. Journal of Computational Acoustics 2009;**17**(01): 45–69. doi:doi:10.1142/S0218396X09003811

[29] Hanss M, Klimke A. On the reliability of the influence measure in the transformation method of fuzzy arithmetic. Fuzzy Sets and Systems. 2004;**143**(3):371–390. doi:http://dx.doi.org/10.1016/S0165-0114(03)00163-5

[30] Allahviranloo T, Kiani NA, Motamedi N. Solving fuzzy differential equations by differential transformation method. Information Sciences. 2009;**179**(7):956–966. doi:http://dx.doi.org/10.1016/j.ins.2008.11.016

[31] Klimke A. An efficient implementation of the transformation method of fuzzy arithmetic. In: Fuzzy Information Processing Society, 2003. NAFIPS 2003. International Conference of the North American. New York: IEEE Xplore, 2003:468–473

[32] Gauger U, Turrin S, Hanss M, Gaul L. A new uncertainty analysis for the transformation method. Fuzzy Sets and Systems. 2008;**159**(11):1273–1291. doi:http://dx.doi.org/10.1016/j.fss.2007.12.027

[33] Rao SS, Berke L. Analysis of uncertain structural systems using interval analysis. AIAA Journal. 1997;**35**(4):727–735. doi:10.2514/2.164

[34] Rao SS, Chen L. Numerical solution of fuzzy linear equations in engineering analysis. International Journal for Numerical Methods in Engineering. 1998;**43**(3):391–408. doi:10.1002/(sici)1097-0207(19981015)43:3<391::aid-nme417>3.0.co;2-j

[35] Köylüog lu HUu, Elishakoff I. A comparison of stochastic and interval finite elements applied to shear frames with uncertain stiffness properties. Computers & Structures. 1998;**67**(1–3):91–98. doi:http://dx.doi.org/10.1016/S0045-7949(97)00160-0

[36] Möller B, Graf W, Beer M. Fuzzy structural analysis using α-level optimization. Computational Mechanics. 2000;**26**(6):547–565. doi:10.1007/s004660000204

[37] Moens D, Vandepitte D. Fuzzy finite element method for frequency response function analysis of uncertain structures. AIAA Journal. 2002;**40**(1):126–136. doi:10.2514/2.1621

[38] Farkas L, Moens D, Vandepitte D, Desmet W. Application of fuzzy numerical techniques for product performance analysis in the conceptual and preliminary design stage. Computers & Structures. 2008;**86**(10):1061–1079. doi:10.1016/j.compstruc.2007.07.012

[39] Farkas L, Moens D, Vandepitte D, Desmet W. Fuzzy finite element analysis based on reanalysis technique. Structural Safety. 2010;**32**(6):442–448. doi:10.1016/j.strusafe.2010.04.004

[40] Zhou YT, Jiang C, Han X. Interval and subinterval analysis methods of the structural analysis and their error estimations. International Journal of Computational Methods. 2006;**3**(2):229–244. doi:10.1142/S0219876206000771

[41] de Boor C, Ron A. On multivariate polynomial interpolation. Constructive Approximation. 1990;**6**(3):287–302. doi:10.1007/bf01890412

[42] Myers RH, Montgomery DC, Anderson-Cook CM. Response Surface Methodology: Process and Product Optimization Using Designed Experiments. Hoboken, NJ: John Wiley & Sons; 2011.

[43] Jones DR, Schonlau M, Welch WJ. Efficient global optimization of expensive black-box functions. Journal of Global Optimization. 1998;**13**(4):455–492. doi:10.1023/a:1008306431147

[44] Martin JD, Simpson TW. Use of Kriging models to approximate deterministic computer models. AIAA Journal. 2005;**43**(4):853–863. doi:10.2514/1.8650

[45] Kleijnen JPC. Kriging metamodeling in simulation: A review. European Journal of Operational Research. 2009;**192**(3):707–716. doi:http://dx.doi.org/10.1016/j.ejor.2007.10.013

[46] Park J, Sandberg IW. Universal approximation using radial-basis-function networks. Neural Computation. 1991;**3**(2):246–257. doi:10.1162/neco.1991.3.2.246

[47] Chen S, Cowan CFN, Grant PM. Orthogonal least squares learning algorithm for radial basis function networks. IEEE Transactions on Neural Networks. 1991;**2**(2):302–309. doi:10.1109/72.80341

[48] T Sev, Shin YC. Radial basis function neural network for approximation and estimation of nonlinear stochastic dynamic systems. IEEE Transactions on Neural Networks. 1994;**5**(4):594–603. doi:10.1109/72.298229

[49] Klimke A, Nunes RF, Wohlmuth BI. Fuzzy arithmetic based on dimension-adaptive sparse grids: A case study of a large-scale finite element model under uncertain parameters. International Journal of Uncertainty, Fuzziness and Knowledge-Based Systems. 2006;**14**(5):561–577. doi:10.1142/S0218488506004199

[50] Klimke A, Willner K, Wohlmuth BI. Uncertainty modeling using fuzzy arithmetic based on sparse grids: Applications to dynamic systems. International Journal of Uncertainty, Fuzziness and Knowledge-Based Systems. 2004;**12**(6):745–759. doi:10.1142/S0218488504003181

[51] Nunes RF, Klimke A, Arruda JRF. On estimating frequency response function envelopes using the spectral element method and fuzzy sets. Journal of Sound and Vibration. 2006;**291**(3–5):986–1003. doi:http://dx.doi.org/10.1016/j.jsv.2005.07.024

[52] Hurty WC. Dynamic analysis of structural systems using component modes. AIAA Journal. 1965;3(4):678–685. doi:10.2514/3.2947

[53] Xia B, Yu D. Modified sub-interval perturbation finite element method for 2D acoustic field prediction with large uncertain-but-bounded parameters. Journal of Sound and Vibration. 2012;**331**(16):3774–3790. doi:http://dx.doi.org/10.1016/j.jsv.2012.03.024

[54] Wang C, Qiu Z, Li Y. Hybrid uncertainty propagation of coupled structural–acoustic system with large fuzzy and interval parameters. Applied Acoustics. 2016;**102**:62–70. doi:http://dx.doi.org/10.1016/j.apacoust.2015.09.006

[55] Massa F, Tison T, Lallemand B. A fuzzy procedure for the static design of imprecise structures. Computer Methods in Applied Mechanics and Engineering. 2006;**195**(9–12):925–941. doi:http://dx.doi.org/10.1016/j.cma.2005.02.015

[56] Giannini O, Hanss M. The component mode transformation method: A fast implementation of fuzzy arithmetic for uncertainty management in structural dynamics. Journal of Sound and Vibration. 2008;**311**(3–5):1340–1357. doi:http://dx.doi.org/10.1016/j.jsv.2007.10.029

[57] Moens D, Vandepitte D. An interval finite element approach for the calculation of envelope frequency response functions. International Journal for Numerical Methods in Engineering. 2004;**61**(14):2480–2507. doi:10.1002/nme.1159

[58] De Gersem H, Moens D, Desmet W, Vandepitte D. A fuzzy finite element procedure for the calculation of uncertain frequency response functions of damped structures: Part 2—Numerical case studies. Journal of Sound and Vibration. 2005;**288**(3):463–486. doi:10.1016/j.jsv.2005.07.002

[59] Moens D, Vandepitte D. A fuzzy finite element procedure for the calculation of uncertain frequency-response functions of damped structures: Part 1—Procedure. Journal of Sound and Vibration. 2005;**288**(3):431–462. doi:10.1016/j.jsv.2005.07.001

[60] De Munck M, Moens D, Desmet W, Vandepitte D. A response surface based optimisation algorithm for the calculation of fuzzy envelope FRFs of models with uncertain properties. Computers & Structures. 2008; **86**(10):1080–1092. doi:10.1016/j.compstruc.2007.07.006

[61] Laszlo F, David M, Gersem HD, Dirk V. Efficient FE reanalysis method for fuzzy uncertainty analysis of a composite wing. In: 10th AIAA Non-Deterministic Approaches Conference, Schaumburg 2008

Chapter 4

Epistemic Uncertainty Quantification of Seismic Damage Assessment

Hesheng Tang, Dawei Li and Songtao Xue

Additional information is available at the end of the chapter

http://dx.doi.org/10.5772/intechopen.68153

Abstract

The damage-based structural seismic performance evaluations are widely used in seismic design and risk evaluation of civil facilities. Due to the large uncertainties rooted in this procedure, the application of damage quantification results is still a challenge for researchers and engineers. Uncertainties in damage assessment procedure are important consideration in performance evaluation and design of structures against earthquakes. Due to lack of knowledge or incomplete, inaccurate, unclear information in the modeling, simulation, and design, there are limitations in using only one framework (probability theory) to quantify uncertainty in a system because of the impreciseness of data or knowledge. In this work, a methodology based on the evidence theory is presented for quantifying the epistemic uncertainty of damage assessment procedure. The proposed methodology is applied to seismic damage assessment procedure while considering various sources of uncertainty emanating from experimental force-displacement data of reinforced concrete column. In order to alleviate the computational difficulties in the evidence theory-based uncertainty quantification analysis (UQ), a differential evolution-based computational strategy for efficient calculation of the propagated belief structure in a system with evidence theory is presented here. Finally, a seismic damage assessment example is investigated to demonstrate the effectiveness of the proposed method.

Keywords: damage model, epistemic uncertainty, uncertainty quantification, evidence theory, differential evolution algorithm

1. Introduction

With widespreading of the concept and applications of performance-based earthquake engineering (PBEE) and performance-based seismic design (PBSD), the effective measures for assessing the performance state of structural components or entire structure have been deeply investigated in seismic engineering. In consistence with the different performance assessment criteria, the evaluation and measurements of damage states for structural components are divided into three main branches (e.g., displacement-based approach, energy-based measure and the combination of both). Due to the simplicity and convenience of observation and description for structural damage states, the displacement-based approach and corresponding damage index (e.g., inelastic displacement, maximum inter story drift ratio, and ductility demand, etc.) have been widely documented in building seismic evaluation and retrofit of existing building guidelines [1]. Notwithstanding the prevalent application of displacement method in damage assessment, the defect of lacking the influence of low cyclic fatigue of structural components is obvious. The hysteretic energy dissipation is considered as a more reasonable indicator for seismic structural damage, because it is a cumulative parameter involved cyclic-plastic deformations in a structure during earthquakes [2]. Despite the effectiveness of hysteretic energy, experimental observations demonstrate that the expression of energy would be significantly affected by the exceedance plastic deformation [3]. And the cumulative laboratory experimental data on structural members and structures indicate the fact that the structure is damaged by a combination of the excessive deformation and hysteretic energy. Park–Ang damage model [4], which takes into account the effects of both the first exceedance failure and cumulative damage failure in low-cycle-fatigue for a structural component during seismic load, is served as a baseline for many researches. Due to intrinsic simplicity as well as calibrations against a significant amount of observed seismic damages, the Park-Ang model and its modified version have been extensively implemented in seismic performance evaluation of structures [5–7].

Although the applicability and practicability of using the Park-Ang model and its modified versions have been supported by many researchers [8, 9], it should be noted that the Park-Ang-damage-index-based performance evaluation is still a challenging task due to the large uncertainties associated with the damage model parameters [10]. With the influence of these uncertainties [11, 12], the evaluation results of structural damage state are always represented with the empirical interval value (e.g., the minor damage state is represented by $0.25<D<0.4$ or $0.11<D<0.4$, etc. [13]). Some of these uncertainties stem from factors that are inherently random (or aleatory) in engineering or scientific analysis (e.g., material properties such as Young's modulus of steel; compression strength of concrete). Others arise from a lack of knowledge, ignorance, or modeling (e.g., simplification of mathematical model of buildings for structural analysis purposes). The large uncertainties associated with the Park-Ang damage model are derived from limited experimental data and approximate modeling (lack of knowledge) [2, 4, 5, 10]. Considering the importance of damage model in assessment of damage state for a structure, the epistemic uncertainty shall be taken into account in seismic damage state assessment with great care. Hence, it is significant to present a comprehensive uncertainty analysis methodology to quantify the epistemic uncertainty and obtain more reliable results.

The traditional probability theory, based on the sufficient statistical information, is used to model the objective uncertainty (random), which is inherent in physical variability of materials and environment. Unfortunately, the limited number of experimental data set cannot support the strong assumption of probability theory, and the process of collecting data is always costly and time consuming. These shortcomings lead the assessment result of damage state of structures are not aleatory but epistemic. In the past decades, several alternative approaches have been developed to deal with epistemic uncertainty. Some of the potential uncertainty theories are the theory of fuzzy set [14], possibility theory [15], the theory of interval analysis [16], imprecise probability theory [17], and evidence theory [18, 19]. Among these promising uncertainty representation models, evidence theory with the ability of handling aleatory and epistemic uncertainty is used for UQ, risk assessment, and reliability analysis.

With two complementary measures of uncertainty such as belief and plausibility, using evidence theory to UQ is flexible and effective. In comparison with the calculation of single probability density function (PDF) in probability theory, the computationally intensive problem involves computing the bound values over all possible discontinuous sets which is a main shackle of wide application for evidence theory. In order to break the computational barriers in the evidence theory-based UQ, the differential-evolution-based interval optimization is employed to enhance the computational efficiency as described by the authors [20].

2. Sources of uncertainty in seismic damage assessment

To effectively describe the damage state of structural components or entire structure, the original Park-Ang damage model and modified model were developed. The original Park-Ang damage model was presented here to access the uncertainty influence of the evaluation on the damage state of column components. There are various methods to estimate constants in Park-Ang damage model in different studies. In addition to diverse combination measures, the empirical estimation value and calibration value dispersed in a large range. Using the classification method proposed by Oberkampf and Helton [21], the aleatory and epistemic uncertainties involved in Park-Ang damage model are listed as:

1. The random uncertainties rooted in experimental materials, e.g., the material composition of concrete and the strength test results in single compositional material.
2. The objective and subjective uncertainties of experimental condition. e.g., the environmental factor, the loading error of machine, and measurements error.
3. The subjective uncertainties of fitting measures of parameters in Park-Ang damage model and mathematical representation of model itself.

In consideration of these aleatory and epistemic uncertainties in Park-Ang damage model, the quantification influence of uncertainties is indispensable. To achieve this goal, a series of empirical expressions are summarized. Then, the Structural Performance Database of Pacific Earthquake Engineering Research Center (PEER) is used to construct the uncertain sources of parameters of damage assessment models. Using these calibration results of column set, the parameter uncertainties are represented by the fluctuation of ratio of empirical values and calibration values.

2.1. Park-Ang model and empirical expression of its constants

The Park-Ang damage model [4] combines the first exceedance failure and cumulative damage failure with a linear expression as:

$$D = \delta_{\mathrm{m}}/\delta_{\mathrm{u}} + \beta \int dE/F_{\mathrm{y}}\delta_{\mathrm{u}} \tag{1}$$

where δ_{m} is the maximum deformation under earthquake, δ_{u} is the ultimate deformation under monotonic load, $\int \mathrm{d}E$ is the cumulative energy under earthquake, β is the energy coefficient, and F_{y} is the yield strength. In order to simplify the analysis procedure, the value of F_{y}, δ_{u}, and β are always assumed as the constants and have nothing to do with the loads pattern. Following above assumption, the value of damage index D for per-load stage can be computed by only using the current value of δ_{m} and $\int \mathrm{d}E$. Furthermore, the damage evolution of structures and components can be described and this evolution index is supported to estimate the true damage stage of structure and components.

In the last two decades of the twentieth century, a set of experimental results were conducted and some illuminate-, empirical-, or mechanical-based expression of F_{y}, δ_{u}, and β were successively generated. Park et al. [4] computed the value of β as given in Eq. (2):

$$\beta = (-0.447 + 0.073l/d + 0.24n_0 + 0.314\rho_{\mathrm{t}}) \times 0.7^{\rho_{\omega}} \tag{2}$$

where l and d denote the length span and effective height of cross section, n_0 is the axial load ratio, ρ_{t} is the longitude tension steel ratio (%), and ρ_{w} is the confinement ratio (%). Kunnath et al. [5] used 260 beams and columns data to fit the value of β as given in Eq. (3):

$$\beta = [0.37n_0 + 0.36(k_{\mathrm{p}} - 0.2)^2]0.9^{\rho_{\mathrm{w}}} \tag{3}$$

where $k_{\mathrm{p}} = \rho_{\mathrm{t}} f_{\mathrm{y}}/0.85 f_{\mathrm{c}}$ is normalized steel ratio and ρ_{w} is confinement ratio. Similarly, δ_{u} can be determined with statistical approach or fundamental method using the mechanics of concrete and steel. Using the typical statistical measure, Park [6] evaluated the ultimate displacement as:

$$\delta_{\mathrm{u}} = 0.52(l/d)^{0.93}\rho^{-0.27}\rho_{\omega}^{0.48}n_0^{-0.48}f_{\mathrm{c}}^{-0.15} \times \delta_{\mathrm{y}} \tag{4}$$

where ρ is normalized steel ratio and δ_{y} is the yield displacement of components that can be computed with [4] and other factors are same as above. Compared to above statistical calculation model, EU 8 [22] and Fardis and Biskinis [23] presented two different models with the mechanics of concrete and steel:

$$\delta_{\mathrm{u}} = \frac{1}{\gamma_{\mathrm{el}}} 0.016(0.3)^{n_0} \left[\frac{\max(0.01, \omega')}{\max(0.01, \omega)} f_{\mathrm{c}}\right]^{0.225} \left[\min\left(9, \frac{l}{h}\right)\right]^{0.35} 25^{\left(\alpha\rho_{\mathrm{sx}}\frac{f_{\mathrm{yw}}}{f_{\mathrm{c}}}\right)} \times l \tag{5}$$

$$\delta_{\mathrm{u}} = \alpha_{\mathrm{st}}(1 - 0.4\alpha_{\mathrm{cyc}})(1 + 0.5\alpha_{\mathrm{sl}})(0.3)^{n_0} \left[\frac{\max(0.01, \omega')}{\max(0.01, \omega)} f_{\mathrm{c}}\right]^{0.175} \left(\frac{l}{h}\right)^{0.4} 25^{\left(\alpha\rho_{\mathrm{s}}\frac{f_{\mathrm{yw}}}{f_{\mathrm{c}}}\right)} \times l \tag{6}$$

where γ_{el} is coefficient of primary and secondary elements, ω' and ω are mechanical steel ratio of compression and tension reinforcement, respectively, h is cross-section height, α is confinement effective factor, ρ_{sx} is confinement steel ratio, f_{yw} is yield strength of stirrup, and α_{st}, α_{cyc}, and α_{sl} are coefficients for type of steel, loading, and anchorage slip. For the yield strength of concrete components, the expression is given by Panagiotakos and Fardis [24]:

$$F_y = \frac{bd^3}{l}\phi_y\left\{E_c\frac{k_y^2}{2}\left(0.5(1+\delta') - \frac{k_y}{3}\right) + \frac{E_s}{2}\left[(1-k_y)\rho + (k_y-\delta')\rho' + \frac{\rho_v}{6}(1-\delta')\right]\right\}(1-\delta') \quad (7)$$

Conventionally, the damage index D can be obtained by using above expressions to obtain the nominal value of Park-Ang constants. Owing to limited statistical data and incomplete knowledge of mathematical model to predict these constants, the large convergence is reported as in [4–6, 23, 24]. Furthermore, these uncertainties will influence the quantification result of Park-Ang damage index. In order to verify the impact of damage quantification result derived from uncertainty of Park-Ang model constants, we present the structural performance database of PEER [25] to calibrate these constants and determine the uncertainty fluctuation range of each constant.

2.2. Comparison between the calibration results and empirical results

In this work, the calibration set is selected from the structural performance database of PEER and the selection criteria are such as (1) the cross section of column is rectangle; (2) the column is loaded cyclically until failure and the corresponding failure model is dominated by flexure; (3) the longitude bars in column should not be spliced and the column should experience more than two hysteretic cycles. In conformity with these criteria, 185 specimens are selected. Using these column load-displacement data, the performance points on the backbone curve of column under cyclic load are calibrated.

Similar to the most studies [23], the ultimate deformation under monotonic load δ_u is defined as a distinct reduction on the negative stiffness slope of backbone curve and 80% of maximum strength which is always assumed as F_u. Unfortunately, the missing monotonic load experiments oblige us to employ the statistical relationship of ultimate displacement under cyclic load and monotonic load to characterize the ultimate displacement. Herein, the failure displacement under typical load histories is assumed as 60% of their ultimate deformation capacity, which is firstly observed by Panagiotakos and Fardis [24]. For yield force, we defined that the value is 75% of the maximum force. Following above definitions, the energy coefficient β is computed with the assumption that damage index D is 1 at the ultimate state. In light with above definitions, the performance point is marked on the backbone of columns as depicted in **Figure 1**.

As shown in **Figure 1**, the column backbone curves are divided into two categories: one with obvious ultimate state point (the 80% maximum force) like in **Figure 1a**, the other with the largest displacement in backbone curve (e.g., **Figure 1b**). In order to yield the uncertainty distribution of empirical model, the attention is concentrated on the first category. Using the selected force-displacement data, the comparison of empirical model results and calibration results is given in **Figure 2**.

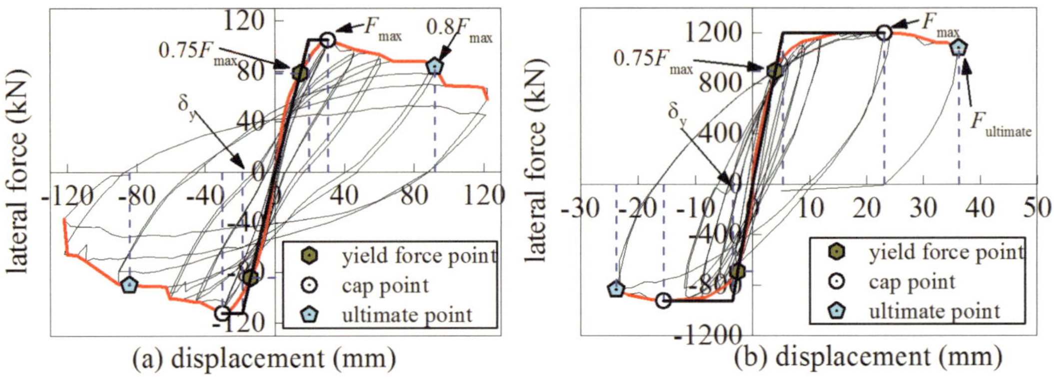

Figure 1. Performance point of backbone curve with obvious ultimate state point (a) and with the largest displacement point (b).

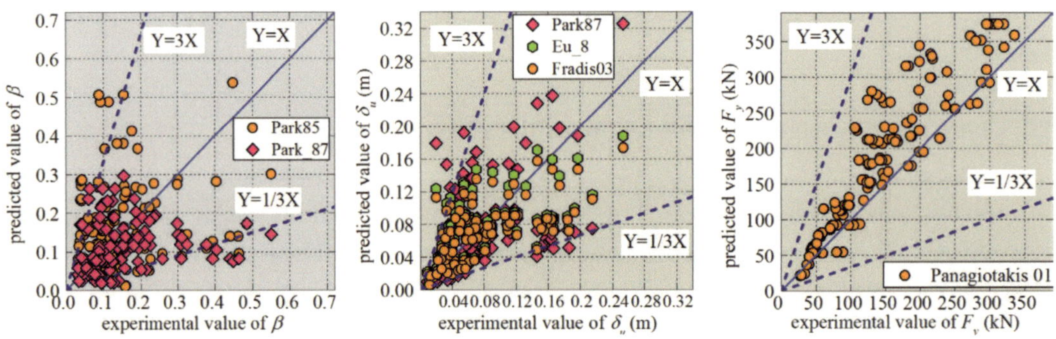

Figure 2. Comparison of predicted results and experimental results of β, δ_u and F_y.

As shown in **Figure 2**, the predicted and experimental values are scattered in a wide range, and this means the researchers should carefully handle the uncertainty derived from the empirical model in the process of evaluating damage state with Park-Ang model. Employing the parameter ε to represent the variability of predicted model deviation, the experimental value V_{exp} can be expressed as $V_{exp} = V_{pre} \times \varepsilon$. Taking into account the major fluctuation range of ε and the number of experimental samples, the ε which is located in the interval [1/3, 3] is selected and the range of data points which located less than 1/3 or more than 3 are discarded. In the light of above rules, the uncertainty source of β, δ_u, and F_y consists of 83, 111, and 173 specimen, respectively.

Along with classical concept, probability theory plays a key role in the UQ of physical model, and the distribution type is determined by the hypothesis test and related parameter are calibrated by enough experimental data. However, the limited data of experimental set and large variation restricted the ability of probability theory. As a generalized UQ measure, evidence theory is compatible with both aleatory and epistemic uncertainties. So, the evidence theory is adopted in this work to handle the epistemic uncertainty rooted in parameters of Park-Ang damage model.

3. Evidence theory and differential evolution-based UQ for seismic damage assessment

3.1. Basic of the evidence theory

Evidence theory is a theoretical framework for reasoning with partial and unreliable information. It was proposed by Dempster [18] and further improved by Shafer [19]. Compared to the classical uncertain model theory, it offers the possibility to explicitly represent doubt and conflict. As the most basic concept of the evidence theory, the fame of discernment **Ω** is defined as a set of mutually exclusive elementary propositions. Due to limited information, the propositions can be scattered, nested, or partially overlapped. Thus, the mutually exclusive elementary propositions construct the power set $F = 2^{\Omega}$. Given the measureable sample space (Ω, F), the basic belief assignment (BBA) on F, m is a mapping $F \rightarrow [0, 1]$ that satisfies the following axioms:

$$m(A) \geq 0 \quad m(\varnothing) = 0 \quad \sum m(A) = 1 \quad \text{for each } A \subseteq \Omega . \tag{8}$$

An element $A \in F$ for which $m(A) > 0$ is named a focal element. Corresponding to the scattered, nested, or partially overlapped propositions in F, it seems more reasonable to make use only of this available information to produce two uncertain measures, the Belief (*Bel*) and the Plausibility (*Pl*) functions (**Figure 3**).

Similar to the additive rule in probability, belief and plausibility measures of proposition A can be calculated from following formula:

$$Bel(A) = \sum\nolimits_{B \subseteq A} m(B) \quad \text{for all } B \subseteq 2^{\Omega} \tag{9}$$

$$Pl(A) = \sum\nolimits_{B \cap A \neq \varnothing} m(B) \quad \text{for all } B \subseteq 2^{\Omega} \tag{10}$$

where A represents different elements in F. In terms of two complementary sets A and $\tilde{A}$, the sum of belief and plausible function is not required to be one. But the weaker rule $Pl(A)+Bel(\tilde{A})=1$ is satisfied, and this expression is completely different from probability distribution function p in probability theory, that is, $p(A)+p(\tilde{A})=1$. As the most remarkable distinction from probability theory, evidence theory allows evidence stemming from different sources and employs the rules of combination to aggregate [26]. One of the most important combination rules is Dempster's rule which has following formulation. Given two independent BBA $m(B_1)$ and $m(B_2)$, the Dempster's rule can be expressed as:

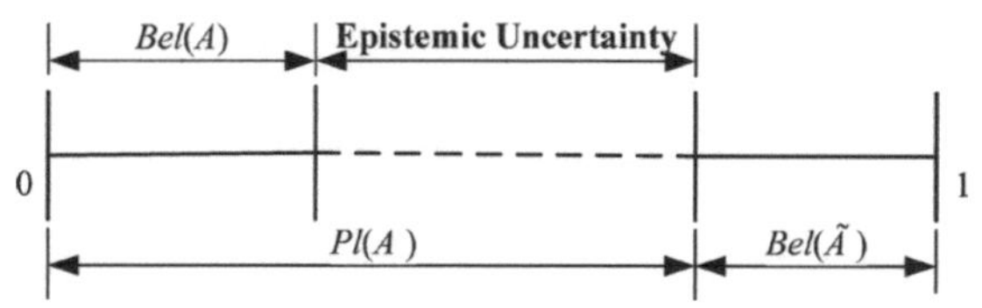

Figure 3. Belief function (*Bel*) and Plausibility function (*Pl*) of proposition A.

$$m(A) = \frac{\sum_{B_1 \cap B_2 = A} m(B_1)m(B_2)}{(1-K)} \quad \text{for all } A \neq \emptyset \tag{11}$$

where $K = \sum_{B_1 \cap B_2 = \emptyset} m(B_1)m(B_2)$ can be viewed as contradiction or conflict among the information given by the independent knowledge sources.

3.2. Evidence theory-based UQ of seismic damage assessment using differential evolution

3.2.1. Evidence-based uncertainty representation

For the purpose of UQ, the first step is the uncertainty representation of parameters using evidence theory, in which separate belief structures for each uncertain parameter should be constructed. In this work, we adopt a general methodology as described previously by Salehghaffari et al. [27] to obtain necessary information from available data and express the uncertain variables in the mathematical framework of evidence theory.

According to Salehghaffari et al. [27], two principle steps are involved in this methodology: (1) representation of uncertain parameters in several intervals through drawing bar charts by using all available data or directly from expert opinions and (2) identification of three relationships between all adjacent intervals and construction of the associated BBA structure. To further illustrate this, assuming that D_1 and D_2 represent the number of data points within two adjacent intervals I_1 and I_2, respectively, and $D_1 > D_2$, three relationships of two adjacent intervals can be identified as agreement ($D_2/D_1 \geq 0.8$), conflict ($0.5 \leq D_2/D_1 < 0.8$), and ignorance ($D_2/D_1 < 0.5$) (see **Figure 4**), the corresponding belief structure and BBA value for these three relationships are calculated by Eqs. (12)–(14), respectively.

$$m(\{I\} = \{I_1, I_2\}) = (D_1 + D_2)/D_T \tag{12}$$

$$m(\{I_1\}) = D_1/D_T, \qquad m(\{I_2\}) = D_2/D_T \tag{13}$$

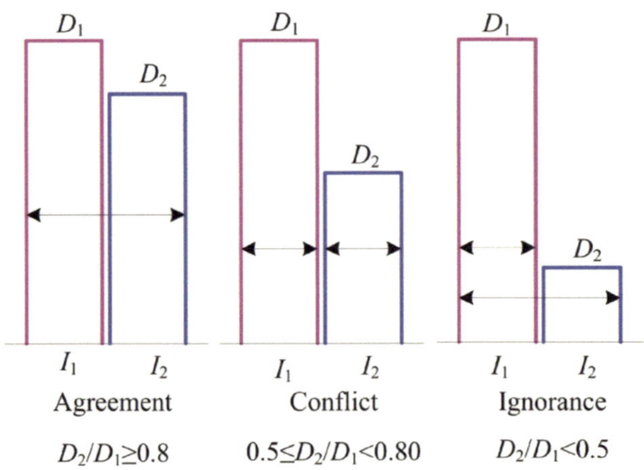

Figure 4. Three relationships of uncertain intervals.

$$m(\{I_1\}) = D_1/D_T, \qquad m(\{I_1, I_2\}) = D_2/D_T \tag{14}$$

where D_T denotes the total number of data points, following this approach, a reasonable BBA structure of uncertain parameter is constructed based on available data and knowledge, a more detailed illustration of uncertainty representation in intervals with assigned BBA value is referred in Salehghaffari et al. [27].

Employing this strategy, the uncertainty of Park-Ang model parameters can be properly represented with the evidence theory. In **Figure 5**, we use $\varepsilon_A(\beta)$, $\varepsilon_B(\beta)$, and $\varepsilon(F_y)$ to denote the variability of the predicted models in Refs. [4, 5] for energy constant β and the one in Ref. [24] for yielding force F_y of columns. The $\varepsilon_C(\delta_u)$, $\varepsilon_D(\delta_u)$, and $\varepsilon_E(\delta_u)$ in **Figure 6** represent the fluctuation of the empirical model for ultimate displacement under monotonic loading in Refs. [6, 22, 23].

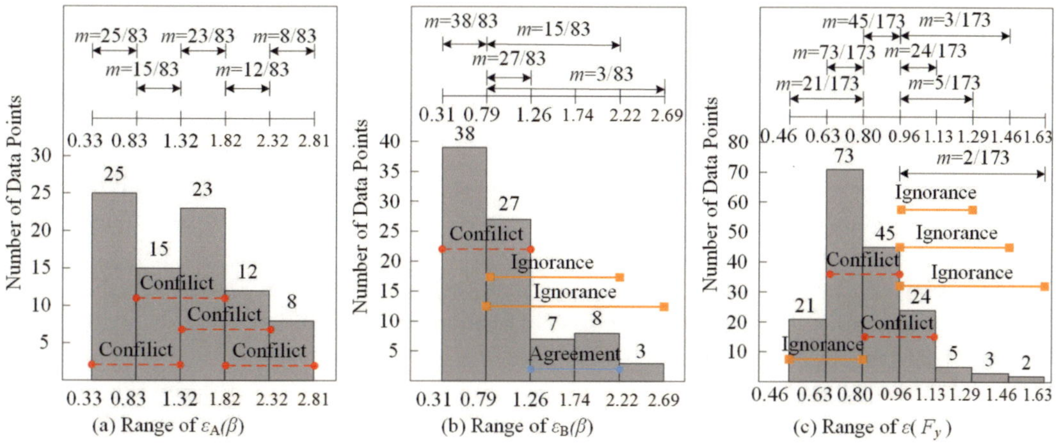

Figure 5. Evidential uncertainty description of $\varepsilon(\beta)$ and $\varepsilon(F_y)$.

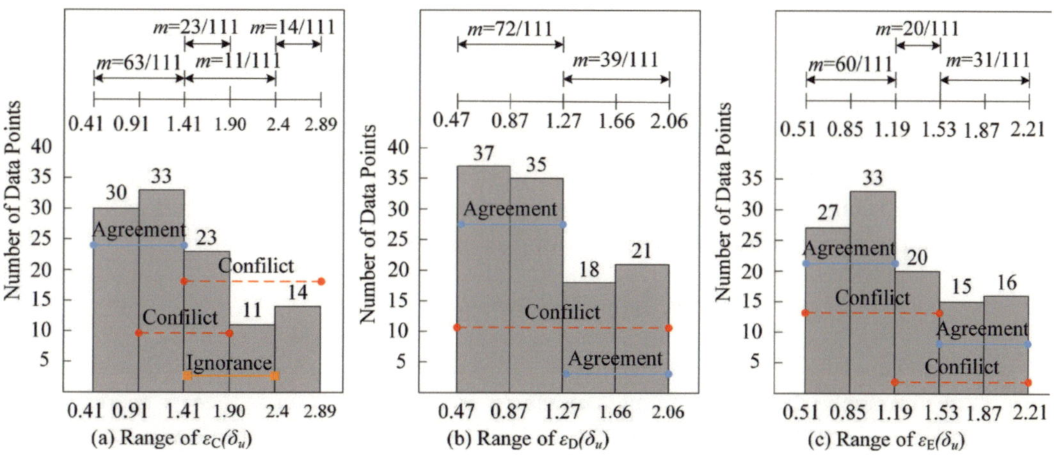

Figure 6. Evidential uncertainty description of $\varepsilon(\delta_u)$.

3.2.2. Uncertainty propagation using differential evolution

In evidence theory community, uncertainty variable is usually expressed to be a series of focal element intervals based on limited information and the joint frame of discernment is composed of the Cartesian products of uncertain intervals, then, the BBA value of each element of joint frame of discernment is also the Cartesian product of BBA value assigned on the corresponding interval. Given two independent uncertain parameters $u_1 \in U_1$ and $u_2 \in U_2$, and corresponding focal element C_1 and C_2, the joint BBA structure of this problem is defined as:

$$C=C_1 \otimes C_2, \qquad \forall u \in U \; \forall u_1 \in U_1 \; \forall u_2 \in U_2 \tag{15}$$

$$m(C) = m(C_1)m(C_2) \tag{16}$$

where the symbol ⊗ denotes the Cartesian products. Using Eqs. (15) and (16), the joint uncertainty input of system can be seemed as the multidimensional hypercube. Therefore, uncertainty propagation is a progress of finding the maximum and minimum of the system response value in each hypercube interval (proposition of the joint belief structure). To propagate the represented uncertainties of Park-Ang damage model constants, the damage index D is considered as system response.

Considering epistemic uncertainty of the system, the belief and plausibility functions of the response are obtained on the basis of the combined BBAs of the input parameters from different information sources using the evidence combination rules. For the prediction response process $D = f(Y)$, whose input parameter vector $\boldsymbol{Y} = (Y_1,\ldots,Y_n)$ has n variables with epistemic uncertainty, the joint proposition C of elementary proposition is constructed for the Park-Ang damage index prediction system model as:

$$C = \{c_k = [x_{1i_1}, x_{2i_2}, \cdots, x_{ni_n}] : x_{1i_1} \in \boldsymbol{X}_1, x_{2i_2} \in \boldsymbol{X}_2, \cdots, x_{ni_n} \in \boldsymbol{X}_n\} \tag{17}$$

where $\boldsymbol{X}_1$, $\boldsymbol{X}_2$, …, $\boldsymbol{X}_n$ denote the intervals sets (frame of discernment) of the n variables Y_1, Y_2, …, Y_n, and the relevant numbers of the intervals are $\boldsymbol{I}_1$, $\boldsymbol{I}_2$,…, $\boldsymbol{I}_n$. $x_{1i_1}, x_{2i_2}, \cdots, x_{ni_n}$ denote the subintervals, $0 \le ji_j \le I_j$ (j = 1,2,…,n); c_k denotes the n-dimensional joint proposition set constructed by several subintervals, and there are $\boldsymbol{I}_1$, $\boldsymbol{I}_2$,…,$\boldsymbol{I}_n$ joint proposition sets $\boldsymbol{c}_k$ in C. The BBA of the joint proposition set C is defined as:

$$m_c(c_k) = m_1(x_{1i_1})m_2(x_{2i_2})\cdots m_n(x_{ni_n}) \tag{18}$$

Thus every element of the Cartesian set C is required to be checked in the evaluation of the belief and plausibility functions by finding the system response bounds. That is to say the minimum and maximum responses of each joint set are needed to calculate:

$$[D_{\min}, D_{\max}] = [\min[f(c_k)], \max[f(c_k)]] \tag{19}$$

As uncertain variable is represented by many discontinuous set instead of smooth and continuous explicit function, time consuming is inevitable in UQ with evidence theory. There are two main approaches to find the bounds of the system response: sampling and optimization. The accuracy of sampling approach is highly dependent on the number of samples and the number of hypercubes, and the process is costly. On the contrary, optimization methods have the potential to dramatically reduce the computational work. To alleviate this computational burden, based on authors' previous work [11], the differential evolution (DE) [28] optimization approach is used to calculate the response bounds of each hypercube and compute the composite BBA of each hypercube, propagation of the represented uncertainty through Park-Ang damage model (Eq. (1)). The characteristics of derivative-free and capability of handling discrete belief structure make DE method to be a good choice for such an interval bound task.

DE is arguably one of the most powerful stochastic real-parameter optimization algorithms for solving complex and computational optimization problems in current use. As a novel evolutionary computation technique, differential evolution resembles the structure of an evolutionary algorithm (EA). However, unlike traditional EAs, the DE-variants perturb the current generation population members with the scaled differences of randomly selected and distinct population members. The characteristics together with other factors of DE make it a fast and robust algorithm and as an alternative to EA. Since late 1990s, DE started to find several significant applications to the optimization problems arising from diverse domains of science and engineering. In a recently published article, Das and Suganthan [29] provided a comprehensive survey of the DE algorithm and its basic concepts, different structures and variants for solving various optimization problems, as well as applications of DE variants to practical optimization problems.

In the context of DE, the individual trial solutions (which constitute a population) are called parameter vectors or genomes. Let $S \in R_n$ be the search space of the problem. Then, the n-dimensional vector can be represented by $\boldsymbol{x}_i = (x_{i1}, x_{i2}, \ldots, x_{in})^T \in S$, $i = 1, 2, \ldots,$ NP, and DE algorithm utilizes NP as a population for each iteration, called a generation of the algorithm. For the damage index assessment response process, its parameter vector is generated by the uncertainty variables (β, F_y, and δ_u) in ranges according to their respective belief structures. DE operates through the same computational steps as employed by a standard EA, including crossover, mutation, crossover, and selection operators, but differs from traditional EAs, DE employs difference of the parameter vectors to explore the objective function landscape. As above brief description, the pseudocode of DE is presented in **Figure 7** and with a detailed survey of the DE family of algorithms can be found in Ref. [29].

Take the pseudocode of DE in mind, the illustration of DE-based computational strategy for finding the propagated belief structure by the example as shown in **Figure 8** (only one uncertain parameter is considered).

The procedure of uncertainty propagation using the DE strategy is as follows:

- Collect all uncertain information and construct corresponding BBA structure of each uncertain parameter, combine the BBA structures under the situation of evidences provided by different sources or experts using combination rules of evidence.
- Use differential evolution algorithm to calculate the bound values of the system response within each joint interval and construct corresponding joint belief structures.
- Given the complete BBA on the output response of interest damage index D, the belief and plausibility functions on D are given and any general subset can be developed by applying Eqs. (9) and (10).

Step1: Set the values of mutation constants F, crossover constants CR, population size NP, maximum numbers of generations G_{max}, object function $f()$ and number of parameters of object function ID

Step 2: Randomly initialize the NP population $\boldsymbol{x}_i^0$ (i<=NP) and select the best competitor $\boldsymbol{x}_{best}^0$

Step3: WHILE $G<=G_{max}$ or convergency criterion is not satisfied

FOR i=1 to NP

3.1 Mutation step: the mutated vector is generated as

$$v_i^{G+1} = x_i^G + F_1\left(x_{best}^G - x_i^G\right) + F\left(x_{r1}^G - x_{r2}^G\right)$$

3.2 Cross step: for each mutated vector, the trial vector is generated using

FOR j=1 to ID

IF rand(j)≤CR or j=randn(i) THEN $u_{ij}^{G+1} = v_{ij}^{G+1}$

OTHERWISE $u_{ij}^{G+1} = x_{ij}^{G+1}$

END IF

END FOR

3.3 Selection step: Evaluate each trial vector $u_i^{(G+1)}$

IF $f(u_i^{G+!}) < f\left(x_i^{G+1}\right)$ THEN $x_i^{G+1} = u_i^{G+1}$

OTHERWISE $x_i^{G+1} = x_i^G$

IF $f(x_i^{G+!}) < f\left(x_{best}^G\right)$ THEN $x_{best}^{G+1} = x_i^{G+1}$

OTHERWISE $x_{best}^{G+1} = x_{best}^G$

END IF

END IF

END FOR

3.4 Increment the generation count G=G+1

END WHILE

Figure 7. Pseudocode of DE.

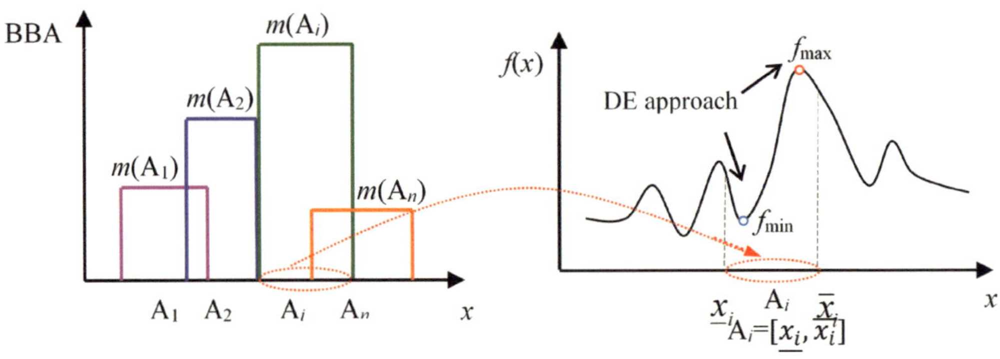

Figure 8. Uncertainty propagation of belief structure of system by DE.

Once the BBA structure of the Park-Ang damage index response is constructed, observed evidence on simulation responses is used in the determination of target propositions to estimate uncertainty measures, i.e., cumulative belief function (CBF) and cumulative plausibility function (CPF).

3.2.3. *Uncertainty measurement for seismic damage assessment*

In evidence theory framework, the plausibility function *Pl* and belief function *Bel* are used to denote the uncertainty measurement. Employing the construction rule proposed by Sentz et al. [30], the CBF and CPF of Park-Ang damage index *D* less than the threshold value are formulated as follows:

$$Pl(D_{\mathrm{thre}}) = \sum\nolimits_{u_D \cap U_D \neq \varnothing} m(u) \quad U_D = \{u_D \leq D_{\mathrm{thre}}\} \tag{20}$$

$$Bel(D_{\mathrm{thre}}) = \sum\nolimits_{u_D \subseteq U_D} m(u) \quad U_D = \{u_D \leq D_{\mathrm{thre}}\} \tag{21}$$

Where $u_D \cap U_D \neq \varnothing$ means that the joint focal element u can be entirely or partially within the threshold domain $u_D \leq D_{\mathrm{thre}}$ and $u_D \subseteq U_D$ means that the joint focal element u_D can be entirely within the threshold domain $u_D \leq D_{\mathrm{thre}}$. Summarized above subparts, the separate stages of UQ framework of evidence theory using differential evolution optimization is shown in **Figure 9**.

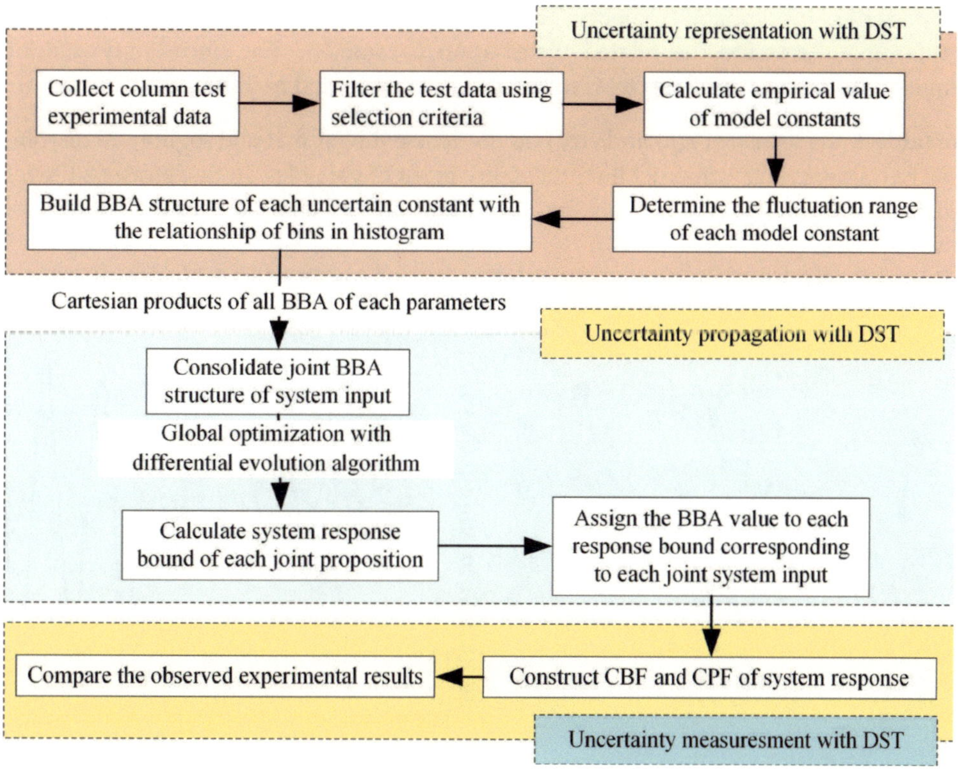

Figure 9. Procedure of UQ of Park-Ang damage model.

4. Case study

In order to investigate the effectiveness and feasibility of the proposed UQ measures, the column "zahn86u7" [31] is selected to compute the Park-Ang damage index in its load step. The backbone curve and load history are shown in **Figure 10**.

As shown in **Figure 10a**, the ultimate cyclic displacement is calibrated by using the average value of 80% maximum force point on the force capacity reduction slope of positive and negative direction. The effective path in **Figure 10b** denotes the load path from initial state to ultimate state and the load path is the global displacement history. Using the properties of column, listed in the webpage of PEER, the nominal value of constants in Park-Ang damage model β, δ_u and F_y can be estimated by the empirical expressions from Eq. (2) to Eq. (7), respectively. In consistent with Section 3.2, the uncertainty distribution of model constants can be depicted as the nominal value multiply the factor ε. Taking the computed results into the evidence representation process, the BBA structures of β, δ_u, and F_y with different models are listed in **Tables 1** and **2**.

Taking above uncertain information into the differential evolution-based uncertainty propagation framework, the evidential UQ results for each load step as shown in **Figure 11**.

To validate the generality of evidence theory, the variability of Park-Ang model parameters is also represented by probability theory. The goodness of fit test is applied to test the distribution type and determine the related distribution parameters. The uncertainty distribution information of model B for β model C for δ_u and F_y is presented in **Table 3**.

From **Table 3**, the values of $\varepsilon(\beta)$ and $\varepsilon(\delta_u)$ do not refuse the normal and lognormal distribution. We use two strategies to construct the probability input of variables. In first strategy, the lognormal distribution is applied to fit all the uncertainty inputs and the cumulative distribution

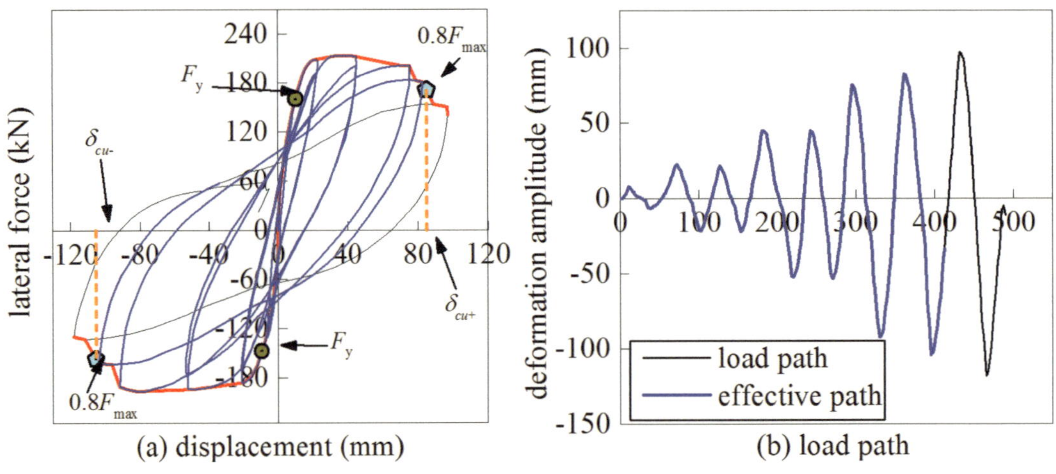

Figure 10. Backbone curve (a) and load path (b) of columns of column test.

β				F_y	
Model A		**Model B**			
Range	**BBA**	**Range**	**BBA**	**Range**	**BBA**
[0.0345, 0.087]	0.301	[0.0266, 0.067]	0.458	[77.40, 133.19]	0.121
[0.0873, 0.139]	0.181	[0.0672, 0.108]	0.325	[105.22, 133.19]	0.422
[0.139, 0.192]	0.277	[0.0672, 0.189]	0.181	[133.19, 161.01]	0.26
[0.192, 0.244]	0.145	[0.0672, 0.230]	0.036	[161.01, 188.82]	0.139
[0.244, 0.296]	0.096			[161.0, 216.63]	0.029
				[161.01, 244.44]	0.017
				[161.01, 272.42]	0.012

Table 1. The BBA structure for multisource of β and F_y.

Model C		**Model D**		**Model E**	
Range	**BBA**	**Range**	**BBA**	**Range**	**BBA**
[0.034, 0.115]	0.568	[0.043, 0.116]	0.649	[0.0442, 0.104]	0.541
[0.115, 0.156]	0.207	[0.116, 0.188]	0.351	[0.104, 0.133]	0.180
[0.115, 0.196]	0.01			[0.133, 0.193]	0.279
[0.196, 0.237]	0.125				

Table 2. The BBA structure for multisource of δ_u.

function of uncertainty response which is indicated as CDF1. In other strategy, the probability distributions of $\varepsilon(\beta)$ and $\varepsilon(\delta_u)$ are assigned as normal distribution, while the distribution of $\varepsilon(F_y)$ is lognormal and corresponding cumulative distribution function of uncertainty result is represented as CDF2. To compare the quantification results of probability and evidence theory, **Figure 12** is presented to describe the damage index evolution in load steps 280 and 412, respectively. To make a further illustration for the damage state evolution in each load step, the point 0.25, 0.5, 0.75, and 1 are used to represent the minor, moderate, severe, and collapse damage state, respectively.

As illustrated in **Figure 12**, the probability theory based UQ results CDF1 and CDF2 are located in the range of curves CPF and CBF, this indicates that evidence theory is compatible to probability theory. The discrepancy of CDF1 and CDF2 demonstrates that probability theory may not be suitable to handle the epistemic uncertainty which is stemmed from limited experimental data. In other words, the probabilistic UQ result is ambiguous due to epistemic uncertainty and the choice of distribution type has a great impact on the quantification result. However, evidential UQ strategy demonstrates its power to quantify the epistemic uncertainty

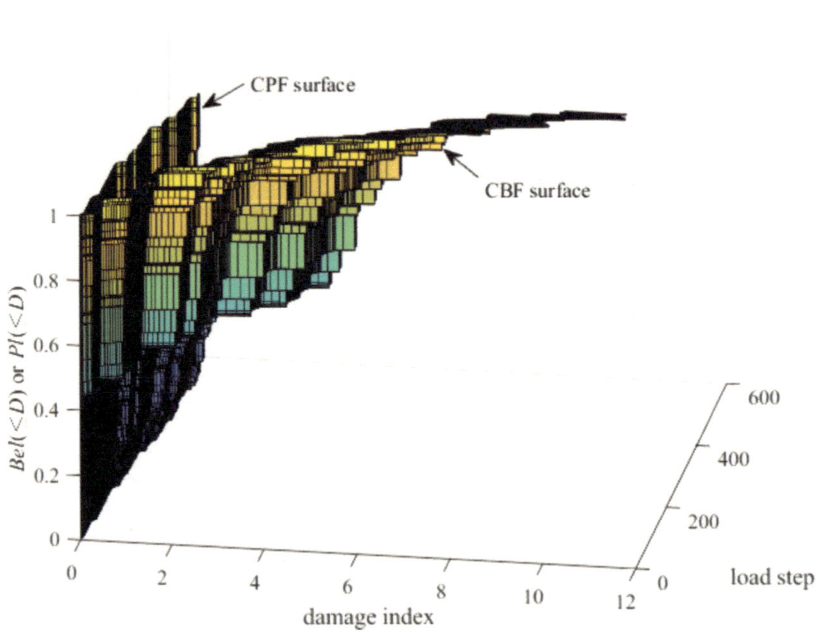

Figure 11. The evidential uncertainty propagation results of Park-Ang damage index.

Constants	Distribution type	m_u	σ
$\varepsilon_B(\beta)$	Normal	0.963	0.529
	Lognormal	-0.171	0.514
$\varepsilon_C(\delta_u)$	Normal	1.404	0.697
	Lognormal	0.206	0.537
$\varepsilon(F_y)$	Lognormal	-0.272	0.225

Table 3. The distribution information of Park-Ang constants.

because of its two uncertain measures belief function and plausibility function. In order to further clarify the influence of epistemic uncertainty, the quantitative results of damage index in **Figures 12a** and **b** are reported in **Table 4**.

As shown in **Table 4**, the belief interval of moderate damage state in steps 280 and 412 are [0.11, 0.447] and [0, 0.026], respectively. This means the exceeding probability of moderate damage state are [0.553, 0.89] and [0.974, 1] in steps 280 and 412, respectively. **Table 5** also displays the cumulative distribution value for moderate damage state for probability-theory-based quantification results. Using the first probability strategy CDF1, the cumulative distribution for moderate damage state are 0.217 and 0 corresponding to steps 280 and step 412. This means the exceeding probabilities of moderate damage state are 0.783 and 1 in steps 280 and 412, respectively. Analogously, the cumulative distribution values of CDF2 for moderate damage state are 0.298 and 0 in steps 280 and 412, respectively. It is worth noting the divergence of the cumulative distribution values of CDF1 and CDF2 in step 280. Furthermore, the

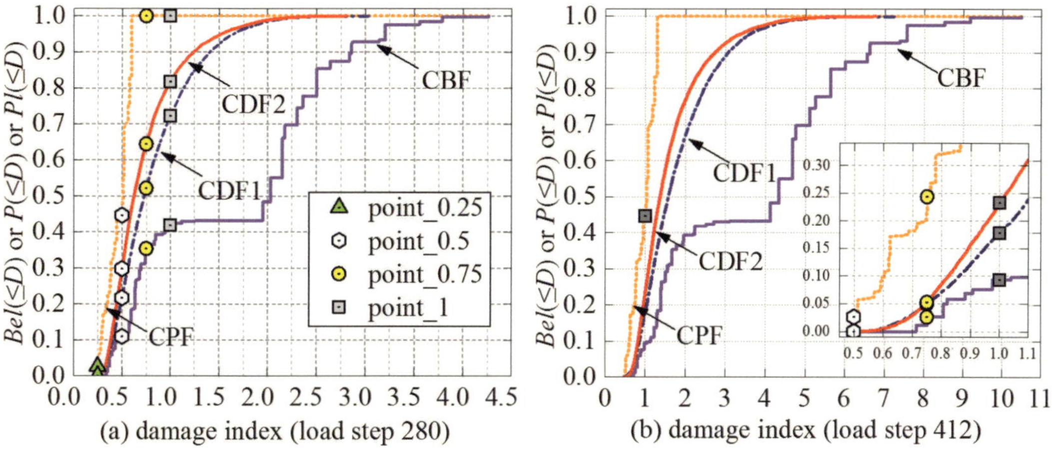

Figure 12. Comparison of propagation results using evidence theory and probability theory. (a) The cumulative distribution of damage index in step 280 and (b) the cumulative distribution of damage index in step 412.

Damage index	Cumulative distribution curve in step 280				Damage index	Cumulative distribution curve in step 412			
	CPF	CDF1	CDF2	CBF		CPF	CDF1	CDF2	CBF
0.25	0.026	0	0	0	0.25	0	0	0	0
0.5	0.447	0.217	0.298	0.11	0.5	0.026	0	0	0
0.75	1	0.522	0.644	0.354	0.75	0.244	0.050	0.053	0.026
1	1	0.722	0.818	0.419	1	0.447	0.178	0.233	0.094

Table 4. The cumulative distribution value of Park-Ang constants in step 280 and 412.

divergence of two kind probability-based quantification results provides the evidence that probability theory is not able to handle the epistemic uncertainty. Comparing the quantification results of collapse damage state, the similar conclusion can be obtained. Especially, the cumulative distribution value for collapse damage state is step 412, the evidence result is [0.094, 0.447], this means the value of damage index larger than 1 is located in the interval [0.453, 0.906]. While the cumulative probabilities of CDF1 and CDF2 are 0.178 and 0.233, respectively. This illustrates that the exceedance probability of collapse state is 0.822 for CDF1 and 0.767 for CDF2. From the view of risk assessment, the evidence theory will give decision maker a more robust UQ result, but the probability cannot.

With the incomplete knowledge of prediction model under the various operation conditions, different expert evidence conflicts are inevitable. To reconcile this task challenge, evidence combination rule is proposed to combine the evidences from multisource. Herein, the Dempster's rule is applied to aggregate the different source of evidence for β, δ_u, and F_y as shown in **Table 5**.

Using the aggregated BBA structures of these three uncertain parameters, the system uncertain response CPF2 and CBF2 are shown in **Figure 13**. To clarify the effectiveness of combination

β		δ_u		F_y	
Range	**BBA**	**Range**	**BBA**	**Range**	**BBA**
[0.035, 0.067]	0.297	[0.044, 0.104]	0.568	[77.40, 133.19]	0.121
[0.067, 0.087]	0.351	[0.104, 0.115]	0.189	[105.22, 133.19]	0.422
[0.087, 0.108]	0.127	[0.115, 0.116]	0.102	[133.19, 161.01]	0.26
[0.087, 0.139]	0.085	[0.116, 0.133]	0.055	[161.01, 188.82]	0.139
[0.139, 0.189]	0.108	[0.133, 0.156]	0.058	[161.01, 216.63]	0.029
[0.139, 0.192]	0.021	[0.133, 0.188]	0.028	[161.01, 244.44]	0.017
[0.192, 0.230]	0.011			[161.01, 272.42]	0.012

Table 5. The combined BBA structure for β, δ_u, and F_y.

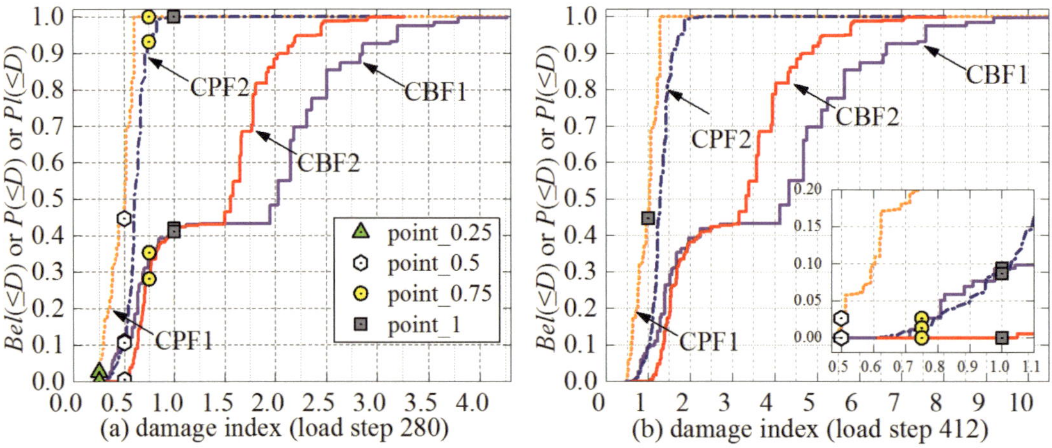

Figure 13. Comparison of propagation results with uncombined and combined BBA input. (a) The cumulative distribution of damage index in step 280 and (b) the cumulative distribution of damage index in step 412.

rule, the uncertainty propagation results CPF1 and CBF1 from the model B of β and model C of δ_u and F_y are also listed in **Figure 13**.

As shown in **Figure 13**, the UQ results of Park-Ang damage index variate in a large range. The distance of CBF and CPF denotes the epistemic uncertainty that is derived from the limited experimental data and lack of knowledge for complicated composite materials (e.g., parameters model hypothesis, material properties) or incomplete knowledge of empirical model. In comparison with the distance of CPF1 and CBF1 for uncombined BBA, the distance of CPF2 and CBF2 for combined BBA is much narrower, and this can be explained as the high conflict information of multisources that are discarded by aggregating the multisources evidence. However, the aggregation rule is not established in probability theory. From this point of view, the evidence theory has great potential to quantify the uncertainty from multisources which are having great existence in civil engineering.

5. Conclusions

UQ of seismic damage model are important for PBSD and performance-based seismic assessment. In this chapter, the epistemic uncertainty of the constants of Park-Ang model is taken into account. The Park-Ang damage model constants are calibrated with column set, selected from PEER column performance database. To effectively represent the uncertainty inherent in Park-Ang model constants with limited experimental data, the UQ measurement that combines evidence theory and differential evolution is presented. In order to further investigate the feasibility and effectiveness of presented UQ measurement, the Monte-Carlo sampling method combined with classical probability distribution, which is fitted with given data, is used. Comparing the propagation results of evidence theory and classical probability theory, we can conclude that the evidence theory is flexible to handle the epistemic uncertainty, which is stemmed from lack of knowledge or sparse experimental data, whereas the classical probability theory may be limited by the selection of distribution type and the determination of value for the distribution parameters. Using the aggregation rules of evidence theory demonstrates that evidence theory is capable to handle the uncertainty from multisources.

Acknowledgements

This study was supported by the Ministry of Science and Technology of China, Grant No. SLDRCE14-B-03 and the National Natural Science Foundation of China, Grant Nos. 51178337 and 51478356.

Author details

Hesheng Tang*, Dawei Li and Songtao Xue

*Address all correspondence to: 02036@tongji.edu.cn

State Key Laboratory for Disaster Reduction in Civil Engineering, Tongji University, Shanghai, China

References

[1] ASCE. ASCE Standard ASCE/SEI41-06: Seismic Rehabilitation of Existing Buildings. American Society of Civil Engineers: Reston, Virginia; 2007

[2] Krätzig WB, Meyer IF, Meskouris K, editors. Damage evolution in reinforced concrete members under cyclic loading. Proceedings of 5th International Conference on Structural Safety and Reliability, San Francisco; 1989:795–804

[3] Teran-Gilmore A, Avila E, Rangel G. On the use of plastic energy to establish strength requirements in ductile structures. Engineering Structures. 2003;**25**(7):965–80

[4] Park YJ, Ang AHS. Mechanistic seismic damage model for reinforced concrete. Journal of Structural Engineering. 1985;**111**(4):722–39

[5] Kunnath S, Reinhorn A, Park Y. Analytical modeling of inelastic seismic response of R/C structures. Journal of Structural Engineering. 1990;**116**(4):996–1017

[6] Park YJ, Ang AHS, Wen YK. Damage-limiting aseismic design of buildings. Earthquake Spectra. 1987;**3**(1):1–26

[7] Park Y-J, Ang AHS, Wen YK. Seismic damage analysis of reinforced concrete buildings. Journal of Structural Engineering. 1985;**111**(4):740–57

[8] Fajfar P. Equivalent ductility factors, taking into account low-cycle fatigue. Earthquake Engineering & Structural Dynamics. 1992;**21**(10):837–48

[9] Chai YH, Romstad KM, Bird SM. Energy-based linear damage model for high-intensity seismic loading. Journal of Structural Engineering. 1995;**121**(5):857–64

[10] Rajabi R, Barghi M, Rajabi R. Investigation of Park-Ang damage index model for flexural behavior of reinforced concrete columns. The Structural Design of Tall and Special Buildings. 2013;**22**(17):1350–1358

[11] Tang HS, Li DW, editors. Uncertainty quantification of the Park-Ang damage model applied to performance based design. Proceedings of the Fifteenth International Conference on Civil, Structural and Environmental Engineering Computing. Stirling shire, UK: Civil-Comp Press; 2015; 170–170.

[12] Williams MS, Sexsmith RG. Seismic assessment of concrete bridges using inelastic damage analysis. Engineering Structures. 1997;**19**(3):208–16

[13] Williams MS, Sexsmith RG. Seismic damage indices for concrete structures: A state-of--the-art review. Earthquake Spectra. 1995;**11**(2):319–49

[14] Zadeh LA. Fuzzy sets. Information and Control. 1965;**8**(3):338–53

[15] Dubois D, Prade HM, Farreny H, Martin-Clouaire R, Testemale C. Possibility theory: An Approach to Computerized Processing of Uncertainty. New York: Plenum press; 1988

[16] Moore RE. Interval Analysis. Englewood Cliffs: Prentice-Hall; 1966.

[17] Walley P. Statistical Reasoning with Imprecise Probabilities. London: Chapman and Hall; 1991

[18] Dempster AP. Upper and lower probabilities induced by a multivalued mapping. The Annals of Mathematical Statistics. 1967;**38**(2):325–39

[19] Shafer G. A Mathematical Theory of Evidence. Princeton: Princeton University Press; 1976

[20] Tang H, Su Y, Wang J. Evidence theory and differential evolution based uncertainty quantification for buckling load of semi-rigid jointed frames. Sadhana. 2015;**40**(5):1611–27

[21] Oberkampf WL, Helton JC, Sentz K, editors. Mathematical Representation of Uncertainty. Non-Deterministic Approaches Forum. American Institute of Aeronautics and Astronautics Seattle, WA, Paper; 2001.

[22] CEN. Eurocode 8: Design of Structures for Earthquake Resistance-Part 3: Assessment and Retrofitting of Buildings; European Committee for Standardization 2005.

[23] Fardis MN, Biskinis DE, editors. Deformation capacity of RC members, as controlled by flexure or shear. Proceedings of International Symposium on Performance-based Engineering for Earthquake Resistant Structures honoring Prof. Shunsuke Otani, University of Tokyo; 2003: 511–530.

[24] Panagiotakos TB, Fardis MN. Deformations of reinforced concrete members at yielding and ultimate. ACI Structural Journal. 2001; **98**(2): 135–148.

[25] University of Washington. The UW-PEER Reinforced Concrete Column Test Database Washington [Internet] 2004 [Available from: http://www.ce.washington.edu/peera1/

[26] Sentz K, Ferson S. Combination of evidence in Dempster-Shafer theory. Callaos N, Ebisuzaki T, Starr B, Abe JM, Lichtblau D, editors. Orlando: International Institute Informatics & Systemics; 2002

[27] Salehgh affari S, Rais-Rohani M, Marin EB, Bammann DJ. A new approach for determination of material constants of internal state variable based plasticity models and their uncertainty quantification. Computational Materials Science. 2012;**55**:237–44.

[28] Storn R, Price K. Differential evolution–a simple and efficient heuristic for global optimization over continuous spaces. Journal of Global optimization. 1997;**11**(4):341–59

[29] Das S, Suganthan PN. Differential evolution: a survey of the state-of-the-art. Evolutionary Computation, IEEE Transactions on. 2011;**15**(1):4–31

[30] Ferson S, Kreinovick V, Ginzburg L, Sentz F. Constructing Probability Boxes and Dempster-Shafer Structures. United States, Albuquerque, NM (US); Livermore, CA (US): Sandia National Labs; 2003. Contract No: SAND2002-4015

[31] Zahn FA. Design of Reinforced Concrete Bridge Columns for Strength and Ductility. University of Canterbury; 1985

Chapter 5

Uncertainty Quantification and Reduction of Molecular Dynamics Models

Xiaowang Zhou and Stephen M. Foiles

Additional information is available at the end of the chapter

http://dx.doi.org/10.5772/intechopen.68507

Abstract

Molecular dynamics (MD) is an important method underlying the modern field of Computational Materials Science. Without requiring prior knowledge as inputs, MD simulations have been used to study a variety of material problems. However, results of molecular dynamics simulations are often associated with errors as compared with experimental observations. These errors come from a variety of sources, including inaccuracy of interatomic potentials, short length and time scales, idealized problem description and statistical uncertainties of MD simulations themselves. This chapter specifically devotes to the statistical uncertainties of MD simulations. In particular, methods to quantify and reduce such statistical uncertainties are demonstrated using a variety of exemplar cases, including calculations of finite temperature static properties such as lattice constants, cohesive energies, elastic constants, dislocation energies, thermal conductivities, surface segregation and calculations of kinetic properties such as diffusion parameters. We also demonstrate that when the statistical uncertainties are reduced to near zero, MD can be used to validate and improve widely used theories.

Keywords: molecular dynamics, molecular statics, uncertainty quantification, model calibration, materials science, thermodynamics, kinetics

1. Introduction

In atomistic simulations, a material is represented by the positions of an assembly of atoms whose energy is represented through a model of the interatomic forces. Molecular dynamics (MD) simulations follow the motion of this collection of atoms. From these simulations, one can extract information about the thermodynamics and kinetics of materials and key material defects. As an example of an MD material simulation, **Figure 1(a)** shows an aluminium crystal

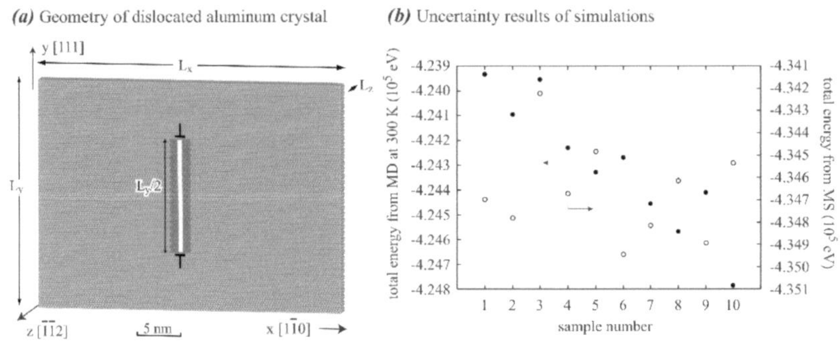

Figure 1. Observation of MD uncertainties. (a) An aluminium crystal containing an edge dislocation dipole and (b) the total energies of the dislocated aluminium crystal obtained from MD and MS simulations of 10 different samples.

whose $[1\bar{1}0]$, $[111]$, and $[\bar{1}\,\bar{1}2]$ crystallographic orientations are aligned respectively with the *x*-, *y*- and *z*- coordinate directions. The initial atom coordinates can be assigned according to structure, orientation and lattice constant of the crystal. To make the system interesting, **Figure 1(a)** also contains two edge dislocations created by removing a $(1\bar{1}0)$ plane as indicated by the white vertical line. The width of the removed region, therefore, equals exactly the Burgers magnitude $b = |\langle 110 \rangle a/2|$. To close the gap of the missing plane, surrounding atoms as indicated by the dark region are shifted towards the gap. The system can also possess a temperature. This is achieved by assigning velocities to all atoms under the Boltzmann distribution condition. Normally, periodic boundary conditions are used to remove free surfaces and infinitely extend the system. This means that the system shown in **Figure 1(a)** is periodically repeated in the *x*-, *y*- and *z*- coordinate directions, with the periodic lengths equal to the corresponding system dimensions L_x, L_y and L_z. Based on an interatomic potential model that can be used to calculate system energy and interatomic forces [1], an MD simulation essentially solves atom positions as a function of time from Newton's equations of motion [2, 3].

The simplest MD simulations conserve energy and do not change system sizes L_x, L_y and L_z. With such NVE (meaning that the number of atoms, system volume and system energy are constant) simulations, constant target temperature and pressure usually cannot be maintained. By using Nose-Hoover dragging forces [4] to increase or decrease atom kinetic energies depending on if the temperature is lower or higher than the desired value, MD simulations can be performed at a constant temperature. By using the Parrinello-Rahman algorithm [5] to allow the periodic lengths L_x, L_y and L_z to increase or decrease depending on if the pressure is higher or lower than the desired value, MD simulations can also be performed at a constant pressure.

Once an interatomic potential is given, the MD methods described above enable many material problems to be computationally studied without any prior knowledge of these problems. For example, MD reveals phonon vibration spectrum and thermal transport properties even when applied to defect-free systems. When systems contain point defects, MD simulates the diffusion of these defects. When systems contain dislocations, such as **Figure 1(a)**, MD computes dislocation core structures and core energies. When external forces/loads are applied to the system, MD explores a variety of other problems including deformation, fracture and structure evolution. When adatoms are continuously added to a surface, MD shows the structure evolution during vapour deposition synthesis processes. Due to the broad applicability and high predictability of MD simulations, the problem of the uncertainty margin of MD results is becoming increasingly important.

In principle, results of molecular dynamics simulations necessarily contain errors as compared with experimental observations. These errors come from a variety of sources, including inaccuracy of interatomic potentials, short length and time scales, idealized problem description and statistical uncertainties of MD simulations themselves. This chapter focuses on quantification and reduction of one important model uncertainty: statistical uncertainty of molecular dynamics simulations.

2. An overview perspective of uncertainty quantification methods

The ultimate goal of evaluating and reducing the statistical uncertainty of MD simulations is to minimize differences between predictions and experimental observations. To establish a useful context, we first briefly describe quantification methods for other uncertainties during multiscale simulations of materials.

Uncertainties are commonly divided into two types: aleatoric uncertainty arising from randomness and epistemic uncertainty arising from lack of knowledge. Examples of the aleatoric uncertainty include head or tail when flipping a coin or a high precision length measured with a coarse scale ruler. Typically, the aleatoric uncertainty can be described by a probability distribution function. Increasing data can result in more accurate characterization of this distribution, but cannot reduce its variance. Examples of the epistemic uncertainty include prediction from an inaccurate (or incorrect) model, or the length measured by a low-quality ruler. Usually, the epistemic uncertainty cannot be described by a probability distribution. This uncertainly, however, can be reduced when additional data or knowledge are incorporated (e.g., when the model is improved or the error of the ruler is calibrated). Note that sometimes the epistemic uncertainty can be treated as the aleatoric uncertainty. For example, due to the thermal expansion, rulers are usually associated with an epistemic error on a given day. This epistemic uncertainty may become an aleatoric uncertainty if the measurements are made throughout the entire year.

There are many issues that influence the comparison of MD results with experimental observations. The most commonly discussed approximation is the accuracy (epistemic uncertainty) of the interatomic potential. Ideally, this represents the true energy of the arrangement of atoms. In practice, a computationally convenient and physically motivated functional form of the potential is assumed and parameterized to match either fundamental electronic structure calculations or experimental data [1]. Only recently have systematic evaluations of these errors begun to be performed [6, 7]. As one practical approach, Moore et al. [7] performed a parameter sensibility study where the parameter of an interatomic potential is varied one at a time and its effects on properties (e.g., lattice constant, elastic constants, cohesive energy and enthalpy of mixing) are determined using MD simulations. Such a study reveals the relative importance of each of the potential parameters. However, it does not provide information on the accuracy of potential.

In principle, we can always image the existence of an ideal potential that will give the exact solution to the problem of our interest, provided that this potential is fitted to the right values of a list of properties $\{k_1, k_2, \ldots, k_n, u_1, u_2, \ldots, u_m\}$, where $k_1, k_2, \ldots, k_n$ are the list of properties that are known to be important (e.g., lattice constant, elastic constants, cohesive energy, etc.), and $u_1, u_2, \ldots, u_m$ are a sufficient list of important properties that will make the potential accurate but are unknown to us as what these properties are due to the lack of knowledge. In practices, however, we will never achieve such an ideal potential because not only we do not know u_i ($i = 1, 2, \ldots, m$), but also no potential can be fitted exactly to the target values of all k_i ($i = 1, 2, \ldots, n$). Based on this recognition, a relevant approach to quantify the epistemic uncertainty of the potential is to create an ensemble of potentials that predict a distribution of properties $\{k_1, k_2, \ldots, k_n\}$ centring around the true experimental values and quantify the effects of this distribution on the target properties computed with MD simulations. This approach may still not yield a satisfactory quantification of the epistemic uncertainty of the potential currently. However, the quantified epistemic uncertainty will continuously improve as more and more u_i properties are understood and become k_i with improved knowledge.

There are additional issues associated with MD simulations. For the study of complex defects, issues can arise from the boundary conditions imposed on the simulations and from the structural idealizations often imposed. For example, in a recent study of faceting of grain boundaries in Fe, there were qualitative differences between the MD-predicted facet length and facet junction geometries and experimental observations [8]. The source of the disagreement was the idealized geometry used in the MD simulations. The simulations assumed an ideal coincident site lattice misorientation between the crystal lattices while the experiment deviated slightly from this ideal misorientation. This deviation introduced interfacial dislocations that fundamentally changed the faceting behaviour. The use of improved geometries, often at the computational cost of using larger systems, can be used to estimate the related epistemic uncertainty. Likewise, the time scales of MD simulations (on the order of nanoseconds) raise issues with processes that occur on longer time scales. For example, in simulations of multi-component systems, diffusive processes of substitutional impurities often occur on time scales beyond direct MD simulations, and simulations of mechanical deformation can be strongly influenced by the high strain-rates required by MD simulation times. Increasing simulation time can provide an estimate of the trends of the related epistemic uncertainty.

To study material problems at engineering scales, multiscale approaches linking models of different scales are needed. Beyond the specific uncertainties associated with MD simulations, there are also initial studies of the broader question of how those uncertainties propagate through a material modelling hierarchy [9–11]. To study how an aleatoric uncertainty of the interatomic potential propagates through the MD to a continuum model, we can perform many MD simulations using different interatomic potentials sampled from the aleatoric uncertainty distribution. Results of each MD simulation are used as inputs to perform a separate continuum simulation of the final material properties. Many continuum simulations then give an aleatoric uncertainty distribution. To yield a highly converged continuous distribution of the final results, thousands or more MD simulations are needed. This is often computationally impractical.

Assume that a continuum scale model requires a list of properties $P_{i,\ MD}$ (i = 1, 2, ..., N) from MD calculations as inputs. If these properties are independent (e.g., thermal conductivities obtained at different temperatures), then the direct Monte Carlo sampling [12] can be used to propagate uncertainties efficiently. First, numerous MD simulations are performed to determine distribution of each $P_{i,\ MD}$. Because only distribution of one property is concerned, the number of MD simulations needed to yield a smooth distribution of that property is significantly reduced. Knowledge of distribution of each of the $P_{i,\ MD}$ properties can then be used to sample as many $\{P_1, P_2, ..., P_N\}$ sets [12] as one may desire. These data sets can be used in continuum simulations to yield a smooth distribution of the final results.

Experimentally, no samples can have exactly the same microstructure in terms of size and population of grains, shape and volume fraction of phases, defect densities, chemical composition and purity. As a result, experimental measurements of mechanical properties of materials always involve uncertainties. Because microstructures obtained from the same processing satisfy a certain distribution, such uncertainties are aleatoric. On the other hand, some properties such as diffusivities are difficult to measure. As a result, there are considerable disagreements for the diffusivity data reported by different groups [13]. Such uncertainties can be considered as epistemic. Note that experimental uncertainties are often the problem of interest, but they are different from model uncertainties. It is possible to use multiscale modelling to predict the experimental uncertainties. For example, MD simulations can be used to determine the cohesive zone laws [14, 15] of different grain boundaries. These cohesive zone laws can be incorporated in continuum models to simulation intergranular fracture. Through a continuum simulation of the intergranular fracture from a large number of realizations of initial grain structures, the experimental uncertainties due to the variation of grain microstructures can be calculated. Because experimental uncertainties are superimposed on model uncertainties, it is required that model uncertainties be reduced (or at least quantified) before experimental uncertainties can be confidently studied. The quantification and reduction of the statistical uncertainty of molecular dynamics simulations are therefore important.

3. Statistical uncertainty of molecular dynamics methods

Due to thermal noises, MD simulations are always associated with a statistical uncertainty. To examine this problem, an MD simulation of the computational system shown in **Figure 1(a)** is performed for a period of 20 ps at a temperature of 300 K using a previously developed Al-Cu interatomic potential [16]. After the first 10 ps is ignored to enable a preliminary equilibration, the total system energy is calculated every 1 ps for the remaining 10 ps. The total energies for these 10 snapshot samples are shown in **Figure 1(b)** using the filled circles. It can be seen that the total energies for the 10 samples are not exactly the same, but rather span a range of nearly 900 eV. Two types of uncertainties can be identified here. First, there is a general decreasing trend with sample number (corresponding to time). This systematic error arises from a continued equilibration with increasing simulation time. Second, there are some occasional fluctuations of the results. This statistical error arises from thermal noises.

Molecular statics (MS) is another frequently applied computational method [2] to study materials. Rather than solving Newton's equation of motion, MS determines equilibrium atom positions by minimizing the total potential energy of the system at the 0 K temperature (i.e., there is no kinetic energy of atoms). To examine if MS simulations have the uncertainty issue when studying dislocations, 10 MS simulations are performed on the configuration of **Figure 1(a)** using different random number seeds. The 10 total system potential energies obtained from the 10 MS simulations are included in **Figure 1(b)** using unfilled circles. Interestingly, MS simulations, which do not involve thermal noises, also involve large uncertainties. In fact, differences among the 10 samples are comparable with the MD simulations (~800 eV or above). This MS error, however, appears to be entirely statistical.

The uncertainty discussed above pertains to total energy of the system. The system considered in **Figure 1(a)** contains 129,600 atoms. As a result, the relative error shown in **Figure 1(b)** is less than 900/129,600 = 0.007 eV/atom. It is important to note that the MS errors revealed in **Figure 1(b)** are larger than one would normally see in literature. This is because literature simulations are usually applied to either defect-free systems or much smaller system dimensions. When defects relax (e.g., a perfect dislocation dissociates into two partials bounding a stacking fault as in the present case), many local energy minimums occur and therefore MS results become uncertain because there are really no robust methods available today to identify the global minimum energy configuration. Furthermore, while current MS methods can achieve high accuracies for relative properties (e.g., energy per atom), it is unrealistic to achieve small global errors for large systems (unless accuracies of relative properties can be infinitely improved when system sizes are increased). Global errors are important to many applications. In **Figure 1(a)**, for example, the dislocation line energy is defined as the total system energy difference between dislocated and perfect crystals, divided by total dislocation length $2L_z$ along the z direction. When L_z is not too big, say, ~25 Å as in the present case, a total energy error of 900 eV will result in meaningless dislocation line energy calculations considering that the line energies of dislocations are usually less than 5 eV/Å [17]. In the following, we will discuss methods to quantify and reduce the statistical uncertainty margin of MD simulations as revealed here.

4. Methods for quantifying molecular dynamics statistical uncertainty

Experimentally measured properties are average behaviour of systems over the time scale of the measurement, which is usually much longer than the MD time scales. To reflect experimental properties, it is appropriate to calculate time-averaged properties during MD simulations. Two different approaches can be used to perform statistical uncertainty quantification for time-averaged MD simulations based on fundamental principles of statistics [18].

The first approach is based entirely on the statistical nature of MD results. Assume that an MD simulation is performed for a total period of t_{tot}. We can divide t_{tot} into N segments with the end point of each segment being $t_i = i\Delta t$ (i = 1, 2, …, N) where $\Delta t = t_{tot}/N$. Any time-averaged property can be calculated for each of the time intervals $\Delta t_i = t_i - t_{i-1} = \Delta t$, and as a result, each MD simulation will produce N values of the property P. If we denote each estimate of P to be P_i ($i = 1, 2, \ldots, N$), the best estimate of the property can be calculated as

$$\overline{P} = \frac{\sum_{i=1}^{N} P_i}{N} \tag{1}$$

The uncertainty of the samples P_i can be quantified by the sample standard deviation defined as

$$\sigma = \sqrt{\frac{\sum_{i=1}^{N} (P_i - \overline{P})^2}{N-1}} \tag{2}$$

The best estimate $\overline{P}$ is also associated with an uncertainty $\overline{\sigma}$. $\overline{\sigma}$ is reduced from σ through the well-known relationship [18]

$$\overline{\sigma} = \frac{\sigma}{\sqrt{N}} \tag{3}$$

Eqs. (1)–(3) are effective in determining the variation of the calculated properties. They do not give direct indication of how physical the results are. In many applications, properties P, Q, R, … are often related through some well-justified physical functions, say, $F(P, Q, R, \ldots) = 0$. The second approach is based on the deviation of the calculated properties from these functions. In particular, a deviation parameter can be defined as ξ

$$\xi = \sqrt{\frac{\sum_{i=1}^{N} F(P_i, Q_i, R_i, \ldots)^2}{N}} \tag{4}$$

As a first example to calculate ξ, elastic constants of single cubic crystals satisfy $C_{11} = C_{22} = C_{33}$, $C_{33} = C_{44} = C_{55}$, $C_{12} = C_{13} = C_{21} = C_{23} = C_{31} = C_{32}$ and C_{ij} ($j = 4, 5, 6$, $i = 1, 2, \ldots, j$-1) = 0. Accordingly, we can define four deviation parameters as

$$\xi_1 = \sqrt{\frac{\sum_{i=1}^{3} [C_{ii} - (C_{11} + C_{22} + C_{33})/3]^2}{3}} \tag{5}$$

$$\xi_2 = \sqrt{\frac{\sum_{j=1}^{3} \sum_{\substack{i=1, \\ i \neq j}}^{3} [C_{ij} - (C_{12} + C_{13} + C_{21} + C_{23} + C_{31} + C_{32})/6]^2}{6}} \tag{6}$$

$$\xi_3 = \sqrt{\frac{\sum_{i=4}^{6}[C_{ii} - (C_{44} + C_{55} + C_{66})/3]^2}{3}} \tag{7}$$

$$\xi_4 = \sqrt{\frac{\sum_{j=4}^{6}\sum_{i=1}^{j-1}(C_{ij}^2 + C_{ji}^2)}{24}} \tag{8}$$

If we want to determine how physical our overall results are, the best MD estimates of C_{ij} can be used in Eqs. (5)–(8) to calculate $\xi_1 - \xi_4$. This simply means that C_{ij} are averaged over the entire simulation time t_{tot} rather than the short time interval Δt. We can also use C_{ij} obtained within different time intervals (multiple of Δt) to examine time convergence of the calculated properties towards the true physical values.

As another example to calculate ξ, diffusivity D is related to pre-exponential factor D_0 and activation energy barrier Q through the Arrhenius equation, $D = D_0\exp\left(\frac{-Q}{kT}\right)$ or $\ln D_0 - \frac{Q}{kT} - \ln D = 0$, where k and T are respectively Boltzmann constant and temperature. If MD can be used to calculate diffusivities D_i at different temperatures T_i (i = 1, 2, …, N), then we can fit the Arrhenius equation to get D_0 and Q. We can then define a deviation error parameter for the calculated diffusivities from true values as

$$\xi = \sqrt{\frac{\sum_{i=1}^{N}\left(\ln D_0 - \frac{Q}{kT_i} - \ln D_i\right)^2}{N}} \tag{9}$$

Note that although the error parameter ξ can validate models, it does not directly measure the uncertainty margin of a property. However, ξ is related to the direct uncertainty margin σ (or $\overline{\sigma}$) because $\xi \to 0$ necessarily leads to $\sigma \to 0$ (or $\overline{\sigma} \to 0$). In the following, we demonstrate specific examples on how to quantify σ (or $\overline{\sigma}$) and ξ in MD simulations.

5. Lattice constant and cohesive energy

We now quantify the uncertainty margins of the finite temperature lattice constant and cohesive energy of aluminium calculated using MD simulations based on a literature interatomic potential [16]. The periodic computational system includes 5 × 5 × 5 unit cells of a face-centred-cubic (fcc) crystal. The initial lattice is intentionally strained in the x-, y- and z- directions by 0.01, −0.01 and 0.02, respectively, and all atoms are randomly disturbed from their lattice sites subjecting to a maximum displacement of 0.05 Å. A zero pressure NPT (number of atoms, pressure, and temperature are constant) MD simulation is then performed at 300 K using a time step size of 0.004 ps. Since the lattice constants (a_x, a_y and a_z) in the three coordinate directions are not the same initially, their geometric mean $a = \sqrt[3]{a_x a_y a_z}$ is used as the overall lattice constant. Here, geometric mean is used instead of arithmetic mean to conserve volume. The short-term average lattice constant and cohesive energy (per atom) are calculated every 10 time steps (i.e., $\Delta t = 0.04$ ps). The best estimates (refer to running averages here) of these properties are calculated using Eq. (1) as a function of simulation time t_{tot}. The results of these best estimates are shown in **Figure 2(a)**. **Figure 2(a)** indicates that despite the initial disturbed crystal that biases the average calculations towards a non-equilibrium structure at short time, the finite temperature lattice constants and cohesive energy calculated from MD approaches convergence rapidly. After 15 ps simulation, both lattice constant and cohesive energy essentially become constant, and as a result, there is no significant uncertainty associated with this simulation.

Note that we do not explicitly show the standard deviation defined by Eq. (3). However, the information is implicitly revealed in **Figure 2(a)**, because the standard deviation must approach zero when the calculated properties become constant. On the other hand, cubic crystal lattice constants satisfy a relation $a_x = a_y = a_z$. This allows us to define a deviation parameter $\xi = \sqrt{\frac{\left(a_x - \sqrt[3]{a_x a_y a_z}\right)^2 + \left(a_y - \sqrt[3]{a_x a_y a_z}\right)^2 + \left(a_z - \sqrt[3]{a_x a_y a_z}\right)^2}{3}}$ to measure how physical the results are. ξ is calculated as a function of t_{tot}, and the results are shown in **Figure 2(b)**. Considering the small scale in the vertical axis, the non-cubic deviation is very small. This further confirms that the calculated values have extremely small uncertainty margin.

This example indicates that the uncertainty margin of time-averaged MD simulations can be easily reduced to a negligible level when calculating simple properties, such as lattice constant and cohesive energy. This is because these quantities are relative properties (i.e., per unit cell for lattice constant and per atom for cohesive energy), do not involve defects (i.e., no large number of local energy minimums) and can be obtained from small systems. More challenging cases will be presented below.

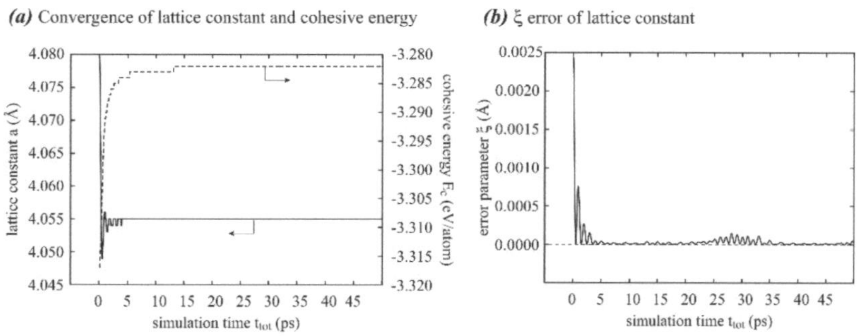

Figure 2. Effect of simulation time on uncertainty of MD calculation of lattice constant and cohesive energy of an fcc aluminium crystal. (a) Lattice constant and cohesive energy and (b) deviation of lattice constant from the cubic relations.

6. Elastic constants

Compared with lattice constant and cohesive energy, calculations of finite temperature elastic constants encounter a bigger uncertainty problem. This is because elastic constants are defined by $C_{ij} = \partial\sigma_i/\partial\varepsilon_j$, where σ_i and ε_j are the stress and strain components in the Voigt notation. Within the finite difference method, elastic constants are calculated as $C_{ij} = \delta\sigma_i/\delta\varepsilon_j$, where $\delta\sigma_i$ is a small change of stress in responding to a small imposed strain $\delta\varepsilon_j$. Accurate calculations can only be achieved when the uncertainty margin of the $\delta\sigma_i$ calculation is significantly smaller than a very small $\delta\varepsilon_j$ value. We now explore this problem using fcc palladium as an example. The simulations employ the literature interatomic potential [19].

First, the equilibrium finite temperature palladium lattice constant that accounts for thermal expansion is calculated using the approach described above. This equilibrium lattice constant is then used to create an fcc palladium crystal containing $4 \times 4 \times 4$ unit cells. Positive and negative small strains of the jth component $\pm\, \delta\varepsilon_j = 10^{-4}$ (j = 1, 2, …, 6) are separately applied to the system. MD simulations using an NVT (number of atoms, volume and temperature are constant) ensemble are performed for 100 ns to relax both the positively and negatively strained systems. An NVT ensemble is needed to maintain the imposed strain. After discarding the first 20 ns, time-averaged stresses σ_i (i = 1, 2, …, 6) are calculated for the remaining t_{tot} = 80 ns. The MD elastic constants C_{ij} are then calculated using a finite-difference scheme

$$C_{ij} = \frac{\sigma_i(\delta\varepsilon_j) - \sigma_i(-\delta\varepsilon_j)}{2\delta\varepsilon_j} \tag{10}$$

By repeating the same process for all i, j = 1, 2, …, 6, we determine all elastic constants. These elastic constants are converted to average values based on the cubic relations, i.e., the bulk modulus $B = (C_{11} + C_{22} + C_{33} + 2C_{12} + 2C_{13} + 2C_{23})/9$, shear moduli $C' = (C_{11} + C_{22} + C_{33} - C_{12} - C_{13} - C_{23})/6$ and $\overline{C}_{44} = (C_{44} + C_{55} + C_{66})/3$. If we divide the 80 ns into 80 segments, B, C' and $\overline{C}_{44}$ are calculated for each segment, and the results are shown in **Figure 3(a)**, where data points are values for some selected segments and lines represent running averages. It can be seen that the uncertainty margin of the averaged elastic constants is very small especially for the running averages, which are virtually constant in the scale of the figure. Note that the data shown in

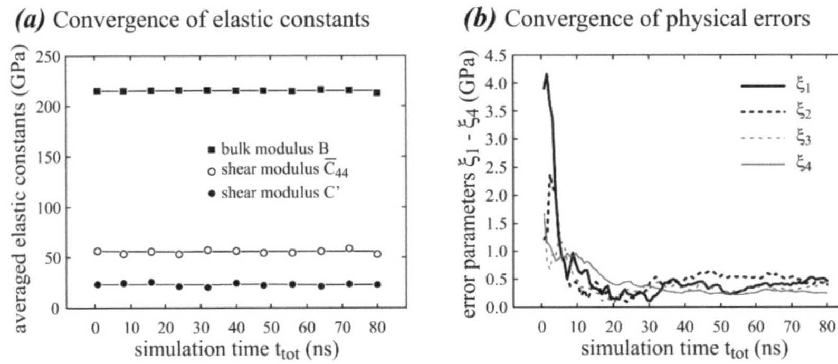

Figure 3. Effect of simulation time on uncertainty of MD calculations of finite temperature elastic constants of an fcc palladium crystal. (a) Cubic-averaged elastic constants and (b) deviation of individual elastic constants from the cubic relations.

Figure 3(a) have been averaged based on the cubic relations. Individual elastic constants C_{ij} may deviate from these relations. The four error parameters $\xi_1 - \xi_4$ for individual elastic constants to deviate from the cubic relations are calculated using Eqs. (5)–(8). If individual elastic constants are calculated as running averages over the entire t_{tot}, then results for $\xi_1 - \xi_4$ are shown in **Figure 3(b)** as a function of t_{tot}. **Figure 3(b)** further reveals that at average time below 20 ns, the calculated elastic constants might have relatively large uncertainties as they have not fully converged to physical values. However, satisfactorily converged results can be achieved when the average time exceeds 20 ns or above.

7. Dislocation energy

Dislocation relaxation causes a large number of local energy minimums, the long elastic field of dislocations requires the use of large systems and dislocation energies are related to total system energies rather than per-atom energy. All of these contribute to large uncertainties as can be seen in **Figure 1(b)**. As a result, reducing uncertainty margin during MD calculations of dislocation energies becomes extremely important. Here, we illustrate this by calculating core energies of edge type of misfit dislocation in zinc-blende CdS [20] using the literature interatomic potential [21]. We also calculated dislocation energies for aluminium using exactly the same geometry as shown in **Figure 1(a)**, and the same results were obtained [22].

The crystals used for the calculations contain n_x (101) planes in x-, n_y (010) planes in y- and $(\bar{1}01)$ n_z planes in z-. At a fixed $n_z = 6$ ($L_z \sim 25$ Å), 10 system dimensions of $n_x \times n_y = 24 \times 86$, 26×92, 28×98, 30×104, 32×110, 34×116, 36×122, 38×128, 40×134 and 42×140 are studied. Under these dimensions, the lengths L_y and L_x roughly satisfy the relation $L_y = 81.7$ (Å) + $4.24\ L_x$, and the smallest ($n_x \times n_y = 24 \times 86$) and the largest ($n_x \times n_y = 42 \times 140$) systems correspond to $L_x \times L_y \sim 100 \times 500$ Å^2 and $\sim 170 \times 820$ Å^2, respectively. Similar to **Figure 1(a)**, a dislocation dipole is created by removing a (101) plane (a thickness of the Burgers magnitude b) of height $d = 40$ (010) planes (~230 Å).

MD simulations are performed at 300 K for 4 ns to equilibrate the systems, and another 16 (= t_{tot}) ns to calculate time-averaged energies of both perfect crystals and crystals containing the dislocation dipoles. Let E_p and N_p represent the energy and total number of atoms in the perfect crystal, and E_d and N_d represent the energy and total number of atoms in the dislocated crystal. Since atoms are equivalent in the perfect crystal, the total energy of a perfect crystal containing the same number of atoms as in the dislocated crystal can be obtained by scaling E_p with the ratio N_d/N_p. Hence, the dislocation line energy is calculated as

$$\Gamma = \frac{E_d - \frac{N_d}{N_p} E_p}{2L_z} \tag{11}$$

where $2L_z$ is the total dislocation length. Based on a time segment of $\Delta t = 16$ ps to calculate sample Γ_i, both best estimate dislocation energies $\overline{\Gamma}$ (simplified as Γ) and their standard deviations $\overline{\sigma}$ are calculated using Eqs. (1)–(3). The results of Γ and $\overline{\sigma}$ are shown in **Figure 4** as unfilled circles and error bars, respectively. In **Figure 4**, the thin light line is obtained from a continuum model [20], and the crosses represent data from MS simulations.

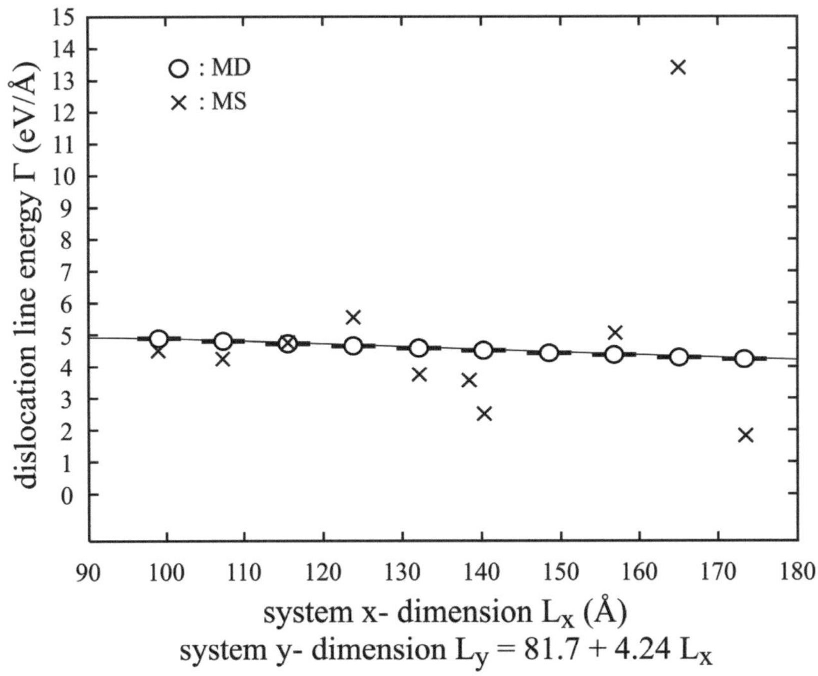

Figure 4. CdS misfit dislocation energy as a function of system dimensions L_x and L_y under the constraint L_y = 81.7 (Å) + 4.24 L_x. Note that error bars of MD data are essentially horizontal lines, indicating negligible uncertainty margins.

Figure 4 indicates that despite the challenge for convergence during short-time MD simulations as seen in **Figure 1(b)**, the uncertainty margin of time-averaged MD results of dislocation energies can be reduced to a negligible level if the average time is increased to 16 ns or above. As a consequence of the high convergence, all the MD data points fall right on top of the continuum line. This means that if constructed from the continuum function, the error parameter ξ would also be near zero. Contrarily, the MS results only approximately agree with the continuum line at small system dimensions (however, our smallest dimension of L_x ~ 100 Å would correspond to 80,000 atoms, which is big according to the literature MS standard) and become meaningless for large systems. The uncertain margin of MS simulations can also be quantified and reduced by performing ensemble averages of a large number of MS simulations with initial configurations taken from various snapshots of an MD simulation (so that they are at different thermally activated states). This is left as an exercise for readers as we only address MD simulations in this chapter.

8. Diffusion parameters

For alloyed systems, or systems involving defects, the number of possible atomic diffusion mechanisms can be tremendous. In such cases, diffusivities can be most effectively calculated from the mean square displacement of the diffusing species obtained from MD simulations. Diffusivities at different temperatures can be further used to derive pre-exponential factor and activation energy of diffusion through an Arrhenius fit. The only challenge of this approach is that it is usually associated with large statistical errors. We now explore this issue using hydrogen diffusion in aluminium as an example. We use the literature Al-H potential [13] in the calculations.

Aluminium fcc crystals containing 8 {100} planes in each of the three <100> coordinate directions are used for simulations. The initial crystals are created based on the room temperature experimental lattice constant $a = 4.05$ Å [23]. The system dimension is therefore around 32 Å, corresponding to 2048 aluminium atoms. For comparison, we also calculate the theoretical lattice constants at finite temperatures following the approach described above, and find $a = 4.05$ Å at 300 K and $a = 4.06$ Å at 700 K. Bulk crystals are simulated using periodic boundary conditions, and a single hydrogen atom is introduced in the computational cell.

First, a warm-up MD simulation is performed for more than 0.1 ns to equilibrate the system at the target temperature T. Following this, an MD simulation is performed for a total period of t_{tot}. If the time step size is dt, the total number of simulated steps $n = t_{tot}/dt$. The time-dependent hydrogen location, $\boldsymbol{r}(t)$, is recorded on a time interval of Δt, i.e., at times $t = i\Delta t$, $i = 1, 2, \ldots, m$ ($m = t_{tot}/\Delta t$), where Δt is a multiple of dt. These locations allow calculations of the relative hydrogen displacement per time interval Δt. For example, if the starting and ending times of the Δt interval are $(i - 1)\Delta t$ and $i\Delta t$, respectively ($i = 1, 2, \ldots, m$), the displacement can be calculated as $\Delta \boldsymbol{r}_i(\Delta t) = \boldsymbol{r}(i\Delta t) - \boldsymbol{r}(i\Delta t - \Delta t)$. Once $\Delta \boldsymbol{r}$ per Δt is known, the relative displacement per larger time intervals of $k\Delta t$, measured between $(i - 1)\Delta t$ and $(i - 1 + k)\Delta t$, can be simply obtained as $\Delta \boldsymbol{r}_i(k\Delta t) = \sum_{j=i}^{i-1+k} \Delta r_j(\Delta t)$, where $i = 1, 2, \ldots, m + 1 - k$. This means that we can calculate $m + 1 - k$ values of $\Delta \boldsymbol{r}_i(k\Delta t)$. Clearly, the number of $\Delta \boldsymbol{r}_i(k\Delta t)$ values is large when $k \ll m$. Under this condition, a highly converged mean square displacement can be obtained from

$$\overline{\lfloor \Delta r(k\Delta t) \rfloor^2} = \frac{\sum_{i=1}^{m+1-k} |\Delta r_i(k\Delta t)|^2}{m + 1 - k} \tag{12}$$

This mean square displacement is a linear function of time t. In particular, $\overline{\lfloor \Delta r(k\Delta t) \rfloor^2} = 6Dt$, where D is diffusivity [24]. Fitting the MD data to $6Dt$ in a small time range $t \ll t_{tot}$ (i.e., $k \ll m$) allows us to determine diffusivity D. Eq. (4) can be used to estimate the uncertainty of this linear fit.

The MD procedures described above can be used to calculate diffusivities at different temperatures. The results can be fitted to the Arrhenius equation to get the pre-exponential factor D_0 and activation energy Q of hydrogen diffusion in aluminium [13]. Eq. (4) can also be used to estimate error of this Arrhenius fit.

Based on an NVT ensemble, MD simulations are performed to calculate the mean square displacement of the hydrogen atom at various temperatures between 400 and 800 K using $t_{tot} = 0.88$ ns, $dt = 0.001$ ps and $\Delta t = 0.0088$ ps. The mean square displacements for a small time range ($t < 15$ ps) are fitted to $6Dt$. A small time range is used to increase the terms in the average sum. For example, for $t = 15$ ps, the total number of terms in Eq. (12) equals $N = m + 1 - k = t_{tot}/\Delta t + 1 - t/\Delta t > 98296$. The MD mean square displacement results and the fitted $6Dt$ lines are shown in **Figure 5(a)** for three chosen temperatures 500, 600 and 700 K. The diffusivities derived from the mean square displacement are fitted to the Arrhenius equation, and the results are shown in **Figure 5(b)**. It can be seen that although the mean square displacement appears to satisfy well the linear function of time, the statistical error for the Arrhenius fit is significant.

To examine convergence of the results with respect to simulation time t_{tot}, extensive MD simulations at a variety of temperatures are performed using $dt = 0.001$ ps and $\Delta t = 4.4$ ps. Arrhenius fits are performed at different total MD simulation time t_{tot}, and the error parameter ξ for the Arrhenius fits is calculated using Eq. (9). The results for the fitted activation energy and the associated error parameter as a function of t_{tot} are shown respectively in **Figure 6(a)** and **(b)**. It can be seen that the activation energy approaches a constant value after the simulation time reaches 10 ns and above. Correspondingly, the Arrhenius error reduces to near zero at $t \geq 10$ ns. To verify that highly converged results are indeed obtained at $t_{tot} = 13.2$ ns, the corresponding mean square displacement as a function of time at selected temperatures and the Arrhenius plot are shown respectively in **Figure 7(a)** and **(b)**. It can be seen that ideally linear plots are obtained for both mean square displacement and Arrhenius fit, indicating

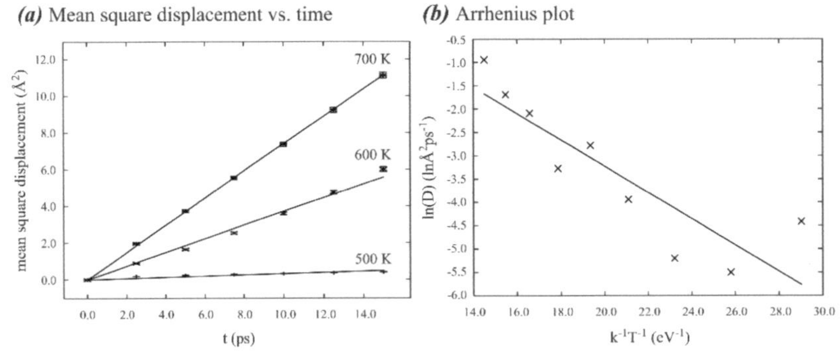

Figure 5. Uncertainty examination of hydrogen diffusion parameters in aluminium calculated from MD simulations at $t_{tot} = 0.88$ ns, $dt = 0.001$ ps and $\Delta t = 0.0088$ ps. (a) Mean square displacement and (b) Arrhenius plot.

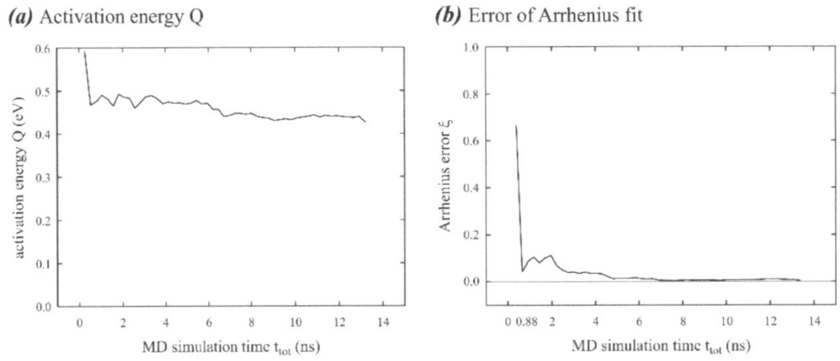

Figure 6. Convergence of diffusion calculation as a function of simulation time. (a) Activation energy and (b) Arrhenius error.

negligible errors. Interestingly, the activation energy determined from the slope of the Arrhenius fit, $Q = 0.43$ eV, is in excellent agreement with MS calculation at 0 K, $Q = 0.41$ eV [13]. Note that MS can only be applied for a single atomic diffusion mechanism as in the present case. MD simulations can be applied to alloyed and defected systems that may involve thousands or more different atomic jump paths.

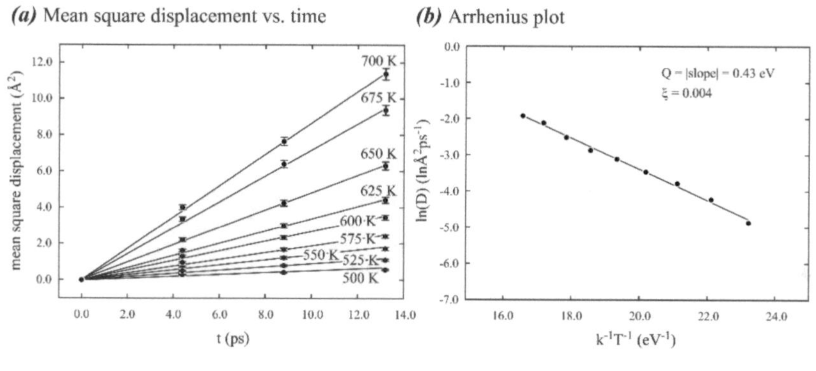

Figure 7. Statistical uncertainty examination of hydrogen diffusion parameters in aluminium calculated from MD simulations at $t_{tot} = 13.2$ ns, $dt = 0.001$ ps and $\Delta t = 4.4$ ps. (a) Mean square displacement and (b) Arrhenius plot.

9. Thermal conductivity

Another good example to examine uncertainty is thermal conductivity calculations which are usually associated with large statistical errors. Here, we explore calculations of thermal conductivities for a bulk GaN crystal using a 'direct method' [12]. The geometry of such a method is illustrated in the left bottom legend of **Figure 8**. Assuming that heat flux is along the x-axis, two regions of width w are created in the cell. One region is in the middle, and the other region is on the two ends (due to the periodic boundary condition, the two regions of width $w/2$ shown in the legend are in fact one region). Through velocity rescaling, a constant heat flux of J (say, in unit eV/ps·Å^2) is continuously removed from the middle region and an exactly the same amount of heat flux is continuously added to the end region. When a steady state is reached, this creates a temperature gradient $\partial T/\partial x$ from the cold (middle) to the hot (end) regions. This temperature gradient can then be used to calculate thermal conductivity κ through the Fourier's law

$$\kappa = \frac{-J}{\partial T/\partial x} \tag{13}$$

Our calculations use the GaN literature potential developed by Bere and Serra [25, 26]. A wurtzite GaN crystal with 500 (0001) planes in the x-direction, 6 $(\bar{1}100)$ planes in the y-direction and 10 $(11\bar{2}0)$ planes in the z-direction is used. The crystal is uniformly divided into

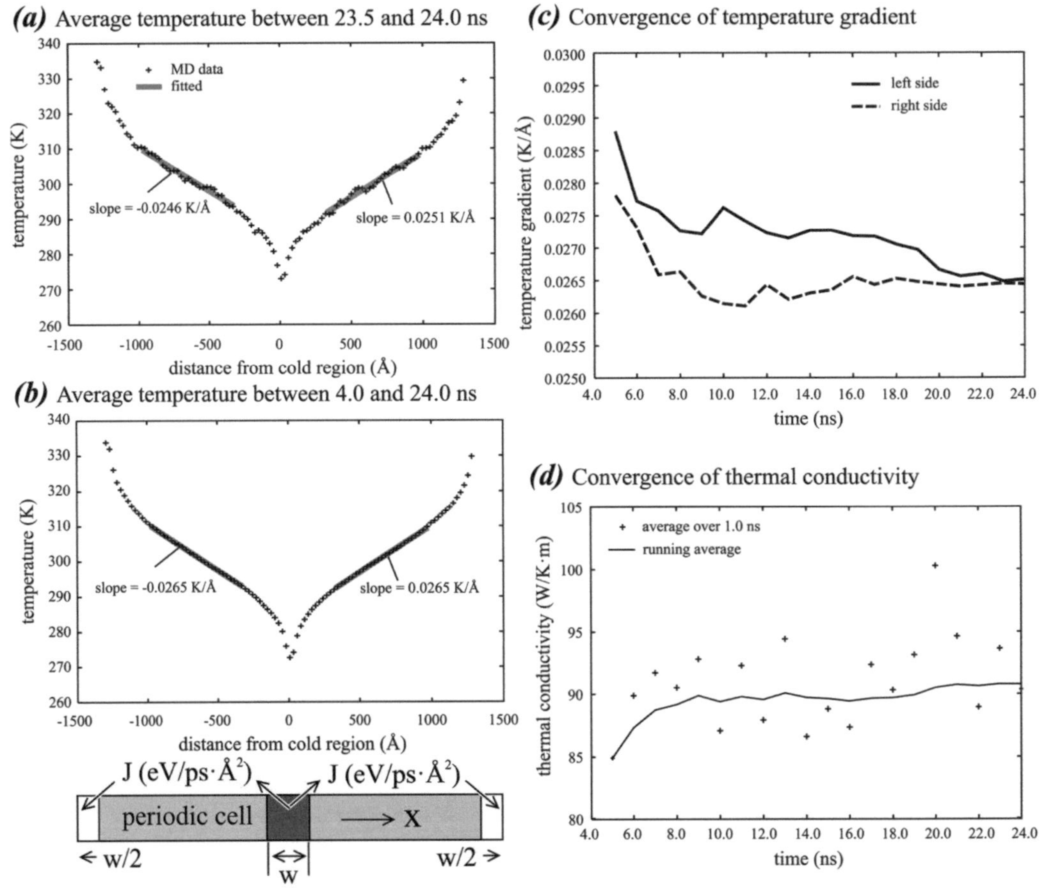

Figure 8. Results of 300 K thermal conductivity calculations. (a) Temperature averaged over a short period of 0.5 ns; (b) temperature averaged over a long period of 20 ns; (c) convergence of temperature gradient and (d) convergence of thermal conductivity.

100 bins along the x-axis so that position-dependent temperature can be calculated as the time-averaged temperature for each of the bins. MD simulation is performed for 24 ns using an NVE ensemble at an initial temperature of 300 K, a heat flux of $J = 0.0015$ W/ps·Å^2, a heat source/sink width of $w = 60$ Å and a time step size of $dt = 0.001$ ps. After the first 4 ns is discarded to enable the temperature gradient to reach a steady state, time-averaged temperatures are calculated for the remaining simulations.

To examine the convergence of the temperature gradient calculations, **Figure 8(a)** and **(b)** compares the temperature profiles obtained from a short average time of 0.5 ns (average between 23.5 and 24 ns) and a long average time of 20 ns (average between 4 and 24 ns). It can be seen that extremely scattered data are obtained at the short average time. A related phenomenon is that the temperature gradients obtained from the left and the right sides of the cold region do not closely match, indicating non-convergence. Contrarily, the data averaged over the longer time are extremely smooth, and the temperature gradients obtained from both sides of the cold region are the same up to the fourth decimal point. This suggests that the statistical margin of the temperature gradients is greatly reduced by increasing the average time. To quantify this, we show the running averages of the left and the right temperature gradients in **Figure 8(c)**. **Figure 8(c)** confirms that although the two temperature gradients differ significantly at short times, they approach the same plateau at $t \rightarrow 24$ ns.

To understand the uncertainty margin of the final thermal conductivity, we divide the 20 ns simulation average time into 20 segments and calculate the thermal conductivities κ_i for each of the segments $i = 1, 2, \ldots, 20$. We also calculate the running average of these conductivities. The results are shown in **Figure 8(d)**. It can be seen that κ_i is associated with a significant uncertainty margin σ, which can be calculated using Eq. (2). However, the running average quickly approaches a saturated value of ~91 W/K·m. Note that the running average at time $t = 20$ ns is exactly the average measurement of the 20 κ_i as defined by Eq. (1). The uncertainty margin of this average is $\overline{\sigma} = \sigma/\sqrt{20}$.

10. Composition profile

Population of chemical species in a material often needs to be studied. For instance, hydrogen segregation to a crack tip causes hydrogen embrittlement. Hydrogen segregation to a surface impacts the adsorption/desorption performance of solid state hydrogen storage materials. Calculation of composition profiles is a good approach to quantify these segregation effects. However, due to the discrete nature of crystals, a snapshot composition profile is not smooth and is hence associated with a significant uncertainty margin. Here, we demonstrate the calculation of uncertainty margin of a composition profile obtained from MD simulations. We use the hydrogen segregation on (111) palladium surface as an example. The literature Pd-H potential [19] is used.

The fcc palladium crystal contains 5040 Pd atoms with 21 $(11\overline{2})$ planes in the x- direction, 20 (111) planes in the y- direction and 12 $(1\overline{1}0)$ planes in the z- direction. Based on an NPT ensemble to relax stresses, an MD simulation is performed at a temperature of $T = 300$ K and a hydrogen composition of $x = 0.1$ (i.e., the chemical formula for the system is $PdH_{0.1}$). The corresponding numbers of H atoms are randomly introduced into the octahedral interstitial sites so that the initial composition is nominally uniform. To simulate the (111) surfaces, periodic boundary conditions are used in the x- and z-directions and a free boundary condition is used in the y- direction. To ensure a full equilibration between the surfaces and bulk, we first perform a pre-conditioning MD simulation that involves 1.5 ns annealing at 600 K, another 1.5 ns to cool the system from 600 K to the target temperature $T = 300$ K, and a final 1.5 ns annealing at the target temperature. With the pre-conditioned sample, a second MD simulation is performed for 33 ns at the target temperature, where 100 snapshots of atom positions are recorded on a time interval of 330 ps. Hydrogen composition is calculated for each atomic layer and is averaged over the 100 snapshots. One snapshot of atomic configuration and the averaged composition profile normal to the surface are shown respectively in **Figure 9(a)** and **(b)**. In **Figure 9(b)**, the error bars represent the standard deviation calculated using Eq. (3).

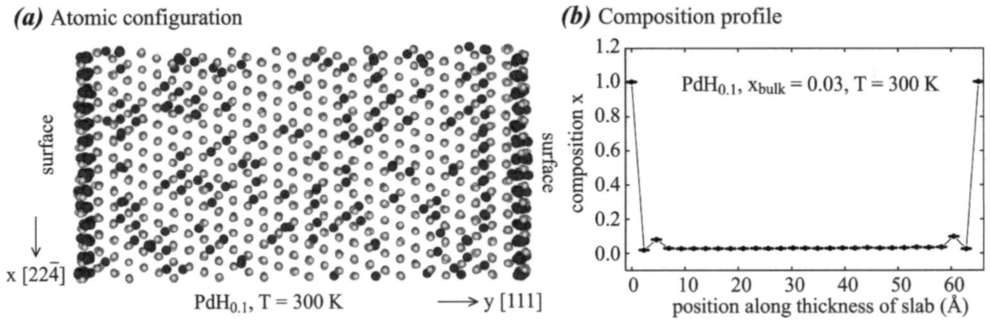

Figure 9. Hydrogen segregation on (111) surfaces. (a) A snapshot configuration and (b) averaged composition profile.

Considering that the initial composition is nominally uniform, **Figure 9(a)** shows visually a strong hydrogen surface segregation effect. This is confirmed in **Figure 9(b)** where the surface composition reaches the saturation value of 1.0 as compared to the bulk value of x_{bulk} ~ 0.03. Interestingly, all data points shown in **Figure 9(b)** have negligible error bars. Also it is important to note that the composition profile is highly symmetric with respect to the two end surfaces and the composition is ideally constant in the bulk region. These further confirm that our high temperature pre-annealing and the ensemble-average of many snapshots have successfully equilibrated the system and reduced the statistical error, resulting in highly converged composition profile.

11. Calibration of continuum models

When the uncertainty margin is reduced to near zero, MD simulations are well suited to validate and calibrate other models. Here, we apply MD to calibrate a continuum misfit dislocation theory. As shown in **Figure 10(a)**, consider that a film is grown on a substrate surface. If the film lattice constant a_f is smaller than the substrate lattice constant a_s, then the film must be stretched by a strain of $\varepsilon = (a_s - a_f)/a_f$ in order to grow on the substrate. This creates a large strain energy. However, if misfit dislocations are formed in the film (i.e., adding a lattice unit in the film), then the strain for the film to match the substrate is reduced to $\varepsilon = (a_s - a_f)/a_f - b/L$, where b is the Burgers magnitude of the dislocation and L is the dislocation spacing. While formation of dislocations reduces lattice mismatch strain energy, it causes additional dislocation energy. The continuum misfit dislocation models express the total system energy as a function of dislocation density so that by minimizing the total energy, the equilibrium dislocation density can be predicted. This concept has been used to develop a variety of continuum misfit dislocation models [27–30].

In previous application of the continuum misfit dislocation models, the dislocation Burgers magnitude b is usually taken from the film lattice constant, and the dislocation spacing L is usually taken from the substrate [31–33]. Referring to **Figure 10(a)**, these mean that $b = a_f$ and $L = L_s$. Despite that these choices appear to be natural, they have not been justified. Questions arise on why the Burgers magnitude should be defined by the film lattice constant because if a

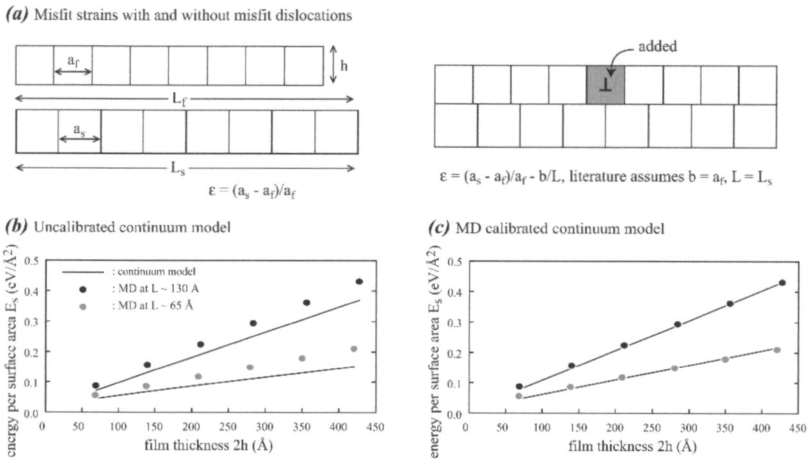

Figure 10. Calibration of a continuum misfit dislocation theory. (a) Misfit strain with and without misfit dislocation; (b) comparison of MD data with an uncalibrated continuum model and (c) comparison of MD data with a calibrated continuum model.

misfit dislocation can be viewed as an extra plane in the film, it can be equally viewed as a missing plane in the substrate. To understand this issue, we have performed MD analyses of a CdS film on a CdTe substrate [20]. Our MD energy (normalized by interfacial area) is compared with the original continuum model [30] in **Figure 10(b)**. It can be seen that MD results do not perfectly match the continuum prediction. Because the uncertainty margin of MD simulations on dislocation energy and strain energy (or equivalently elastic constant) calculations has been reduced to near zero as shown in **Figures 3** and **4**, the results should match perfectly if the MD and the continuum models are consistent. We find, however, that if an approximation of the dislocation interaction energy array assumed in the original continuum model is corrected, and if the Burgers magnitude is taken from substrate rather than film (i.e., $b = a_s$), and the dislocation spacing is taken from the film rather than substrate (i.e., $L = L_f$), then MD results can match the continuum prediction perfectly as shown in **Figure 10(c)**.

The Burger magnitude must be defined from substrate, whereas the dislocation spacing must be defined from the film can be analytically derived. Assume that in a dislocation-free system, n_f planes of film with plane spacing a_f are matched with n_s (assumes that $n_s = n_f$) planes of substrate with plane spacing a_s. If the substrate is much thicker than the film, it can be assumed to be rigid. Then the film is subject to a mismatch strain of $(n_f a_s - n_f a_f)/(n_f a_f) = (a_s - a_f)/a_f$. If we consider a scenario where a half plane is inserted to the film, then the film is subject to a residual strain of $[n_f a_s - (n_f + 1)a_f]/[(n_f + 1)a_f] = (a_s - a_f)/a_f - a_s/L_f$. Obviously, $L_f = (n_f + 1)a_f$ is exactly the length of unstrained film. Alternatively, if we consider a scenario where a half plane is removed from the substrate, then the film is subject to a residual strain of $[(n_f - 1)a_s - n_f a_f]/(n_f a_f) = (a_s - a_f)/a_f - a_s/L_f$. Interestingly, $L_f = n_f a_f$ is again exactly the length of unstrained film. Hence, when the substrate is fixed, a dislocation always causes a consistent residual strain of $(a_s - a_f)/a_f - a_s/L_f$ whether the dislocation is viewed as inserting a half plane in the film or removing a half plane from the substrate. By comparing the residual strain shown in **Figure 10 (a)**, we see that the magnitude of the Burgers vector b should be the substrate value a_s rather than the film value a_f, and the dislocation spacing L should be the film value L_f rather than the substrate value L_s. This can also be understood in a different way. According to the definition of strain $\varepsilon = \Delta L/L_0$ where ΔL is change of sample length and L_0 is the length of unstrained sample, it is clear that the unstrained film length L_f should be used in place of L_0 because in our case, the substrate is fixed and only the film is strained. On the other hand, our fixed substrate represents an infinite substrate thickness so that the thickness weighted average plane spacing equals the substrate plane spacing. As a result, the substrate spacing b_s (or a_s) should be taken as the Burgers vector. This example shows how an MD model with reduced uncertainty margin can reveal errors of widely used theories.

12. Conclusions

A brief overview is given for uncertainty quantification methods of multiscale models. We demonstrate that rigorous quantification of all model uncertainties is still challenging. However, robust methods are already available today to reliably quantify and reduce the statistical uncertainties of molecular dynamics (MD) simulations. In particular, by averaging over time, the statistical uncertainties of MD calculated properties can always be reduced to near zero as long as the MD simulation is sufficiently long. Counterintuitively, the statistical uncertainties of time-averaged MD simulations are significantly smaller than those of molecular statics simulations especially for large systems with many local energy minimums. For instance, the dislocation energies calculated from time-averaged MD simulations match exactly the continuum predictions, whereas the dislocation energies calculated from MS diverge at large system dimensions. It is also demonstrated that the statistical uncertainties in long MD diffusion simulations can be reduced to such a low level that ideally linear Arrhenius behaviour of diffusion is captured. This means that MD simulations can be used to study diffusion for any complex systems containing any number of diffusion paths. This is extremely important considering that the past MS method to calculate diffusion energy barrier is usually only applicable to single, known atomic jump paths. When zero statistical uncertainty margin is achieved, MD simulations have been successfully used to validate and improve a widely-used misfit dislocation theory. Most importantly, zero statistical error means that MD simulations do not introduce additional errors beyond those inherent in the interatomic potential and simplified systems. Such MD simulations, therefore, isolate out other uncertainties, facilitating their quantifications. All these show that when statistical uncertainties are quantified and reduced, MD simulations can impact material research that would be otherwise impossible.

Acknowledgements

The Sandia National Laboratories is a multi-mission laboratory managed and operated by Sandia Corporation, a wholly owned subsidiary of Lockheed Martin Corporation, for the US Department of Energy's National Nuclear Security Administration under contract DE-AC04-94AL85000. The authors gratefully acknowledge research support from the U.S. Department of

Energy, Office of Energy Efficiency, and Renewable Energy, Fuel Cell Technologies Office, under Contract Number DE-AC04-94AL85000.

Author details

Xiaowang Zhou[1]* and Stephen M. Foiles[2]

*Address all correspondence to: xzhou@sandia.gov

1 Sandia National Laboratories, Livermore, California, USA

2 Sandia National Laboratories, Albuquerque, New Mexico, USA

References

[1] Finnis M. Interatomic Forces in Condensed Matter, Oxford Series on Materials Modelling. Oxford: Oxford University Press; 2003.

[2] Plimpton S. Fast parallel algorithms for short-range molecular-dynamics. Journal of Computational Physics. 1995;**117**:1–19.

[3] LAMMPS download site: lammps.sandia.gov

[4] Hoover WG. Canonical dynamics: Equilibrium phase-space distributions. Physical Review A (Atomic, Molecular, and Optical Physics). 1985;**31**:1695–1697.

[5] Parrinello M, Rahman A. Polymorphic transitions in single crystals: A new molecular dynamics method. Journal of Applied Physics. 1981;**52**:7182–7190.

[6] Cailliez F, Pernot P. Statistical approaches to forcefield calibration and prediction uncertainty in molecular simulation. Journal of Chemical Physics. 2011;**134**:054124.

[7] Moore AP, Deo C, Baskes MI, Okuniewski MA, McDowell DL. Understanding the uncertainty of interatomic potentials' parameters and formalism. Computational Materials Science. 2017;**126**:308–320.

[8] Medlin DL, Hattar K, Zimmerman JA, Abdeljawad F, Foiles SM. Defect character at grain boundary facet junctions: Analysis of an asymmetric $\Sigma = 5$ grain boundary in Fe. Acta Materialia. 2017;**124**:383–396.

[9] Koslowski M, Strachan A. Uncertainty propagation in a multiscale model of nanocrystalline plasticity. Reliability Engineering & System Safety. 2011;**96**:1161–1170.

[10] Chernatynskiy A, Phillpot SR, LeSar R. Uncertainty quantification in multiscale simulation of materials: A prospective. Annual Review of Materials Research. 2013;**43**: 157–182.

[11] Dienstfrey A, Phelan Jr FR, Christensen S, Strachan A, Santosa F, Boisvert R. Uncertainty quantification in materials modelling. The Journal of the Minerals, Metals and Materials Society. 2014;**66**:1342–1344.

[12] Zhou XW, Aubry S, Jones RE, Greenstein A, Schelling PK. Towards more accurate molecular dynamics calculation of thermal conductivity: Case study of GaN bulk crystals. Physical Review B (Condensed Matter). 2009;**79**:115201.

[13] Zhou XW, El Gabaly F, Stavila V, Allendorf MD. Molecular dynamics simulations of hydrogen diffusion in aluminum. Journal of Physical Chemistry C. 2016;**120**:7500–7509.

[14] Zhou XW, Moody NR, Jones RE, Zimmerman JA, Reedy ED. Molecular-dynamics-based cohesive zone law for brittle interfacial fracture under mixed loading conditions: Effects of elastic constant mismatch. Acta Materialia. 2009;**57**:4671–4686.

[15] Lloyd JT, Zimmerman JA, Jones RE, Zhou XW, McDowell DL. Finite element analysis of an atomistically derived cohesive model for brittle fracture. Modelling and Simulation in Materials Science and Engineering. 2011;**19**:065007.

[16] Zhou XW, Ward DK, Foster ME. An analytical bond-order potential for the aluminium copper binary system. Journal of Alloys and Compounds. 2016;**680**:752–767.

[17] Hirth JP, Lothe J. Theory of Dislocations. New York: McGraw-Hill; 1968.

[18] Mandel J. Statistical Analysis of Experimental Data. Weinheim: Wiley; 1964.

[19] Zhou XW, Zimmerman JA. An embedded-atom method interatomic potential for Pd-H alloys. Journal of Materials Research. 2008;23:704–718.

[20] Zhou XW, Ward DK, Zimmerman JA, Cruz-Campa JL, Zubia D, Martin JE, van Swol F. An atomistically validated continuum model for strain relaxation and misfit dislocation formation. Journal of the Mechanics and Physics of Solids. 2016;**91**:265–277.

[21] Zhou XW, Ward DK, Martin JE, van Swol FB, Cruz-Campa, JL, and Zubia D. Stillinger-Weber potential for the II-VI elements Zn-Cd-Hg-S-Se-Te. Physical Review B (Condensed Matter). 2013;**88**:085309.

[22] Zhou XW, Sills RB, Ward DK, Karnesky RA. Atomistic calculations of dislocation core energy in aluminium. Physical Review B (Condensed Matter). 2017;**95**:054112.

[23] Donnay JDH, Ondik HM, editors. Crystal Data, Determinative Tables. 3rd ed. Vol. 2 (Inorganic Compounds). USA: U. S. Department of Commerce, National Bureau of Standards, and Joint Committee on Power Diffraction Standards; 1973.

[24] Reif F. Fundamentals of Statistical and Thermal Physics. New York: McGraw-Hill; 1965.

[25] Bere A, Serra A. Atomic structure of dislocation cores in GaN. Physical Review B (Condensed Matter). 2002;**65**:205323.

[26] Bere A, Serra A. On the atomic structures, mobility and interactions of extended defects in GaN: Dislocations, tilt and twin boundaries. Philosophical Magazine. 2006;**86**:2159–2192.

[27] Jain SC, Gosling TJ, Willis JR, Totterdell DHJ, Bullough R. A new study of critical layer thickness, stability and strain relaxation in pseudomorphic Ge_xSi_{1-x} strained epilayers. Philosophical Magazine A: Physics of Condensed Matter Structure Defects and Mechanical Properties. 1992;**65**:1151–1167.

[28] Jain SC, Harker AH, Cowley RA. Misfit strain and misfit dislocations in lattice mismatched epitaxial layers and other systems. Philosophical Magazine A: Physics of Condensed Matter Structure Defects and Mechanical Properties. 1997;**75**:1461–1515.

[29] Willis JR, Jain SC, Bullough R. The energy of an array of dislocations—Implications for strain relaxation in semiconductor heterostructures. Philosophical Magazine A: Physics of Condensed Matter Structure Defects and Mechanical Properties. 1990;**62**:115–129.

[30] Nix WD. Mechanical-properties of thin films. Metallurgical Transactions A: Physical Metallurgy and Materials Science. 1989;**20**:2217–2245.

[31] Maroudas D, Zepeda-Ruiz LA, Weinberg, WH. Interfacial stability and misfit dislocation formation in InAs/GaAs(110) heteroepitaxy. Surface Science. 1998;**411**:L865–L871.

[32] Payne AP, Nix WD, Lairson BM, Clemens BM. Strain relaxation in ultrathin films - a modified theory of misfit-dislocation energetics. Physical Review B (Condensed Matter). 1993;**47**:13730–13736.

[33] Pizzagalli L, Cicero G, Catellani A. Theoretical investigations of a highly mismatched interface: SiC/Si(001). Physical Review B (Condensed Matter). 2003;**68**:195302.

Section 3

Model Calibration

Chapter 6

Bayesian Uncertainty Quantification for Functional Response

Xiao Guo, Yang He, Binbin Zhu, Yang Yang,
Ke Deng, Ruopeng Liu and Chunlin Ji

Additional information is available at the end of the chapter

http://dx.doi.org/10.5772/intechopen.69385

Abstract

This chapter addresses the stochastic modeling of functional response, which is a major concern in engineering implementation. We first introduce a general framework and several conventional models for functional data, including the functional linear model, penalized regression splines, and the spatial temporal model. However, in engineering practice, a naive mathematical modeling of functional response may fail due to the lack of expressing the underlying physical mechanism. We propose a series of quasiphysical models to handle the functional response. A motivating example of metamaterial design is thoroughly discussed to demonstrate the idea of quasiphysical models. In real applications, various uncertainties have to be taken into account, such as that of the permittivity or permeability of the substrate of the metamaterial. For the propagation of uncertainty, simulation-based methods are discussed. A Bayesian framework is presented to deal with the model calibration in the case of functional response. Experimental results illustrate the efficiency of the proposed method.

Keywords: functional response, meta model, Bayesian uncertainty quantification, model calibration, metamaterial design

1. Introduction

In recent years, computer experiments have become widely adopted in both engineering applications and scientific research to replace or support their physical counterparts. Functional response is the mathematical representation of system behaviors, where the data are collected over an interval of some input indices. With the advance of modern simulation and experiment technology, accessing functional data becomes easier. Functional response can be in the form of one-dimensional data such as a curve or higher dimensional data such as an image, which can provide better physical insights. However, even with the advancement of computer technology, full simulation based on a finite element method or a finite difference method still takes an extensive amount of time. To reduce the amount of simulation time, historical simulated data are usually used to build a cheaper metamodel [1], in which the functional response of unobserved input can be predicted by either regression or interpolation. The simplest representation of functional data can be considered basis expansion, where polynomials are used to formulate the input-output relation [2]. For frequency response analysis, Fourier series are usually applied to replace the polynomials [3]. Both methods are categorized as linear regression, which requires parameter estimations. Nonparametric approaches were also used to analyze functional data in many scientific and engineering fields [4]. The purpose of building these models is to provide the "best" estimate regarding the given data, while providing a statistical scheme for prediction at unobserved inputs.

In this chapter, we provide a more sophisticated approach to naturally analyze functional responses, which may suggest more insightful conclusions that may not be apparent otherwise. We introduce one motivating example of functional response in computer experiments. In the design of metamaterial, the goal is to establish a relationship between the physical dimensions of a unit cell and its electromagnetic (EM) frequency response [5]. In practice, designers usually evaluate the EM properties of a metamaterial microstructure via full-wave simulation data, such that corresponding adjustments are constantly made to the design (dielectric architecture, microstructure topologies, etc.) until a desired performance is achieved. **Figure 1** depicts an example of unit cell design whose response phases differ on a frequency span along with the varying geometric parameter. Naïve regression-based metamodels fail in dealing with such a problem

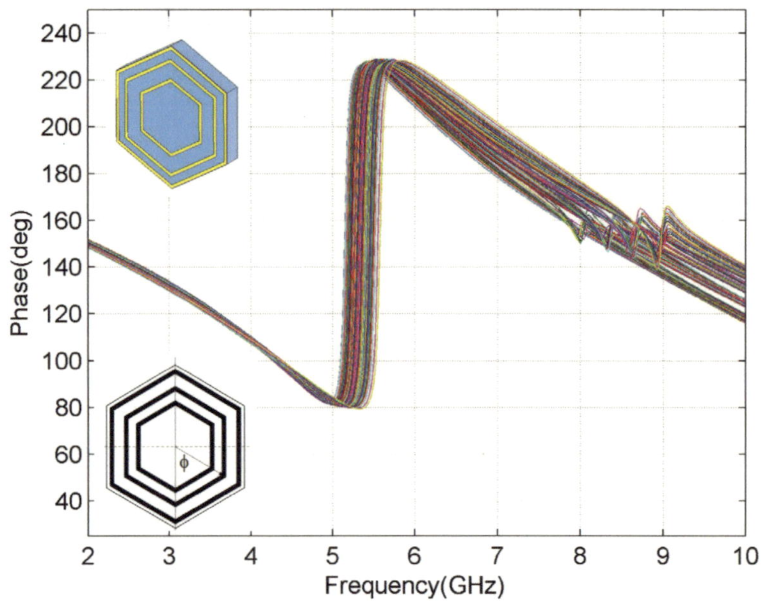

Figure 1. Example of functional response in metamaterial unit cell design-phase shift between different physical dimension inputs.

because they require building regressions for each output, which could be very expensive and leaves the correlation between different frequencies unutilized. Moreover, when resonance is involved, the functional data cannot be well described by polynomials or splines. However, this can be overcome by some quasiphysical models, which explore the essential physical mechanism. In addition, a more general two-stage modeling scheme can be applied, where in Stage I, we approximate the response with rational functions. This allows us to decompose the continuous response into a few discrete parameters. Stage II consists of a nonparametric metamodel to capture the input dependence.

2. General models for functional response

Various statistical models, including the spatial temporal model, functional linear model, and penalized regression splines, have been widely discussed in the past. Most models share a unified expression that sums up a mean function $\mu(f, \mathbf{x})$ and a random term $\varepsilon(f, \mathbf{x})$, written as

$$y(f, \mathbf{x}) = \mu(f, \mathbf{x}) + \varepsilon(f, \mathbf{x}) \tag{1}$$

where y is the response, $\mathbf{x} = \{\mathbf{x}_1, \ldots, \mathbf{x}_p\}$ is the input variables with dimensionality p, and f represents some index, which could be the frequency of an electromagnetic wave or the time of a time series. Despite the shared form, these models differ in the way the mentioned terms are estimated.

2.1. Functional linear model

To model the functional response, the primary task is to estimate the mean function $\mu(f, \mathbf{x})$, on which a certain form is often imposed. As a generalization of linear regression models, the functional linear model is in the form of

$$\mu(f, \mathbf{x}) = \boldsymbol{\beta}_0(f) + \mathbf{x}^T \boldsymbol{\beta}(f), \tag{2}$$

with basis functions $\boldsymbol{\beta} = \{\boldsymbol{\beta}_0(f), \boldsymbol{\beta}(f)\}$ ($\boldsymbol{\beta}(f) = (\boldsymbol{\beta}_1(f), \ldots, \boldsymbol{\beta}_p(f))^T$ has the same dimensionality to the input variable), which incorporate the index dependence, and can be seen as an extension to the parameters of linear regression models. Therefore, by substituting the mean function into Eq. (1), we obtain the resulting output

$$y(f, \mathbf{x}) = \beta_0(f) + \mathbf{x}^T \boldsymbol{\beta}(f) + \varepsilon(f, \mathbf{x})\,. \tag{3}$$

Given a certain index f, this model is a universal linear model. Furthermore, it contains an underlying index-varying effect of $\mathbf{x}$, whereas $\boldsymbol{\beta}$ is assumed to be a smooth function of f. Thus, the model is referred to as a functional linear model. To estimate the coefficients $\beta_0(f)$ and $\beta(f)$, it is straightforward to apply the least squares method, which adopts the data collected at f. However, smoothing over f componentwise, using penalized splines, can enhance the efficiency of estimates [6].

Penalized regression splines implement estimation of smoothing basis functions in functional linear models by minimizing the penalized least squares. They are widely adopted in modeling functional responses due to their easy implementation and low computational cost [6].

Noted that the primary purpose of applying penalized regression splines is to estimate the basis function $\boldsymbol{\beta}$. Suppose we have n data $\{(f, y_i), i = 1, \ldots, n\}$, and the basis function is a random sample from

$$\beta_j = m(f) + \delta_j, \tag{4}$$

with $j = 1, \ldots, p$. $m(f)$ is an unspecified smooth mean function of $\boldsymbol{\beta}$ and δ_j is a zero mean random error. In practice, $m(f)$ can be estimated by a series of power-truncated spline basis $1, f, f^2, f^p, (f - \kappa_1)_+^p, \ldots, (f - \kappa_K)_+^p$, where $\{\kappa_1, \ldots, \kappa_K\}$ is a given set of knots and a_+ denotes the positive part of a, i.e., $a_+ = (a + |a|)/2$. Therefore, the model in Eq. (4) can be approximately written as

$$\beta_j \approx \alpha_0 + \sum_{l=1}^{p} \alpha_l f^l + \sum_{k=1}^{K} \alpha_{k+p} (f\text{-}\kappa_k)_+^p + \delta_j, \tag{5}$$

where α_j represents coefficients whose values can be obtained via least squares estimates. Generally, overfitting in the approximation of $m(f)$ may occur, which leads to high variance and poor prediction. To avoid large modeling bias, the trade-off between model bias and overfitting requires careful consideration. In order to resolve such a problem, variable selection procedures should be applied to the linear regression model. However, when the number of involved basis functions is very large, variable selection would encounter great computational difficulty [7]. Alternatively, α_j is estimated by minimizing the penalized least squares function in the form of

$$\sum_{i=1}^{n} \left[y_i - x_{ij} \left\{ \alpha_0 + \sum_{l=1}^{l} \alpha_l f^l + \sum_{k=1}^{K} \alpha_{k+p} (f\text{-}\kappa_k)_+^p \right\} \right]^2 + g \sum_{\text{k}=1}^{K} \alpha_{k+p}^2, \tag{6}$$

where g is a tuning parameter determined by cross-validation or generalized cross-validation [8].

The smoothing method with penalized splines estimates also requires selection of the number of knots and the order p, which may vary from case to case. Fortunately, the estimates are not sensitive to these choices; and cubic splines are suggested in most cases [6], which ensure continuous second-order and piecewise continuous third-order derivatives at the knots. Meanwhile, knots are usually selected from the interval over which f is evenly distributed, or κ_k is taken to be the $100k/(K + 1)$th percentile from the unevenly distributed f.

2.2. Spatial temporal model

The spatial temporal model is defined by the sum of a mean function, $\mu(f, \mathbf{x})$, and $\varepsilon(f, \mathbf{x})$ of a zero-mean Gaussian random field. It is a generalization of the Gaussian processes (GP) model, which has been widely adopted for spatial statistic problems [4, 9].

Both of the preceding models aim to represent the functional data in terms of their mean functions. In contrast, the spatial temporal model utilizes the property of the normal distribution of the residuals; thus, the output can be seen as a realization of a Gaussian random field. We assume a mean function $\mu(f, \mathbf{x})$ in the form of

$$\mu(f, \mathbf{x}) = \sum_{i=0}^{n} h_i(\mathbf{x})\beta_i(f) \overset{def}{=} \mathbf{h}(\mathbf{x})^T \boldsymbol{\beta}(f), \tag{7}$$

where $\mathbf{h}(\mathbf{x})$ and $\boldsymbol{\beta}(f)$ are two series of basis functions of the input variable and index variable, respectively. Such an assumption leads to a spatial temporal model

$$y(f, \mathbf{x}) = \mathbf{h}(\mathbf{x})^T \boldsymbol{\beta}(f) + \varepsilon(f, \mathbf{x}), \tag{8}$$

where $\varepsilon(f, \mathbf{x})$ is a zero-mean Gaussian random field, and the covariance function follows the form

$$cov\{\varepsilon(f, \mathbf{x}), \varepsilon(f, \mathbf{x}')\} = \mathrm{K}(\kappa_f; |\mathbf{x}\text{-}\mathbf{x}'|), \tag{9}$$

where $\mathbf{K}(\kappa_f)$ denotes the covariance matrix, whose *(i,j)* element $K(\kappa_f; |\mathbf{x}_i - \mathbf{x}_j|)$ measures the covariance between $\mathbf{x}_i$ and $\mathbf{x}_j$. κ_f is an *f*-dependent hyperparameter that controls the properties of the covariance.

Suppose we have obtained observation $y(f_j, \mathbf{x}_i)$ at input sites $(f_j, \mathbf{x}_i)$ with $j = 1, \ldots, J$ and $i = 1, \ldots, n$, where J and n are the length of indices and input settings. $\boldsymbol{\beta}(f)$ and κ_f can be calculated following the hyperparameter estimation procedure within a standard Gaussian processes model [4]. The spatial temporal model also allows predictions at unobserved sites f_* and $\mathbf{x}_*$. The procedures for prediction are summarized in the following algorithm.

Step 1: For $j = 1, \ldots, J$, calculate the best estimates of $\hat{\boldsymbol{\beta}}(f)$ and κ_f for $f = f_j$ by maximizing the (log) likelihood, given by

$$\log p(\mathbf{y}|\mathbf{X}) = -\frac{1}{2}[(\mathbf{y} - \mathbf{h}(\mathbf{x})\boldsymbol{\beta})^T \mathbf{K}^{-1}(\kappa_f)(\mathbf{y} - \mathbf{h}(\mathbf{x})\boldsymbol{\beta})] - \frac{1}{2}\log|\mathbf{K}| - \frac{N}{2}\log 2\pi$$

Step 2: According to the data $\{\mathbf{x}_i, y(f_j, \mathbf{x}_i)\}$, obtain estimates $\mu(f, \mathbf{x})$, and $\hat{\kappa}_f$. Calculate prediction $y(f_j, \mathbf{x}_*)$, at $f = f_j$, with the best linear unbiased prediction [2]

$$y(f_j, \mathbf{x}_*) = \mathbf{h}(\mathbf{x}_*)^T \hat{\boldsymbol{\beta}} + \mathbf{K}^T(\hat{\kappa}_f; |\mathbf{x}_*\text{-}\mathbf{x}|)\ \mathbf{K}^{-1}(\hat{\kappa}_f; |\mathbf{x} - \mathbf{x}'|)(\mathbf{y} - \mathbf{h}(\mathbf{x})^T \hat{\boldsymbol{\beta}})$$

Step 3: For new index $f_* \in [f_1, f_J]$ and given outputs at two existing indices $y(f_0)$ and $y(f_1)$, use linear interpolation to make predictions for $y(f_*, \mathbf{x}_*)$, as

$$y(f_*, \mathbf{x}_*) = y(f_0, \mathbf{x}_*) + (f_* - f_0)\frac{y(f_1, \mathbf{x}_*) - y(f_0, \mathbf{x}_*)}{f_1 - f_*}$$

2.3. Quasiphysical model

Metamaterial frequency response, for example, modeling the resonance response is often quite challenging and cannot be achieved with the models introduced above. This is due to that the above models are based upon linear regression and simply encode the index dependence within the linear index-dependent smooth basis functions. However, when distinct resonance peaks exist, a common scenario in radio frequency engineering, fitting to these smooth basis functions often, leads to poor accuracy [10]. To deal with these problems, we tend to utilize some underling physical mechanism and establish a quasiphysical modeling method. For example, the mean function $\mu(f, \mathbf{x})$ is represented by the combination of some link function $\mathbf{L}(f, \bullet)$, which follows certain physical mechanisms, and a set of low-dimensional scaling variables $\varphi(\mathbf{x})$, i.e.,

$$\mu(f, \mathbf{x}) = \mathrm{L}(f, \varphi(\mathbf{x})). \tag{10}$$

Then, we have $y(f, \mathbf{x}) = \mathrm{L}(f, \varphi(\mathbf{x})) + \varepsilon(f, \mathbf{x})$. Instead of finding a single function with respect to both frequency index and input variables, the functional response is separated into two parts: a physical meaningful link function $\mathbf{L}(f, \bullet)$ contains the functional features, whereas the other captures the relationship between input variables $\mathbf{x}$ and scaling variables $\varphi(\mathbf{x})$. This separation often leads to dimension reduction in statistical models. In the example of metamaterial design, the functional response is represented by the effective permittivity of a unit cell, which can be well fitted by a Drude-Lorentz form [11],

$$\mathbf{L}(f, \varphi(\mathbf{x})) = \varepsilon_a \left(1 - \frac{F_e f^2}{f^2 - f_0^2 + i\gamma_e f} \right). \tag{11}$$

where $\varphi(\mathbf{x}) \equiv \{\varepsilon_a, F_e, f_0, \gamma_e\}$ is the intermediate variable which can be estimated via fitting the functional response by Eq. (11), meanwhile $\varphi(\mathbf{x})$ is a function of input variables. Here, we choose the Gaussian processes (GP) regression model for interpolate new φ^* given previous obtained pairs $\{\mathbf{x}, \varphi(\mathbf{x})\ \}$7D and new $\mathbf{x}^*$. Once the new φ^* is obtained, it can then be used to evaluate the new functional response by Eq. (11). **Figure 2** displays a smooth surface of f_0 and an example of predicted effective permittivity.

The aforementioned Drude-Lorentz model allows high accuracy only when the metamaterial system works in a static or quasistatic regime, such that the metamaterial architecture can be seen as a single piece of effective medium. However, for complex metamaterial systems, the working regime is beyond static; thus, approximation accuracy by such a model is severely deteriorated. We noted that EM waves propagate through each layer of metamaterial like a current on transmission lines. Such a perspective transfers the EM field problems to circuit problems. Hence, function response to a continuous spectrum is reduced to discrete LRC (short form of inductor, resistor and capacitor) networks. We propose a two-stage modeling scheme, where in the first stage, a vector fitting (VF) technique is adopted to provide accurate rational approximation to frequency responses with distinct resonances. Its results are easily interpreted as an equivalent circuit. The approximation accuracy to a frequency response and its corresponding equivalent circuits are shown in part (a) and (b) of **Figure 3**, respectively. And in

http://dx.doi.org/10.5772/intechopen.69385

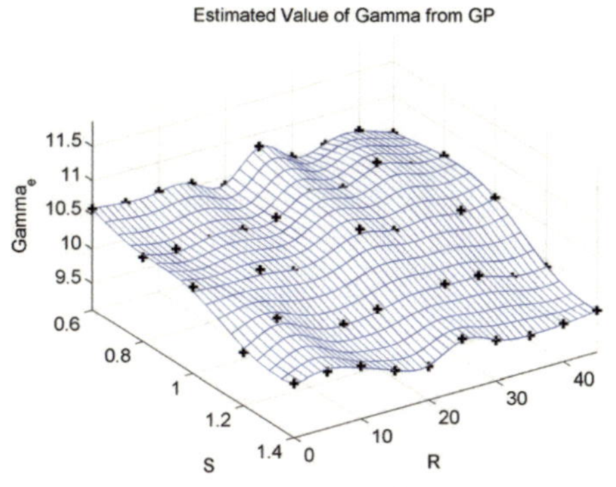

(a)

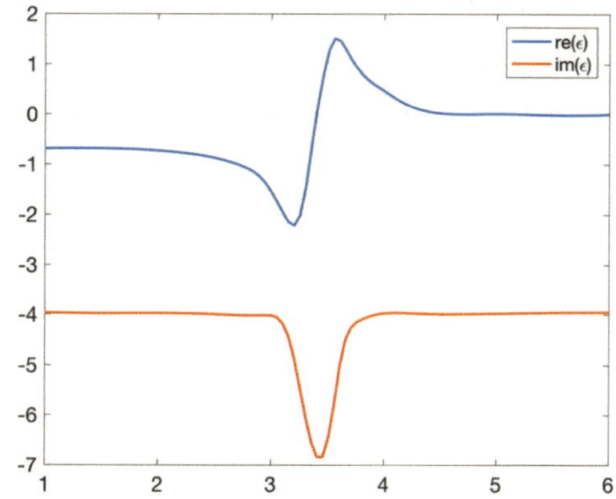

(b)

Figure 2. Example of modeling functional response assisted by the physical model: (a) Gaussian process surface of a scaling variable; (b) predicted functional response.

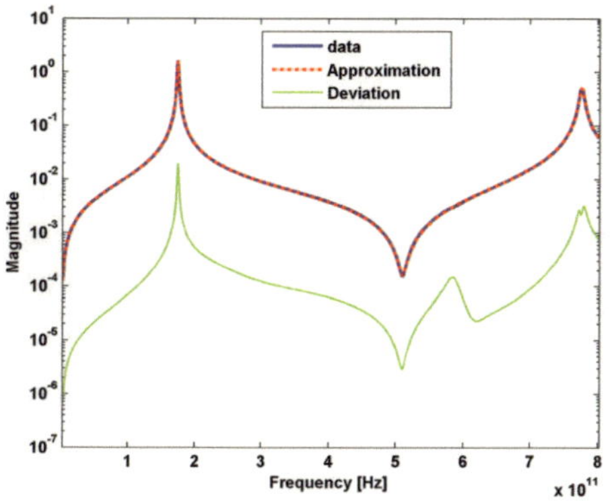

(a)

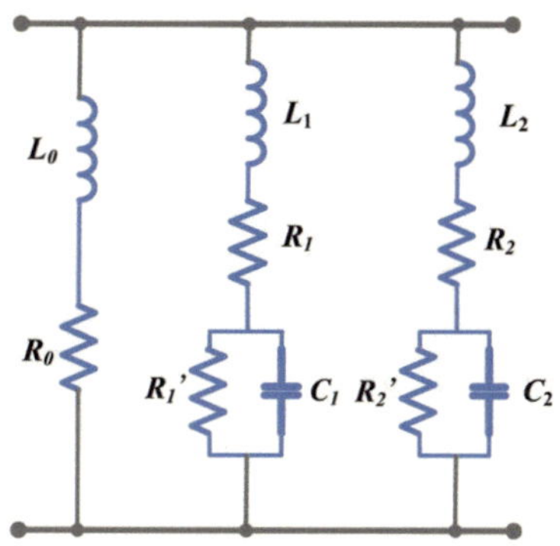

(b)

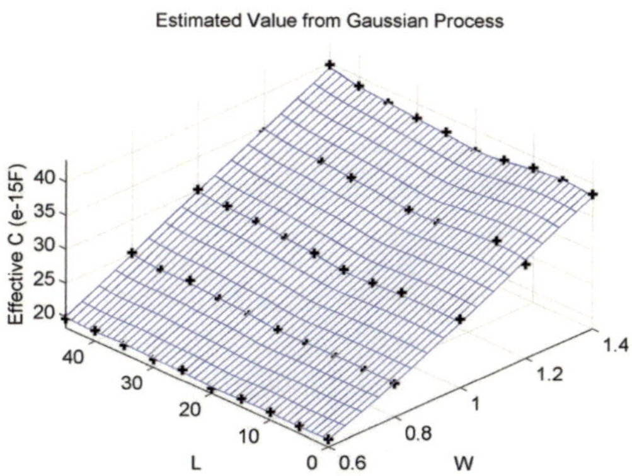

(c)

Figure 3. Example of modeling frequency response via (a) vector fitting, (b) equivalent circuit, and (c) GP regression.

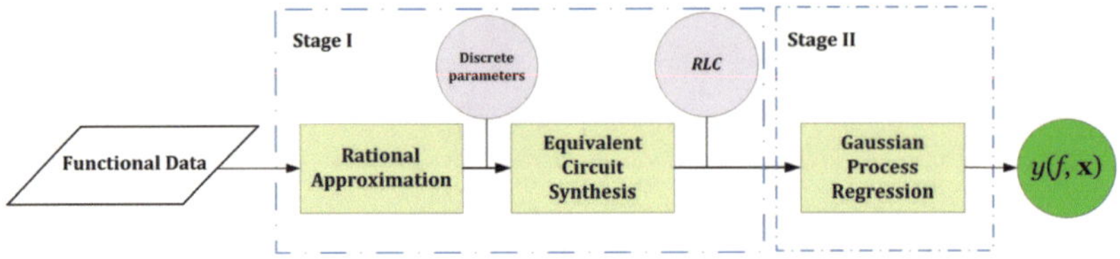

Figure 4. Flowchart of the two-stage modeling approach.

Stage II, the empirical circuit elements are then taken as the target response in statistical models to establish the mapping input-output relation by performing regression, which also allows predictions at unobserved input sites. Part (c) of **Figure 3** presents the GP surface built of circuit parameters over two input variables. A graphical display of this two-stage approach is illustrated in **Figure 4**. To predict functional response at unobserved input, it is implemented by first predict the presenting circuit elements and then recover the response.

3. Uncertainty quantification

In the engineering modeling and design, uncertainty is ubiquitous, due to the inability to specify a "true" input or model parameter. Quantifying the uncertainty of the model, e.g., in the form of predictive confidence intervals, is of great importance for decision making and advanced design [1]. In general, uncertainty quantification can be divided into two major types of problem: forward uncertainty propagation and inverse assessment of model and parameter uncertainties [12].

The full relationship between experimental output $z(f, \mathbf{x})$ and simulation output $y(f, \mathbf{x})$ can be expressed as

$$z(f, \mathbf{x}) = y(f, \mathbf{x}) + \varepsilon'(f) = \mathrm{L}(f, \varphi(\mathbf{x}, \theta) + \eta(\mathbf{x})) + \varepsilon(f, \mathbf{x}) + \varepsilon'(f), \tag{12}$$

where $\varphi(\mathbf{x}, \boldsymbol{\theta})$ denotes the GP regression model, which depends on the input variable $\mathbf{x}$ and several unobservable calibration parameters θ. $\eta(\mathbf{x})$ is the additive discrepancy function (or model bias function), which does not depend upon the calibration parameters. To reduce the complexity of the analysis, we assume that $\varepsilon(f, \mathbf{x})$ is a zero-mean Gaussian random field and being independent of $\mathbf{x}$. And then we can merge $\varepsilon(f, \mathbf{x})$ and $\varepsilon'(f)$ together, which is denoted by $\varepsilon(f)$. Thus, the model becomes

$$z(f, \mathbf{x}) = \mathrm{L}(f, \varphi(\mathbf{x}, \theta) + \eta(\mathbf{x})) + \varepsilon(f) \tag{13}$$

where $\varepsilon(f)$ is assumed to be a zero-mean Gaussian noise with known variance λ, $\varepsilon(f_i) \sim \mathcal{N}(0, \lambda)$.

In forward problems, with an uncertain input $\mathbf{x}$ and given model parameters $\boldsymbol{\theta}$, the model output y and other quantities of interest are to be calculated. On the other hand, the inverse problem is to estimate the values of model parameters $\boldsymbol{\theta}$ such that it makes the model's output fit the experimental data as accurate as possible (or satisfy some precision requirements).

3.1. Metamodel-based uncertainty propagation

The main problem in analyzing uncertainty propagation is obtaining an analytical representation of the metamodel for any arbitrary (uncertain) input values. Given its probability density, the Bayesian framework can provide a probability measure of random inputs on the output field. The purpose of such an operation is to evaluate the influence of an uncertain input on the model response.

Assume that the Gaussian process regression model is trained on a dataset with the input $\mathbf{X} = \{\mathbf{x}_1, \ldots, \mathbf{x}_N\}$ and the corresponding intermediate variable $\Psi = (\varphi(\mathbf{x}_1), \ldots, \varphi(\mathbf{x}_N))^{\mathrm{T}}$ which is obtained by fitting algorithm in Stage I. The GP hyperparameters learned from the data are denoted by γ. The uncertainty of the input variable $\mathbf{x}^*$ is captured by a probability density function,

$$\mathbf{x}^* \sim p(\mathbf{x}^*) \tag{14}$$

At a deterministic test input $\mathbf{x}^*$, the predictive distribution of the function, $p(\varphi^*|\mathrm{x}^*, \mathbf{X}, \Psi, \gamma)$ (for simplicity, we use φ^* to denote $\varphi(\mathbf{x}^*)$, the output of the metamodel.), is Gaussian with mean

$$\tilde{\varphi}* = \mathbf{E}(\varphi^*|\mathrm{x}^*, \mathbf{X}, \Psi, \gamma) = \sum_{i=1}^{N} \zeta_i \mathrm{C}(\mathbf{x}_i, \mathrm{x}^*), \tag{15}$$

and variance

$$cov(\phi^*) = \mathbf{C}(\mathrm{x}^*, \mathrm{x}^*) - \sum_{i,j=1}^{N} (\mathbf{C} - \sigma^2\mathbf{I})^{-1}\mathrm{C}(\mathrm{x}^*, \mathbf{x}_i)\mathbf{C}(\mathrm{x}^*, \mathbf{x}_j) \tag{16}$$

where ζ_i is the ith element of column vector $\zeta = [\mathbf{C}+\sigma^2\mathbf{I}]\Psi$. $\mathbf{C}$ denotes the covariance matrix of the Gaussian process, whose ijth element is given by $C_{ij} = \mathbf{C}(\mathbf{x}_i, \mathbf{x}_j)$.

The final goal is to propagate uncertainty through the link function $\mathrm{L}(f, \varphi^*)$. The computation of the statistics is implemented by integrating over the uncertainty with the mean

$$\mu_{\mathrm{L}^*} = \int \mathrm{L}(f, \varphi^*) p(\varphi^*|\mathrm{x}^*, \mathbf{X}, \Psi, \gamma) p(\mathbf{x}^*) d\varphi^* d\mathbf{x}^*. \tag{17}$$

and the variance

$$\sigma^2_{\mathrm{L}^*} = \int [\mathrm{L}(f, \varphi^* - \mu_{\mathrm{L}^*})]^2 p(\varphi^*|\mathbf{x}^*, \mathbf{X}, \Psi, \gamma) p(\mathbf{x}^*) d\varphi^* d\mathbf{x}^*. \tag{18}$$

The uncertainty propagation is induced by the variability of the input variable. For example, in metamaterial engineering, the dimension of a design parameter, say the thickness of the metallic microstructure layer, could differ from what has been instructed during the manufacturing processes. From measurements, the value of such a variable would rather follow a distribution than be pre-specified as an exact value. Therefore, the analysis of uncertainty propagation is needed to be in the metamaterial design process.

3.2. Bayesian calibration

Compared to uncertainty forward propagation, the inverse problem is more difficult yet of great importance in enhancing the fidelity of metamodels. Two major aspects concerning the inverse problem are measuring model discrepancy and model calibration. In this chapter, we use the formulation to address both issues within an updating process, similar to that proposed in Ref. [12].

3.2.1. The model

In this section, we introduce the details of performing Bayesian calibration with regard to Eq. (13). The calibration parameters, denoted by $\boldsymbol{\theta}$, are defined as any physical parameters that can be specified as an input to the statistical model given by Eq. (13). The fundamental difference between $\mathbf{x}$ and $\boldsymbol{\theta}$ is that the former refers to design inputs whose value can be specified by the user during experiment and simulation, whereas the latter cannot be controlled and its true value is not directly observable [12]. In the previous chapter, the calibration parameter is not explicitly specified. However, we here include it in the framework to quantify its uncertainty, which completes the full cycle of metamaterial design and modeling. Suppose $\boldsymbol{\theta}$ represent a constitutive parameter, say permittivity, of a dielectric used to fabricate the metamaterial system, which cannot be accurately measured directly.

Before offering the detailed statistics for uncertainty quantification, we must note that the purpose of parameter calibration is to provide an accurate prediction with the metamodel with a small amount of data. An even smaller amount of experimental data is acquired to calibrate and validate the main model. To select the "best" experiment samples, uniform experimental design techniques are usually applied [6]. A Latin hypercube sampling, for example, is widely used for such cases, mainly due to its good coverage property [13].

The data corresponding to the metamodel φ are obtained at $D_1 = \left\{(\mathbf{x}_1^{'}, \theta_1), \ldots, (\mathbf{x}_N^{'}, \theta_N)\right\}$, where $\{\mathbf{x}_1^{'}, \ldots, \mathbf{x}_N^{'}\}$ and $\{\theta_1, \ldots, \theta_N\}$ are the set of design inputs and calibration parameters. Although the notation is included, the true values of the calibration parameters are unknown throughout the entire calibration process. The inverse problem of uncertainty quantification is implemented in an updated formulation with a Bayesian approach [1]. In model (13), the metamodel, $\boldsymbol{\varphi}(\mathbf{x}, \boldsymbol{\theta})$, and discrepancy function, $\eta(\mathbf{x})$, are both Gaussian processes:

$$\varphi(\mathbf{x}, \theta) \sim \mathcal{N}(m_1(\mathbf{x}, \theta), C_1((\mathbf{x}, \theta), (\mathbf{x}', \theta'))), \tag{19}$$

$$\eta(\mathbf{x}) \sim \mathcal{N}(m_2(\mathbf{x}), C_2(\mathbf{x}, \mathbf{x}')), \tag{20}$$

where $m_1(\mathbf{x}, \theta) = \mathbf{h}_1(\mathbf{x}, \theta)^{\mathrm{T}}\beta_1$ and $m_2(\mathbf{x}) = \mathbf{h}_2(\mathbf{x})^{\mathrm{T}}\beta_2$ [12]. $C_1((\cdot,\cdot),(\cdot,\cdot))$ and $C_2(\cdot,\cdot)$ are covariance functions, which can be parameterized by some hyperparameters, denoted by Γ_1 and Γ_2, respectively. Let us denote these hyperparameters with $\Gamma = (\Gamma_1, \Gamma_2)$, collectively. There are many candidates of covariance functions from which one can chose. For example, as one of the most applied covariance functions, squared exponential function, in form of

$$C_1((\mathbf{x},\theta),(\mathbf{x}',\theta')) = \sigma_1^2 \exp\left\{-(\mathbf{x}-\mathbf{x}')^{\mathrm{T}}\mathbf{V}_{1x}(\mathbf{x}-\mathbf{x}')\right\}\exp\left\{-(\theta-\theta')^{\mathrm{T}}\mathbf{V}_{\theta}(\theta-\theta')\right\},$$
$$C_2(\mathbf{x},\mathbf{x}') = \sigma_2^2 \exp\left\{-(\mathbf{x}-\mathbf{x}')^{\mathrm{T}}\mathbf{V}_{2x}(\mathbf{x}-\mathbf{x}')\right\}, \tag{21}$$

can provide smooth samples to infer the latent function variable. In Eq. (21), the value of hyperparameters can be inferred via Markov Chain Monte Carlo (MCMC) techniques.

3.2.2. *Data and prior distribution*

Let us denote the matrix of basis functions $\mathbf{H}_1(D_1)$ with rows $\left\{\mathbf{h}_1(\mathbf{x}_1^{'},\theta_1)^T,\ldots,\mathbf{h}_1(\mathbf{x}_N^{'},\theta_N)^T\right\}$, which leads to the expectation of φ as $\mathbf{H}_1(D_1)\beta_1$. Similarly, from the experimental observations we can obtain $\hat{\varphi}$, the estimation of φ by Eq. (13). It can be further augmented by the calibration parameter at each $\mathbf{x}$, with $D_2(\theta) = \{(\mathbf{x}_1,\boldsymbol{\theta}),\ldots,(\mathbf{x}_n,\boldsymbol{\theta})\}$. In contrast to the simulation output $\{\mathbf{x}_1^{'},\ldots,\mathbf{x}_N^{'}\}$, the experimental data are usually acquired with much smaller size, i.e., $n << N$, which is in accordance with the purpose of reducing the amount of physical experiments with calibrated models. Meanwhile, we use $\mathbf{x}_i$ and $\mathbf{x}_i{}'$ to describe that the observation points could be different between two datasets. The expectation $\hat{\varphi}$ of can be represented by $\mathbf{H}_1\{D_2(\theta)\}\beta_1 + \mathbf{H}_2(D_2)\beta_2$. We write the full data vector $\Omega^T = \{\varphi^T,\hat{\varphi}^T\}$, which is obtained via *Stage I* given the simulation and observation of functional response. Meanwhile, they are normally distributed given the full set of parameters $\{\boldsymbol{\theta},\boldsymbol{\beta},\boldsymbol{\phi}\}$ ($\beta = (\beta_1^T,\beta_2^T)^T$, $\boldsymbol{\phi} = (\lambda,\Gamma)$).

The goal of calibration is to obtain $p(\boldsymbol{\theta}|\Omega)$, the posterior distribution of conditional only on the full data Ω. To derive the posterior distribution of parameters, we begin with the normal distribution of the full set of data, during which the likelihood function will yield a Gaussian [14], with mean

$$E(\Omega|\boldsymbol{\theta},\boldsymbol{\beta},\boldsymbol{\varphi}) = \mathbf{m}_d(\boldsymbol{\theta}) = \mathbf{H}(\boldsymbol{\theta})\boldsymbol{\beta}, \tag{22}$$

where

$$\mathbf{H}(\theta) = \begin{pmatrix} \mathbf{H}_1(D_1) & 0 \\ \mathbf{H}_1\{D_2(\theta)\} & \mathbf{H}_2(D_2) \end{pmatrix}. \tag{23}$$

To specify the variance matrix of Ω, we need the variance matrix of φ, denoted by $\mathbf{V}_1(D_1)$, whose (i,i') element is $C_1\left((\mathbf{x}_i^{'},\theta_i),(\mathbf{x}_{i'}^{'},\theta_{i'})\right)$. Similarly, we can define $\mathbf{V}_1\{D_2(\boldsymbol{\theta})\}$ and $\mathbf{V}_2(D_2)$. Let $\mathbf{C}_1\{D_1,D_2(\boldsymbol{\theta})\}$ be the matrix with (i,j) element $C_1\left\{(\mathbf{x}_i^{'},\theta_i),(\mathbf{x}_j^{'},\theta_j)\right\}$. Therefore,

$$Var(\Omega|\boldsymbol{\theta},\boldsymbol{\beta},\boldsymbol{\varphi}) = \mathbf{V}_d(\boldsymbol{\theta}) = \begin{pmatrix} \mathbf{V}_1(D_1) & \mathbf{C}_1\{D_1,D_2(\boldsymbol{\theta})\}^T \\ \mathbf{C}_1\{D_1,D_2(\boldsymbol{\theta})\} & \lambda\mathbf{I}+\mathbf{V}_1\{D_2(\boldsymbol{\theta})\}+\mathbf{V}_2(D_2) \end{pmatrix}, \tag{24}$$

where $\mathbf{I}$ is the $n \times n$ identity matrix.

To derive the posterior distribution under the Bayesian framework, the prior distributions of parameters, $\{\boldsymbol{\theta},\boldsymbol{\beta},\boldsymbol{\phi}\}$, must also be independently specified. Following the suggestion of [12], we chose conjugate prior for $\boldsymbol{\theta}$ and $\boldsymbol{\phi}$, and a weak prior for β, specifically $p(\beta_1, \beta_2) \propto 1$, then we have $p(\boldsymbol{\theta}, \boldsymbol{\beta}, \boldsymbol{\phi}) = p(\boldsymbol{\theta})p(\boldsymbol{\phi})$, where $p(\boldsymbol{\phi}) = p(\lambda)p(\Gamma_1)p(\Gamma_2)$. Meanwhile, Bayesian inference with MCMC requires specification of proper prior distributions to perform Bayesian statistics. For such purpose, conjugate priors are specified, e.g.

$$\begin{aligned} &\sigma_1^2, \sigma_2^2 \sim \mathcal{IG}(\mathrm{a}, \mathrm{b}), \\ &\mathbf{V}_{1x}, \mathbf{V}_{2x} \sim \mathcal{W}(\rho, \nu), \\ &\theta \sim \mathcal{N}(\mu_\theta, \mathrm{V}_\theta). \end{aligned} \tag{25}$$

where $\mathcal{IG}$, $\mathcal{W}$, and $\mathcal{N}$ are inverse gamma, Wishart, and normal distributions, respectively [15].

3.2.3. Posterior distribution

Conditional on full data, the independence of parameters leads to the full joint posterior distribution

$$\begin{aligned} p(\boldsymbol{\theta}, \boldsymbol{\beta}, \boldsymbol{\phi}|\Omega) &\propto p(\boldsymbol{\theta})p(\boldsymbol{\phi})p(\boldsymbol{\beta})p(\Omega|\mathbf{m}_d(\boldsymbol{\theta}), \mathbf{V}_d(\boldsymbol{\theta})) \\ &\propto p(\boldsymbol{\theta})p(\boldsymbol{\phi})|\mathbf{V}_d^{-1}(\boldsymbol{\theta})|^{-1/2} \\ &\times \exp\left[-\frac{1}{2}\left\{(\Omega - \mathbf{m}_d(\boldsymbol{\theta}))^T \mathbf{V}_d^{-1}(\boldsymbol{\theta})(\Omega - \mathbf{m}_d(\boldsymbol{\theta}))\right\}\right]. \end{aligned} \tag{26}$$

To obtain $p(\boldsymbol{\theta}|\Omega)$, it is required to integrate out β and hyperparameters $\boldsymbol{\phi}$ from Eq. (26). Integrating β yields

$$\begin{aligned} p(\boldsymbol{\theta}, \boldsymbol{\phi}|\Omega) &\propto p(\boldsymbol{\theta})p(\boldsymbol{\phi})|\mathbf{V}_d^{-1}(\boldsymbol{\theta})|^{-1/2}|\mathbf{W}(\boldsymbol{\theta})|^{1/2} \\ &\times \exp\left[-\frac{1}{2}\left\{\left(\Omega - \mathbf{H}(\boldsymbol{\theta})\hat{\beta}(\boldsymbol{\theta})\right)^T \mathbf{V}_d^{-1}(\boldsymbol{\theta})\left(\Omega - \mathbf{H}(\boldsymbol{\theta})\hat{\beta}(\boldsymbol{\theta})\right)\right\}\right], \end{aligned} \tag{27}$$

where

$$\hat{\boldsymbol{\beta}}(\boldsymbol{\theta}) = \mathbf{W}(\boldsymbol{\theta})\mathbf{H}(\boldsymbol{\theta})^T \mathbf{V}_d(\boldsymbol{\theta})^{-1}\Omega, \tag{28}$$

$$\mathbf{W}(\boldsymbol{\theta}) = \left(\mathbf{H}(\boldsymbol{\theta})^T \mathbf{V}_d(\boldsymbol{\theta})^{-1}\mathbf{H}(\boldsymbol{\theta})\right)^{-1}. \tag{29}$$

3.2.4. Calibration and prediction

Since the posterior distribution specified in Eq. (27) is a highly intractable function of $\boldsymbol{\phi}$, we need Monte Carlo method to integrate out $\boldsymbol{\phi}$ and get the numerical estimation for the posterior distribution of the calibration parameters θ. The formulation is given by

$$p(\theta|\Omega) = \frac{1}{M}\sum_{i=1}^{M} p(\theta, \boldsymbol{\phi}^i|\Omega). \tag{30}$$

However, the purpose of calibration of parameters is to predict the real process rather than achieve their values. Therefore, in practice, we are rather more interested in expressing the posterior distribution of $\boldsymbol{\phi}$, which is a Gaussian process as well, conditional on the calibration parameters and estimated hyperparameters. The mean and covariance function of this GP is given by

$$E(\boldsymbol{\varphi}(\mathbf{x})|\boldsymbol{\theta}, \boldsymbol{\phi}, \Omega) = \mathbf{h}(\mathbf{x}, \boldsymbol{\theta})^T\hat{\boldsymbol{\beta}}(\boldsymbol{\theta}) + \mathbf{t}(\mathbf{x}, \boldsymbol{\theta})^T\mathbf{V}_d^{-1}(\boldsymbol{\theta})\left(\Omega - \mathbf{H}(\boldsymbol{\theta})\hat{\boldsymbol{\beta}}(\boldsymbol{\theta})\right), \tag{31}$$

where $\mathbf{h}(\mathbf{x}, \theta) = \begin{pmatrix} \mathbf{h}_1(\mathbf{x}, \boldsymbol{\theta}) \\ \mathbf{h}_2(\mathbf{x}) \end{pmatrix}, \mathbf{t}(\mathbf{x}, \boldsymbol{\theta}) = \begin{pmatrix} \mathbf{V}_1((\mathbf{x}, \boldsymbol{\theta}), D_1) \\ \mathbf{V}_1((\mathbf{x}, \boldsymbol{\theta}), D_2(\boldsymbol{\theta})) + \mathbf{V}_2(\mathbf{x}, D_2) \end{pmatrix},$

and covariance

$$\begin{aligned} cov(\varphi(\mathbf{x}), \varphi(\mathbf{x}')|\boldsymbol{\theta}, \boldsymbol{\phi}, \Omega) &= c_1((\mathbf{x}, \boldsymbol{\theta}), (\mathbf{x}', \boldsymbol{\theta})) + c_2(\mathbf{x}, \mathbf{x}') - \mathbf{t}(\mathbf{x}, \theta)^T\mathbf{V}_d^{-1}(\boldsymbol{\theta})\mathbf{t}(\mathbf{x}', \theta) \\ &+ \left(\mathbf{h}(\mathbf{x}, \boldsymbol{\theta}) - \mathbf{H}(\boldsymbol{\theta})^T\mathbf{V}_d^{-1}(\boldsymbol{\theta})\mathbf{t}(\mathbf{x}, \boldsymbol{\theta})\right)^T\mathbf{W}(\boldsymbol{\theta})\left(\mathbf{h}(\mathbf{x}', \boldsymbol{\theta}) - \mathbf{H}(\boldsymbol{\theta})^T\mathbf{V}_d^{-1}(\boldsymbol{\theta})\mathbf{t}(\mathbf{x}', \boldsymbol{\theta})\right). \end{aligned} \tag{32}$$

Inference about $\boldsymbol{\phi}(\mathbf{x})$ can be implemented again numerically with its posterior mean $E[\varphi(\mathbf{x})|\boldsymbol{\theta}, \boldsymbol{\phi}, \Omega]$ at estimated $\boldsymbol{\theta}$ and $\boldsymbol{\phi}$, by integrating Eq. (31) with regard to Eq. (28). Given the estimation of $\phi(\mathbf{x})$, the analysis of z becomes straightforward by applying the link function $\mathrm{L}(\cdot)$ as described in model (13).

So far, we have accomplished calibrating a metamodel in the Bayesian framework using the experimental data, which accounts for parameter uncertainty and corrects the model discrepancy and experimental uncertainty.

4. Simulation study

This section demonstrate the results obtained using the Bayesian uncertainty quantification framework for the metamaterial design problem with the models described in Sections 2 and 3, with examples. Of both propagation and inverse assessment, the overall model is formulated in Eq. (13), where geometric variable $\mathbf{w}$ and incident angle α are input variables specified in the simulation, i.e., $\mathbf{x}^T = \{\mathbf{w}, \alpha\}^T$. Thus, the model is expressed as

$$\begin{aligned} z(\mathbf{x}) &= y(\mathbf{x}, \boldsymbol{\theta}) + \eta(\mathbf{x}) + \varepsilon \\ &= \mathbf{L}(f, \varphi(\{\mathbf{w}, \alpha\}, \boldsymbol{\theta}) + \eta(\mathbf{w}, \alpha)) + \varepsilon', \end{aligned} \tag{33}$$

To demonstrate parameter calibration within the metamaterial modeling and design, we consider an example where the real part of the permittivity of a dielectric material, ε_d, is defined as the calibration parameters $\theta = \varepsilon_d$, and its prior is given normal distribution as model (25), with mean $\mu_\theta = 3$ and variance $V_\theta = 0.5$. **Figure 5** illustrates the probability density function of this prior distribution. We demonstrate a measure of uncertain propagation in **Figure 6**, where

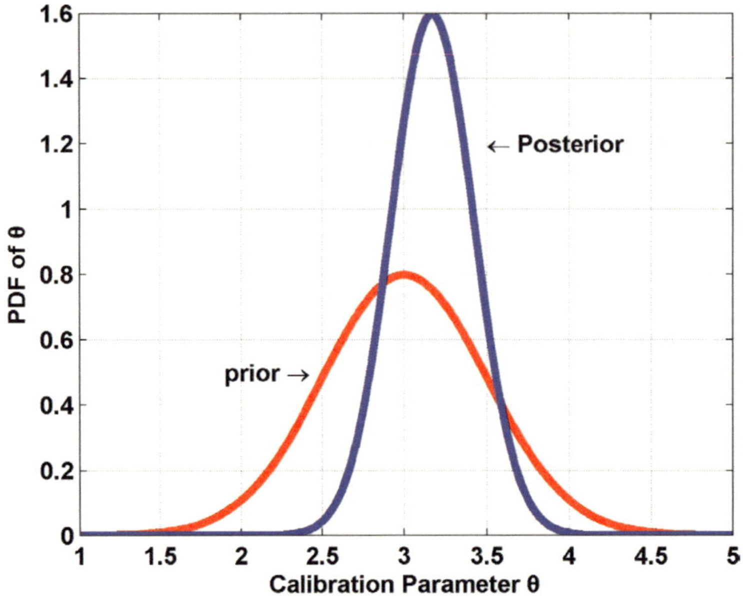

Figure 5. Comparison of prior and posterior distributions of the calibration parameter. The mean of the Gaussian distribution shifts from 3 to 3.17, and the variance is much smaller after Bayesian calibration.

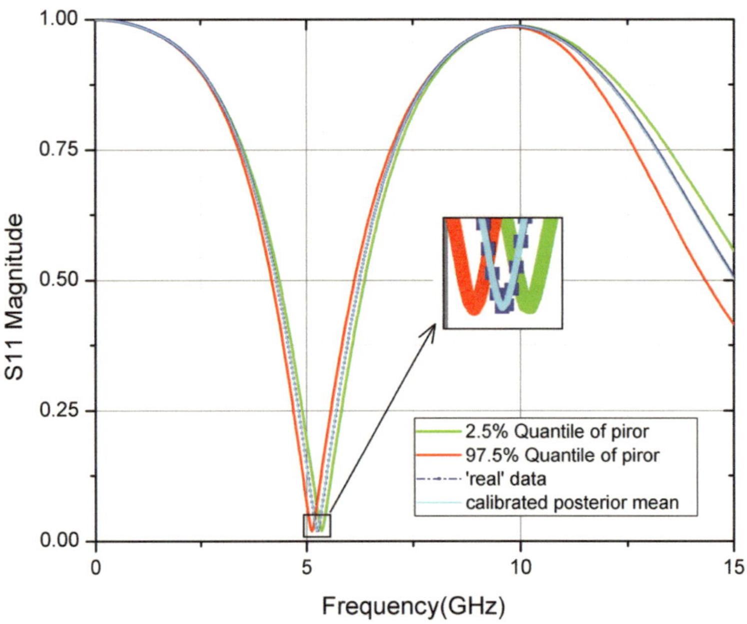

Figure 6. The effect of uncertainty propagation and results of parameter calibration.

predictions with 2.5% quantile (green or light gray) and 97.5% quantile (red or dark gray) of the samples are depicted to show the discrepancy induced by the uncertain input. Following the methodology introduced in Section 3, metamodels can be established for the simulation data and discrepancy function, with Gaussian process regression models. In our example, we obtained 92 simulation data to build GPs and 20 observations for calibration. The posterior distribution of the calibration parameter is also displayed in **Figure 5**. After calibration, the distribution of calibration parameter has a much smaller variance. The comparison between the prediction at posterior mean (cyan curve) and "real data" (blue dash) is shown in **Figure 6**, where the discrepancy reduction is remarkable.

5. Conclusion

In this chapter, we review several conventional model for functional response and present the quasiphysical model for functional response. Compared with the conventional models, this model can reveal the physical insight more clearly and make better use of historical experience. The two-stage method was presented to model the frequency response of metamaterial and facilitate the design process. Using this approach, we decomposed the complex modeling problem into a vector fitting-based equivalent circuit modeling process and a GP regression process, which can easily generate the mapping function from the structure's geometric design. The predictive property of this model enables the massive reduction of time-consuming simulations.

Another important topic with this chapter was the development and application of a Bayesian uncertainty quantification approach in dealing with functional response. Both forward uncertainty propagation and inverse assessment of the model were discussed, and a Bayesian framework was presented with simulation experimental results to deal with the model calibration for functional response. We envision that our two-stage approach can be generalized to model any functional responses of a rational form. With the Bayesian framework for the functional data of computer experiments, we were able to incorporate our prior knowledge into the model and obtain a probabilistic measure of the uncertainty associated with metamaterial system design. This general methodology enables researchers and designers to achieve high efficiency and accuracy in modeling functional response with a considerably small amount of data. With a Bayesian calibration framework, we are able to constantly increase the precision of predictions of the functional response at unobserved sites, thus replacing expensive physical experiments.

Acknowledgements

This work was supported by the Shenzhen Key Laboratory of Data Science and Modeling.

Author details

Xiao Guo[1], Yang He[1], Binbin Zhu[1], Yang Yang[2], Ke Deng[2], Ruopeng Liu[1] and Chunlin Ji[1]*

*Address all correspondence to: chunlin.ji@kuang-chi.org

1 Kuang-Chi Institute of Advanced Technology, Shenzhen, China

2 Center for Statistical Science, Tsinghua University, Beijing, China

References

[1] Kennedy M, O'Hagan A. Predicting the output from a complex computer code when fast approximations are available. Biometrika. 1998;**87**:1–13. DOI: 10.1093/biomet/87.1.1

[2] Hastie T, Tibshirani R, Friedman J. The Elements of Statistical Learning. New York: Springer; 2001. p. 745. DOI: 10.1007/978-0-387-84858-7

[3] Ramsay J, Silverman B. Applied functional data analysis: Methods and case studies. New York: Springer; 2002. DOI: 10.1007/b98886

[4] Cressie A. Statistics for spatial data. Terra Nova. 1992;**4**(5):613–617. DOI: 10.1002/978111 9115151

[5] Liu R, Ji C, Mock J, Chin J, Cui T, Smith D. Broadband ground-plane cloak. Science. 2009;**323**(5912):366–369. DOI: 10.1126/science.1166949

[6] Fang KT, Li R, Sudjianto A. Design and modeling for computer experiments. Boca Raton, FL, USA: Chapman and Hall/CRC Press. 2005. DOI: 10.1201/9781420034899

[7] Ruppert D, Carroll R. Theory & methods: Spatially-adaptive penalties for spline fitting. Australian & New Zealand Journal of Statistics. 2000;**42**(2):205–223. DOI: 10.1111/1467-842X.00119

[8] Graven P, Wahba G. Smoothing noisy data with spline functions. Numerische Mathematik. 1979;**31**:377–403. DOI:10.1007/BF01404567

[9] Carroll R, Chen R, George E, Li T, Newton H, Schmiediche H, et al. Ozone exposure and population density in Harris County, Texas. Journal of the American Statistical Association. 1997;**92**(438):392–404. DOI: 10.2307/2965684

[10] Liu B, Ji C. Bayesian nonparametric modeling for rapid design of metamaterial microstructures. International Journal of Antennas & Propagation. 2014;**2014**:187–187

[11] Cui T J, Smith D, Liu R. Metamaterials: Theory, Design, and Applications. New York: Springer Publishing Company, Incorporated; 2009. DOI: 10.1007/978-1-4419-0573-4.

[12] Kennedy M, O'Hagan A. Bayesian calibration of computer models. Journal of the Royal Statistical Society: Series B (Statistical Methodology). 2001;**63**(3):425–464. DOI:10.1111/1467-9868.00294

[13] McKay M, Beckman R, Conover W. A comparison of three methods for selecting values of input variables in the analysis of output from a computer code. Technometrics. 1979;**21**(2):239–245. DOI:10.2307/1271432

[14] Kennedy M, O'Hagan A. Supplementary details on Bayesian calibration of computer. Technical Report., University of Nottingham. Statistics Section; 2001

[15] Neal RM, Probabilistic inference using Markov Chain Monte Carlo methods. 1997

Chapter 7

Fitting Models to Data: Residual Analysis, a Primer

Julia Martin, David Daffos Ruiz de Adana and
Agustin G. Asuero

Additional information is available at the end of the chapter

http://dx.doi.org/10.5772/68049

"Since all models are wrong the scientist cannot obtain a "correct" one by excessive elaboration. On the contrary following William of Occam he should seek an economical description of natural phenomena. Just as the ability to devise simple but evocative models is the signature of the great scientist so overelaboration and overparameterization is often the mark of mediocrity".

(Box, G.E.P. Science and Statistics, J. Am. Stat. Ass. 1976, 71, 791–796)

Abstract

The aim of this chapter is to show checking the underlying assumptions (the errors are independent, have a zero mean, a constant variance and follows a normal distribution) in a regression analysis, mainly fitting a straight-line model to experimental data, via the residual plots. Residuals play an essential role in regression diagnostics; no analysis is being complete without a thorough examination of residuals. The residuals should show a trend that tends to confirm the assumptions made in performing the regression analysis, or failing them should not show a tendency that denies them. Although there are numerical statistical means of verifying observed discrepancies, statisticians often prefer a visual examination of residual graphs as a more informative and certainly more convenient methodology. When dealing with small samples, the use of the graphic techniques can be very useful. Several examples taken from scientific journals and monographs are selected dealing with linearity, calibration, heteroscedastic data, errors in the model, transforming data, time-order analysis and non-linear calibration curves.

Keywords: least squares method, residual analysis, weighting, transforming data

1. Introduction

The purpose of this chapter is to provide an overview of checking the underlying assumptions (errors normally distributed with zero mean and constant variance (σ_i^2), being independent one of each other) in a regression analysis, via the use of basic residual plot, such as plots of residuals versus the independent variable x. Compact formulae for the weighted least squares calculation of the a_0 (intercept) and a_1 (slope) parameters and their standard errors [1, 2] are shown in **Table 1**. The similarity with simple linear regression is obvious, simply making the weighting factors $w_i = 1$. A number of selected examples taken from scientific journals and monographs are subject of study in this chapter. No rigorous mathematical treatment will be given to this interesting topic. Emphasis is mainly placed on a visual examination of residuals to check for the model adequacy [3–7] in regression analysis. The role of residuals in regression diagnostics is vital, being necessary with their thorough examination to consider an analysis as complete [8–10].

The residuals are geometrically the distances calculated in the y-direction [1, 2, 11, 12] (vertical distances) between the points and the regression line (error free in the independent variable)

$$r_i = y_i - \hat{y}_i \tag{1}$$

The calculated regression line

$$\hat{y}_i = a_0 + a_1 x_i \tag{2}$$

corresponds to the model

$$y_i = \alpha_0 + \alpha_1 x_i + \varepsilon_i \tag{3}$$

where ε_i is the random error (a_0 and a_1, Eq. (2), are the estimates of the true values α_0 and α_1), leading to a sum of squares of the residuals minimum

$$Q_{\min} = \left[\sum r_i^2\right]_{\min} \tag{4}$$

Note that the model error is given by

$$\varepsilon_i = y_i - E(y_i) \tag{5}$$

where $E(y_i)$ is the expected value of y_i [6]. Thus, the residuals r_i may be viewed as the differences between what is really observed, and what is predicted by the model equation (i.e. the amount that the regression equation is not able to explain). The residuals r_i may be thought as the observed errors [10] in correct models. The residuals reveal the existing asymmetry [13] in the functions of the response and the independent variable in regression problems. A number of assumptions concerning the errors [14, 15] have to be made when performing a regression analysis, for example, normality, independence, zero mean and constant variance (homoscedasticity property).

http://dx.doi.org/10.5772/68049

Equation: $\hat{y}_i = a_0 + a_1 x_i$	Slope: $a_1 = S_{XY}/S_{xx}$
Weights: $w_i = 1/s_i^2$	Intercept: $a_0 = \overline{y} - a_1 \overline{x}$
Explained sum of squares: $SS_{\mathrm{Reg}} = \sum w_i(\hat{y}_i - \overline{y})^2$	Weighted residuals: $w_i^{1/2}(y_i - \hat{y}_i)$
Residual sum of squares: $SSE = \sum w_i(y_i - \hat{y}_i)^2$	Correlation coefficient: $r = S_{XY}/\sqrt{S_{XX}S_{YY}}$
Mean: $\overline{x} = \sum w_i x_i / \sum w_i$ $\overline{y} = \sum w_i y_i / \sum w_i$	Standard errors: $s^2_{y/x} = \frac{SSE}{n-2} = \frac{S_{YY} - a_1^2 S_{XX}}{n-2}$
Sum of squares about the mean: $S_{XX} = \sum w_i(x_i - \overline{x})^2$ $S_{YY} = \sum w_i(y_i - \overline{y})^2$ $S_{XY} = \sum w_i(x_i - \overline{x})(y_i - \overline{y})$	$s^2_{a_0} = s^2_{y/x}\frac{\sum w_i x_i^2}{S_{XX}\sum w_i}$ $s^2_{a_1} = \frac{s^2_{y/x}}{S_{XX}}$ $\mathrm{cov}(a_0, a_1) = -\overline{x}s^2_{y/x}/S_{XX}$

Table 1. Formulae for calculating statistics for weighted linear regression (WLR).

An assumption that the errors are normally distributed is not required to obtain the parameter estimates by the least squares method. However, for inferences and estimates (standard errors, *t*- and *F*-test, confidence intervals) to be made about regression, it is necessary to assume that the errors are normally distributed [11]. The assumption of normality, nevertheless, is plausible as in many real situations errors tend to be normally distributed due to the central limit theorem. The assumption that no residual term is correlated with another, combined with the normality assumption, means [10] the errors are also independent. Constructing a normal probability plot of the residuals [16–18] is a way to verify the assumption of normality. Residuals are ordered and plotted against the corresponding percentage points from the standardized normal distribution (normal quantities). If the residuals are then situated along a straight line, the assumption of normality is satisfied.

A standardized residual is the residual divided by the standard deviation of the regression line

$$e_{r_i} = \frac{r_i}{s_{y/x}} \tag{6}$$

The standardized residuals are normally distributed with a mean value of zero and (approximately) unity variance [10, 19]

$$\begin{aligned}\mathrm{Var}(r_i) &= \mathrm{Var}(y_i) - \mathrm{Var}(\hat{y}_i) = \sigma^2 - \sigma^2\left(\frac{1}{\sum w_i} + \frac{(x-\overline{x})^2}{S_{XX}}\right)\\ &= \sigma^2\left(1 - \frac{1}{\sum w_i} - \frac{(x-\overline{x})^2}{S_{XX}}\right) = \sigma^2(1 - h_{ii})\end{aligned} \tag{7}$$

$$\mathrm{Var}(e_{r_i}) = 1 - h_{ii} \tag{8}$$

The h_{ii} term may be regarded as measuring the leverage of the data point (x_i, y_i) (see below). The estimated residuals are correlated [10], but this correlation does not invalidate the residual plot when the number of points is large in comparison with the number of parameters estimated by the regression. As pointed out by Behnken and Draper [20]: '*In many situations little is lost by failing to take into account the differences in variances*'. Standardized residuals are useful in looking for outliers. They should have random values, the 95% falling between −2 and 2 for normal distribution.

The tendencies followed by the residuals should confirm the assumptions we have previously made [21], or at least do not deny them. Remember the sentence of Fischer [22, 23]: '*Every experiment may be said to exist only in order to give the facts a chance of disproving the null hypothesis*'. Conformity assays of the assumptions inherent to regression fall mainly in the examination of residual pattern. Although there are statistical ways of numerically measuring some of the observed discrepancies [24], graphical methods play an important role in data analysis (**Table 2**) [25–31]. A quick examination of residuals often allows obtaining more information than significance statistical tests of some limited null hypothesis. Nevertheless, objective, unambiguous determination should be based on standard statistical methodology. This chapter is mainly focused on residual plots rather than on formulas, or hypothesis testing. As we will see in the selected examples, the plots easily reveal violations of the assumptions if they are severe enough as to warrant any correction.

The main forms of representation [10] of residuals are (i) global; (ii) in temporal sequence, if its order is known; (iii) faced to the adjusted values, y-hat; (iv) facing the independent variable x_{ji} for $j = 1,2\ldots k$; and (v) in any way that is sensitive to the problem subject of analysis.

The following points can be verified in the representation of the residuals: (i) the form of the representation, (ii) the number of positive and negative residuals should be equivalent of vanishing median, (iii) the sequence of residual signs must be randomly distributed between + and −, and (iv) it is possible to detect spurious results (outliers); their magnitudes are greater than the rest of the residuals.

Residual plots appear more and more frequently [32–39] in papers published in analytical journals. In general, these plots as well as those discussed in this chapter are very basic and

Sentence	Author(s)/reference
'Most assumptions required for the least squares analysis of data using the general linear model can be judged using residuals graphically without the need for formal testing'	Darken [25]
'Graphical methods have an advantage over numerical methods for model validation because they readily illustrate a broad range of complex aspects of the relationship between the model and the data'.	NIST/ SEMATECH [26]
'There is no single statistical tool that is a powerful as a well-chosen graph'	Huber [27]
'Although there are statistical ways of numerically measuring some of the observed discrepancies, statistician themselves prefer a visual information of the residual plots as being more informative and certainly more convenient'	Belloto and Sokoloski [28]
'Eye-balling can give diagnostic insights no formal diagnostic will ever provide'	Chambers et al. [29]
'Graphs are essential to good statistical analysis'	Anscombe [30]
'One picture says more than a thousand equations'	Sillen [31]

Table 2. Sentences of some authors about the use of graphical methods.

can undergo some criticism. For example, the residuals are not totally distributed independent of x, since [10, 19] the substitution of the estimates by the parameters introduces some dependence. However, more sophisticated methods have been developed [40–44] based on standardized, studentized, jack-knife, predictive, recursive residuals, and so on (**Table 3**). In spite of their importance, they are considered beyond the scope of this contribution.

Despite the frequency with which the correlation coefficient is referred to in the scientific literature as a criterion of linearity, this assertion is not free from reservations [1, 45–49] as evidenced several times throughout this chapter.

The study of linearity not only implies a graphic representation of the data. It is also necessary to carry out a statistical check, for example, the analysis of the variance [50–54], which requires repeated measurements. This implies the fulfilment of two requirements: the homogeneity (homoscedasticity) of the variances and the normality of the residuals. Incorporating replicates to the calibration estimation offers a possibility to look at the calibration not only in the context of fitting but also of the uncertainty of measurements [15]. However, if replicate measurements are not made, and an estimate of the mean square error (replication variance) is not available, the regression variance

$$s_{y/x}^2 = \frac{\sum (y_i - \hat{y}_i)^2}{n-2} = \frac{\sum r_i^2}{n-2} \tag{9}$$

may be compared with the estimated variance around the mean of the y_i values [55]

$$s_y^2 = \frac{\sum (y - \overline{y})^2}{n-1} \tag{10}$$

by means of an F-test. The goodness of fit of non-linear calibration curves is improved by raising the degree of the fitting polynomial, performing then an F-test (quotient of the residual variance for the kth to $k+$ first-polynomial degree) [56]. A suitable test can also be carried out according to Mandel [56, 57]. However, this contribution is essentially devoted to the use of basic graphical plots of residuals, a simple and at the same time a powerful diagnostic tool, as we will have the occasion to claim through this chapter.

Symbol	Name	Formula	Comments
e_i	Classical residuals	e_i	
e_{N_i}	Normalized residuals	$\frac{e_i}{s_{y/x}}$	
e_{S_i}	Standardized residuals	$\frac{e_i}{s_{y/x}\sqrt{1-h_{ii}}}$	Identification of heteroscedasticity
e_{J_i}	Jack-knife residuals	$e_i\sqrt{\frac{n-m-1}{n-m-e_{S_i}^2}}$	Identification of outliers
e_{P_i}	Predicted residuals	$\frac{e_i}{1-h_{ii}}$	
e_{R_i}	Recursive residuals		Identification of autocorrelations

Table 3. Types of residuals and suitability for diagnostic purposes [42–44].

Several examples taken from scientific journals and monographs are selected in order to illustrate this chapter: (1) linearity calibration methods: fluorescence data [58] as an example; (2) calibration graphs: the question of intercept [59] or non-intercept; (3) errors are not in the data, but in the model: the CO_2 vapour pressure [59] versus temperature dependence; (4) the heteroscedastic data: high-performance liquid chromatography (HPLC) calibration assay [60] of a drug; (5) transforming data: preliminary investigation of a dose-response relationship [61, 62]; the microbiological assay of vitamin B_{12}; (6) the variable that has not yet been discovered; the solubility of diazepan [28] in propylene glycol; and (7) no models perfect: nickel(II) by atomic absorption spectrophotometry.

2. Linearity in calibration methods: fluorescence data as example

Calibration is a crucial step, an essential part, the key element, the soul of every quantitative analytical method [38, 40, 63–69], and influences significantly the accuracy of the analytical determination. Calibration is an operation that usually relates an output quantity to an input quantity for a measuring system under given condition (The International Union of Pure and Applied Chemistry (IUPAC)). The topic has been the subject of a recent review [67] focused on purely practical aspects and obviating the mathematical and metrological aspects. The main role of calibration is transforming the intensity of the measured signal into the analyte concentration in a way as accurate and precise as possible. Guidelines for calibration and linearity are shown in **Table 4** [70–81].

Linearity is the basis of many analytical procedures. It has been defined as [78] the ability (within a certain range) to obtain test results that are directly proportional to the concentration (amount) of analyte in the sample. Linearity is one of the most important characteristics for the

Scientific Association or Agency	Reference
Calibration	
International Union of Pure and Applied Chemistry (IUPAC)	Guidelines for calibration in analytical chemistry [70]
International Organization for Standardization (ISO)	ISO 8466-1:1990 [70]; ISO 8466-2:2001 [71]; ISO 11095:1996 [72]; ISO 28037:2010 [73]; ISO 28038:2014 [74]; ISO 11843-2: 2000 [75]; ISO 11843-5: 2008 [76]
LGC Standards Proficiency Testing	LGC/VAM/2003/032 [77]
Linearity	
International Conference on Harmonization (ICH)	Guideline Q2A [78]
Clinical Laboratory Standard Institute (CLSI)	EP6-A [79]
Association of Official Analytical Chemists (AOAC)	AOAC Guidelines 2002 [80]
European Union	EC 2002/657 [81]

Table 4. Scientific organizations that approve calibration guidelines [70–81].

evaluation of accuracy and precision in assay validation, and as seldom is the case where a calibration curve is perfectly linear, it is crucial to access linearity during method validation. Such evaluation is also recommended in regulatory guidelines [78–81]. Although it may seem that everything has been said on the subject of linearity, it is still an open question and subject to debate. It is therefore not surprising that some proposals are made from time to time to resolve this issue [54, 82–92].

However, in calibration, statistical linearity tests between the variables are rarely performed in analytical studies. When dealing with regression models, the most convenient way of testing linearity beside a visual assessment is plotting the residual sequence in the concentration domain. A simple nonparametric statistical test for linearity, known as 'the sign test' [9, 16, 28], is based on the examination of the residuals (r_i) sign sequence.

The residuals should be distributed in a random way. That is, the number of plus and minus residuals sign should be equal with the error symmetrically distributed (null hypothesis for the assay) when the variables are connected through a true linear relationship. The probability to get a random residual signs pattern is related to the number of runs in the sequence of signs. Intuitively and roughly speaking, the more these changes are randomly distributed [93] the best is the fit. A run is a sequence of the same sign with independence of its length. A pattern of residual signs of the kind [+ - - + + - + - + - +], from independent measurements, is considered as random, whereas a pattern like this [- - - + + + + + + - -] is not. Though a formal statistical test may carry out [94] with the information afforded by the residual plot, it is necessary a number of points greater than is usual in calibrate measurements.

The fluorescence in arbitrary units of a series of standards is shown in **Table 5**. To these data that appear to be curved, a straight line may be fitted (**Figure 1**, top) which results in an evident lack of fit, though the correlation coefficient (R) of the line is equal to 0.995 2. A plot of the resulting residuals r_i against the x-values (reduced residuals on the secondary axis) is also shown in **Figure 1** (top), and allows checking for systematic deviations between data and model.

The pattern of the sign of the residuals indicates that fitting the fluorescence data by a straight-line equation is inadequate, higher-order terms should possibly be added to account for the curvature. Note that the straight-line model is not adequate even though the reduced residuals are less than 1.5 in all cases. When an erroneous equation is fitted to the data [95–97], the

Concentration (μM)	Fluorescence (arbitrary units)	Concentration (μM)	Fluorescence (arbitrary units)
0	0.2	6	20.4
1	3.6	7	22.7
2	7.5	8	25.9
3	11.5	9	27.6
4	15	10	30.2
5	17		

Table 5. Calibration fluorescence data [58].

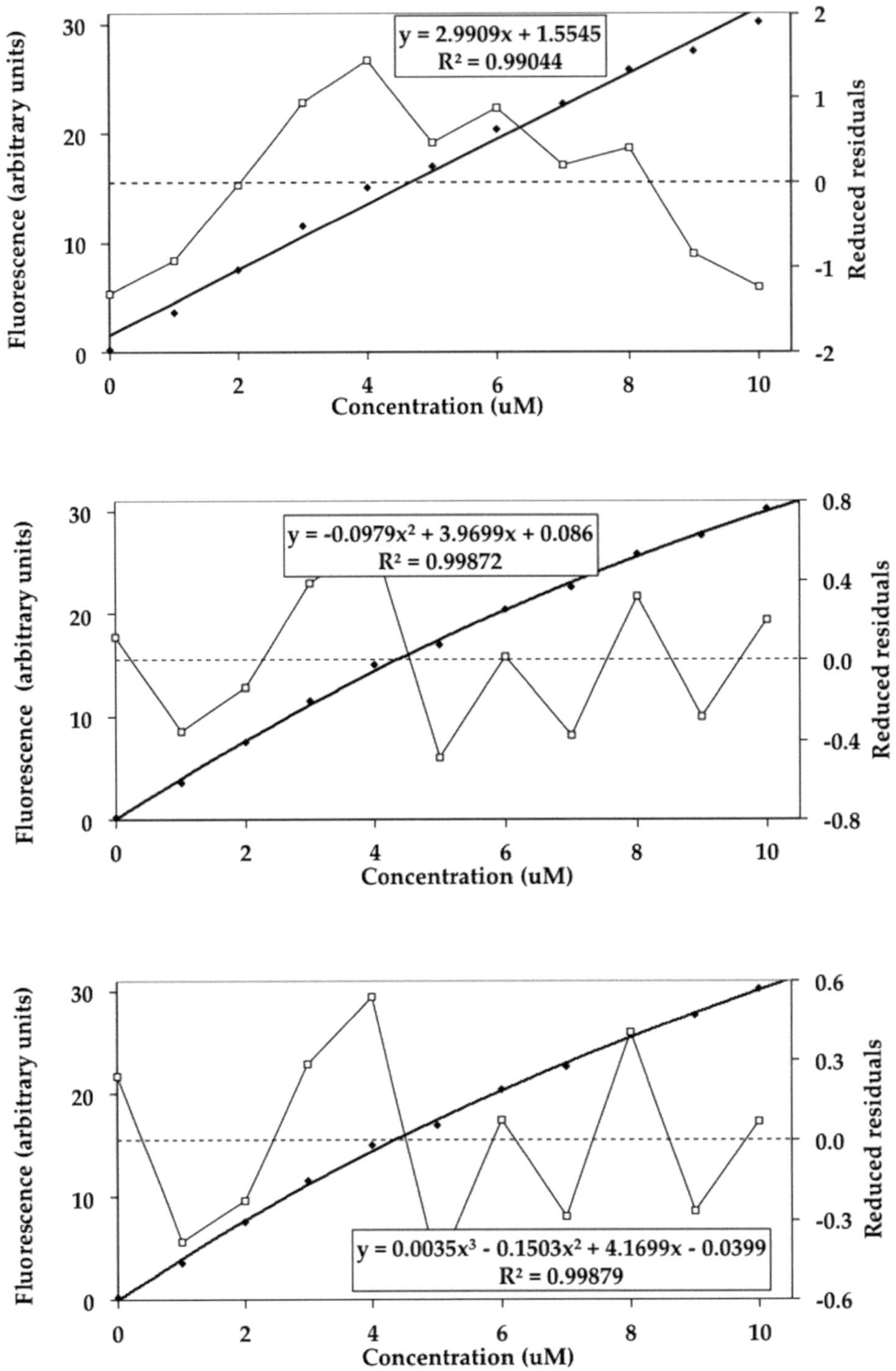

Figure 1. Fitting a straight line (top), a quadratic function (middle) and a cubic function (bottom) to fluorescence data compiled in **Table 5**.

information contained in the form of the residual plots is a valuable tool, which indicates how the model equation must be modified to describe the data in a better way. A curved calibration line may be fitted to a power series. The use of a quadratic (second-degree) equation is enough in this case to obtain a good fit: the scattering of the residuals above and below the zero line is similar, as shown in **Figure 1** (middle). Then, when no obvious trends in the residuals are apparent, the model may be considered to be an adequate description of the data. The simplest model or the model with the minimum number of parameters that adequately fit the data in question is usually the best choice. '*Non sunt multiplicanda entia praeter necessitatem*' (Occam's razor) [98]. In fact, the order of the polynomial (k) must not rise above 2 since $[s_{y/x}]k = 2 = 0.3994 < [s_{y/x}]k = 3 = 0.4142$.

In summary, when it is assumed a correct relationship between the response and the independent variable (s), the residual plot should resemble that of **Figure 2** (left). All residuals should fall into the gravelled area, with a non-discernable pattern, that is, random. If the representation of the residuals resembles that of **Figure 2** (right), where curvature is appreciated, the model can probably be improved by adding a quadratic term or higher-order terms, which should better describe the model with the required curvature.

Calibration curves with a non-linear shape also appear in analytical chemistry [99–104]. When the data in the x-range (calibration) vary greatly as it does in many real problems, the response becomes non-linear (**Table 6**) [101, 105–107] at sufficiently large x-values. The linear range of liquid chromatography-tandem mass spectrometry (LC-MS/MS) is typically about three orders of magnitude. The analyst's usual response in this case is to restrict sometimes the concentration range with the purpose of using a linear response, thus introducing biases in the determination, since the choice of the 'linear region' is usually done in an arbitrary way. The use of a wider range in standard curve is preferred in order to avoid the sample dilution, saving time and labour [108]. An acceptable approach to extend the dynamic range of the standard curve is the use of quadratic regression. Among the possible causes of standard curve non-linearity are saturation at high concentration during ionization, the formation of dimer/multimer/cluster ions, or detector saturation. It has been established that when the analyte concentration is above $\sim 10^{-5}$ M, its response starts to saturate providing non-linear response.

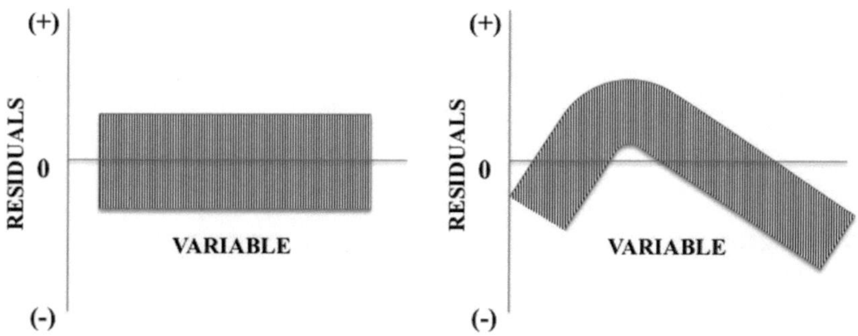

Figure 2. Residuals in a random (left) and parabolic (right) form.

Response function	Name	Technique
$y = a_0 + a_1x$	Beer law	Absorption spectrophotometry
$y = A + B\log x$	Nernst equation	Electrochemistry
$y = ax^n$ $(\log y = n \log x + \log a)$	Scheibe-Lomakin	Emission spectroscopy ESI-MS; ELSD; CAD
$y = a\,x^n + a_0 \quad (0 < y < y')$ $y = k\,x + y_0 \quad (y > y')$		TLC-densitometry"
$b_ny^n + b_1y = x$		DAD
$b\sqrt{y} + b_0 = \sqrt{x}$		ESI-MS
$y = a_0 + a_1x + a_2x^2$	Wagenaar et al.	Atomic absorption spectrophotometry, liquid chromatography/MS/MS
$\log y = a_0 + a_1\log x + a_2\log x^2$		CAD
$y = a_0 + a_1x + a_2x^2 + a_3x^3$		Ion-Trap-MS
$y = A + B(1 - \exp^{-Cx})$	Andrews et al.	Atomic absorption spectrophotometry
$y = \frac{A-D}{1+\left(\frac{x}{C}\right)^B} + D$	Rodbard	Radioimmunoassay

ESI-MS: electrospray ionization mass spectrometry; TCD: thermal conductivity detector; TLC-densitometry: TLC with detection by optical densitometry; ELSD: evaporative light scattering detector; CAD: charged aerosol detection.

Table 6. Response functions used in instrumental analysis [105–107].

Quadratic curve-fitting calibration data are more appropriate [104, 109–117] than straight-line linear regression, in the case of some quantification methods. Matrix-related non-linearity is typical of methods such as LC-MS/MS. In order to provide an appropriate validation strategy for such cases, the straight-line fit approximation has been extended to quadratic calibration functions. When such quadratic terms are included [10, 118–120], precautions should be taken because of the consequent multicollinearity problems.

However, the use of quadratic regression model is considered as less appropriate or even viewed with suspicion by some regulatory agencies and, as a result, not often used in regulated analysis. In addition, the accuracy around the upper limit of quantitation (ULOQ) can be affected if the curve range is extended to the point where the top of the curve is flat.

Statistical tests may also be considered for providing linearity, like Mandel's test [57] for comparison errors of residuals of quadratic and linear regression by means of an *F*-test at a determined significance level, or like lack-of-fit test by analysis of variance (ANOVA) or testing homoscedasticity (the homogeneity of variance residuals).

3. Calibration graphs: the question of intercept or non-intercept

Absorption spectrometry is an important analytical technique, and, to be efficient, the calibration must be accomplished with known samples. Data for the calibration of an iron analysis, in which the iron is complexed with thiocyanate, are shown in **Table 7**. The absorption of the iron

Concentration, Fe (ppm)	Absorbance	Concentration, Fe (ppm)	Absorbance
0.3644	0.0268	3.644	0.248
0.7288	0.0506	7.288	0.495
1.083	0.0783	32.8	1.52

Table 7. Absorbance data for Fe^{3+} calibration (as $Fe\text{-}SCN^{2+}$ complex) [59].

complex is measured and depicted versus iron concentration in ppm. The standard deviation of the regression line, $s_{y/x}$, obtained from the experimental data, quantifies the quality of fit and the accuracy of the model to predict the values of y (the measured quantity), for a given value of x (the independent variable).

The regression line is first computed by forcing it to pass through the coordinate origin ($a_0 = 0$), since the absorbance should be directly proportional to the concentration (at zero concentration, a zero absorbance might be expected). However, the adjustment thus obtained is not very good. The representation of residuals shows the pattern of signs + + + + + - (**Figure 3**, lower left). If we compute the regression line with intercept (**Figure 3**, upper right), the correlation coefficient increases from 0.990 8 to 0.994 7, but the pattern of non-random signs persists, that is, - - - + + - (**Figure 3**, lower right). What is a reasonable explanation? If the highest concentration point (32.8 ppm) is discarded, all the other points appear to fall on a straight line. However, this point cannot be discarded on the basis of its deviation from the best-fit line, because it is closer to the line than other calibration points in the series. As a matter of fact, the last point (32.8 ppm) defines where the line must pass: being so distant, it has a great influence (leverage) and forces the least squares regression line in its direction. The non-robustness behaviour is a general weakness of the least squares criterion. Very bad points [59] have a great influence just because their deviation from the true line, which rises to the square, is very large. One has to be aware of dubious data by

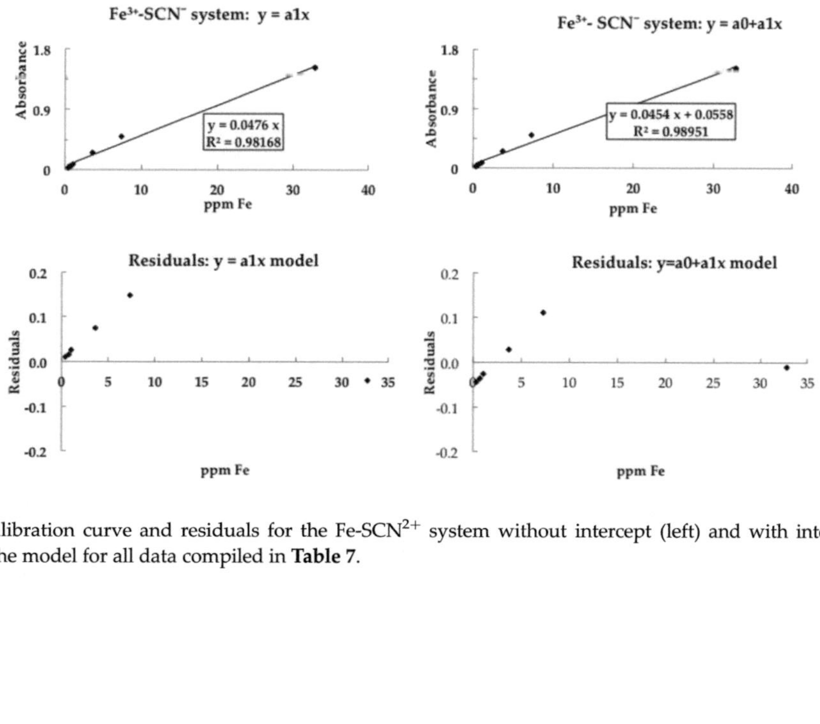

Figure 3. Calibration curve and residuals for the $Fe\text{-}SCN^{2+}$ system without intercept (left) and with intercept (right) included in the model for all data compiled in **Table 7**.

correcting obvious copying errors and adopting actions coherent with the identified causes. Improper recording of data (e.g. misreading responses or interchange of digits) is frequently a major component of the experimental error [121].

A few high or low points [8] can alter the value of the correlation coefficient in a great extension. Larger deviations present at larger concentrations tend to influence (weight) the regression line more than smaller deviations associated with smaller concentrations, and thus the accuracy in the lower end of the range is impaired. It is therefore very convenient [122–124] to analyse the plotted data and to make sure that they cover uniformly (approximately equally spaced) the entire range of signal response from the instrument (85). Data should be measured at random (to avoid confusing non-linearity with drift). The individual solutions should be prepared from the same stock solution, thus avoiding the introduction of random errors from weighing small quantities from individual standards. Depending on the location of the outliers, the correlation coefficient may increase or decrease. In fact, a strategically situated point can make the correlation coefficient varies practically between −1 and +1 (**Figure 4**), so precautions should be taken when interpreting its value. However, points of influence (e.g. leverage points and outliers) (**Table 8**) are rejected only when there is an obvious reason for their anomalous [125] behaviour. The effect of outliers is greater as the sample size decreases. Duplicate measurements, careful scrutiny of the data while collecting and testing discrepant results with available samples may aid to solve problems [28] with outliers.

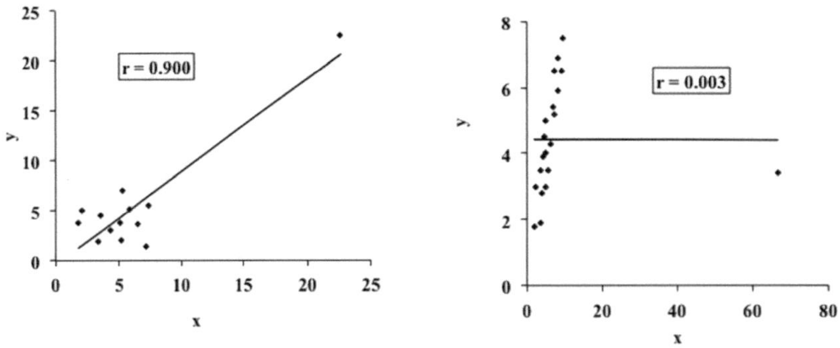

Figure 4. Influence of an anomalous result on the least squares method (solid line) and on the correlation coefficient.

Gross errors	Caused by outliers in the measured variable or by the leverage points extremes
Golden points	Special chosen points which have been very precisely measured to extend the prediction capability of the system
Latently influential points	Consequence of a poor regression model
According to data location	
Outliers	Differs from the other points in values of the y-axis
Leverage points	Differ from the other points in values of the x-axis or in a combination of these quantities (in the case of multicollinearity)

Table 8. Influential points [44].

If the regression analysis is made without the 32.8 ppm influence point forcing to pass through the origin, the correlation coefficient reaches the 0.999 91 value (**Figure 5**, top left). This point was not considered because a high deviation standard values were above the new line. Perhaps, the problem observed with the 32.8 ppm point is due to the fact that sulphocyanide (thiocyanate) is not in enough excess to complex all the iron present. However, the inspection of residuals (+ + + + -) shows systematic, non-random deviations (**Figure 5**, bottom left), which may indicate an incorrect or inadequate model. Systematic errors of analysis translate into (systematic) deviations from the fit equation (negative residuals correspond to low estimated values, and positive residuals to high). An erroneous omission of the intercept term in the model may be the cause of this effect. The standard deviation of the regression line improves notably, from 0.0026 to 0.0017, when the intercept is introduced (**Figure 5**, top right) in the model (correlation coefficient equals 0.999 97), the residual pattern being now random (- - + - +) (**Figure 5**, bottom right). The calibration is then appropriate and linear, at least up to 8 ppm. However, the intercept value, 0.0027, is of the same order of magnitude as the standard deviation, $s_{y/x}$, of the regression line. A calibration problem (of minor order) may be apparent, for example, the spectrophotometer was not properly set to zero or the cuvettes were not conveniently matched.

Residual analysis of small sample sizes has [126] some complications. Firstly, residuals are not totally distributed in an independent way from x, because the substitution of the parameters by the estimators introduces [10, 19] certain dependence. Secondly, a few points far from the bulk of the data may eventually condition the estimators, residuals and inferences.

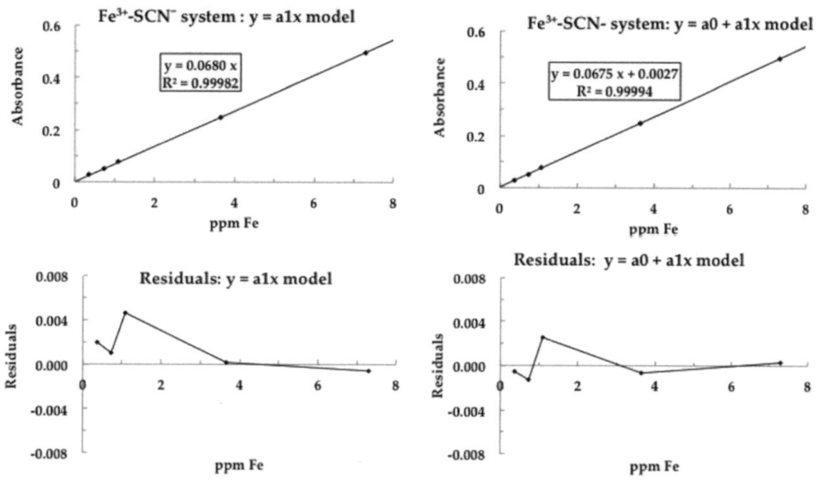

Figure 5. Calibration curve and residuals for the Fe-SCN^{2+} system without intercept (left) and with intercept (right) included in the model (data in **Table 7** with the exception of the 32.8 ppm point).

4. Error is not in the data, but in the model: the CO_2 vapour pressure versus temperature case

The linear variation of physical quantities is not a universal rule, although it is often possible to find a coordinate transformation [18] that converts non-linear data into linear ones. The vapour pressure, *P*, in atmospheres, of carbon dioxide (liquid) as a function of temperature, *T*, in degrees Kelvin, is not linear (**Table 9**). Carbon dioxide found its use in chemical analysis as a supercritical fluid for extracting the caffeine from the coffee. We may expect, on the basis of the Clausius-Clapeyron equation, to fit the data compiled in **Table 9** into an equation of the form

$$\ln P = A + B/T \tag{11}$$

This requires a transformation of the data. If we define

$$Y = \ln P \tag{12}$$

and

$$X = 1/T, \tag{13}$$

this form is linear,

$$Y = A + BX \tag{14}$$

The resulting graph (**Figure 6**, middle solid line) examined, appears to be fine, like calculated statistics, and so there is no reason at first to esteem any problem. Results lead to a correlation coefficient of 0.999 988 76. This almost perfect adjustment is indeed very poor when attention is paid to the potential quality of the fit as shown by the sinusoidal pattern of residuals [+ + - + - + + + + + - -], which are incorporated in the figure to the resulting least squares regression line. As the details of measurements are unknown, it is not possible to test for systematic error in the experiments. The use of an incorrect or an inadequate model is the reason, which explains in this case the systematic deviations. The Clausius-Clapeyron equation does not exactly describe the phenomenon when the temperature range is wide. Results similar to those shown in **Figure 6** are also obtained by applying weighted linear regression by using weighting factors defined by [6, 7, 127–129]

Temperature (°K)	Vapour pressure	Temperature (°K)	Vapour pressure
216.5500	5.11023	266.4944	28.70169
222.0500	6.44393	272.0500	33.39684
227.6056	8.04301	277.6056	38.63636
233.1611	9.92107	283.1611	44.47469
238.7167	12.09853	288.7167	50.93903
244.2722	14.62303	294.2722	58.07022
249.8278	17.50817	299.8278	65.91589
255.3833	20.78797	304.1611	72.76810
260.9389	24.51007		

Table 9. CO_2 vapour pressure versus temperature data [59].

http://dx.doi.org/10.5772/68049

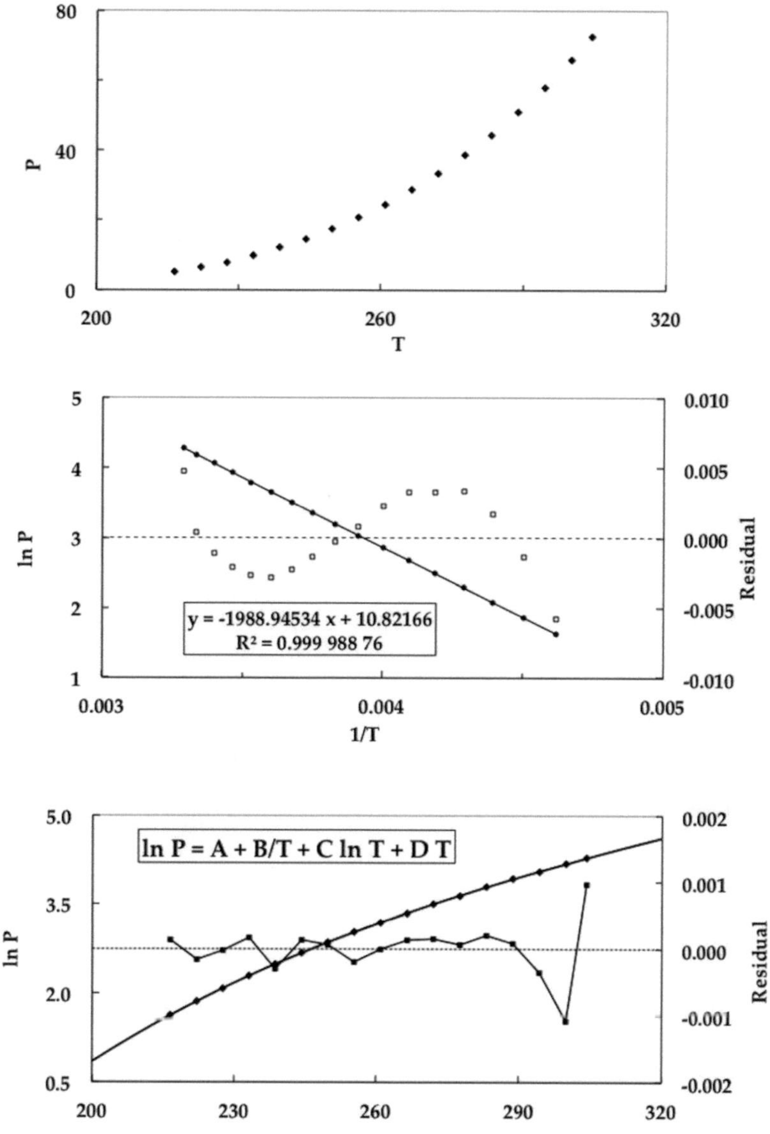

Figure 6. Top: CO_2 vapour pressure against temperature data (top). Middle: representation of ln P against the reciprocal of temperature (Clausius-Clapeyron equation) including the residuals plot. Bottom: CO_2 vapour pressure as a function of temperature according to the expanded (MLR) model.

$$w_i = \frac{1}{\left(\frac{\partial Y_i}{\partial y_i}\right)^2} = \frac{1}{\left(\frac{\partial \ln P_i}{\partial P_i}\right)^2} = P_i^2 \tag{15}$$

on the basis of the transformation used.

The error does not lie in the data then, but in the model. We may try to improve the latter by using a more complete form of the equation

$$\ln P = A + B/T + C\ln T + DT \tag{16}$$

The results now obtained (analysis by multiple linear regression) depicted in **Figure 6** (bottom) are better than those obtained by using the single linear regression equation, with the residuals randomly distributed. Values of ln P may be calculated with an accuracy of 0.001 (or an accuracy level of 0.1%), as suggested by the standard deviation of the regression line obtained. In addition, as T is used as a variable, instead of its inverse, interpolation calculations are carried out in an easier way.

The moral of this section is that there are not perfect models [130, 131], but models that are more appropriate than others.

5. The heteroscedastic data: HPLC calibration assay of a drug

In those cases in which the experimental data to be used in a given analysis are more reliable than others [6, 61, 63], gross errors may be involved when the conventional method of least squares is applied in a direct way. The assumption of uniform or regular variance of y may be no correct when the experimental measurements cover a wide range of x-values. There are two possible solutions to this non-constant, irregular, non-uniform or heteroscedastic variance problem: data transformation or weighted least squares regression analysis.

The squared sum of the weighted residuals [132, 133, 64]

$$Q_{\min, w} = \left[\sum w_i r_i^2\right]_{\min} \tag{17}$$

$$w_i = \frac{1}{\sigma_i^2} \tag{18}$$

is minimized in the weighted least squares procedure. The idea underlying weighted least squares is to attribute the greatest worth [2, 40, 132, 66, 101, 135, 136] to the most precise data. The greater the deviation from the homoscedasticity, the greater the profit that can be extracted from the use of the weighted least squares procedure. The homoscedasticity hypothesis is usually justified in analytical chemistry in the framework of the calibration. However, when the range of abscissa values (concentration) covers several orders of magnitude, for example, in the study of (calibration) drug concentrations in urine or in other biological fluids, the accuracy of y-values is strongly dependent of the x ones. In those cases, the homoscedastic requirement implied in single linear regression is violated, thus the introduction of weighting factors being mandatory. Some typical cases of heteroscedasticity appear [137, 138] involving a constant relative standard deviation (**Figure 7**)

$$RSD = \frac{\sigma_i}{\overline{x}} \tag{19}$$

or a constant relative variance (radioactive accounts, Poisson distribution). Photometric absorbances by Beer's law cover a wide concentration range and like chromatographic analysis in

http://dx.doi.org/10.5772/68049

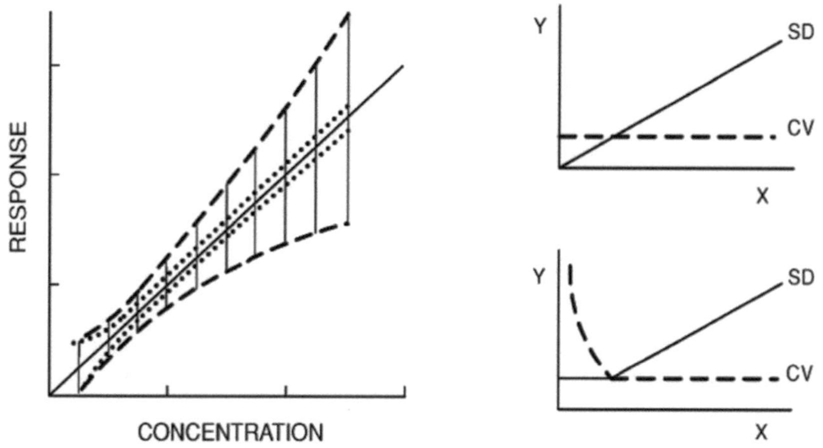

Figure 7. Left: hypothetical HPLC response versus concentration for a typical serum. Right: examples of relationships between concentration of analyte (x), standard deviation (SD), and coefficient of variation (CV).

certain conditions, tend to be heteroscedastic. Inductive plasma-coupling emission spectrometry coupled to mass spectrometry (ICPMS) requires weighted least squares estimates even when the calibration covers a relatively small concentration range. The standard deviation (absolute precision) of measurements σ_i usually increases with the concentration x_i, whereas the relative standard deviation (relative precision, RSD) decreases instead.

It is possible to derive [138] relationships between precision and concentration through the concentration range essayed so that chemical methods are applied to found analytes present at varying concentrations. A number of different relationships [2, 139–142] have been proposed (**Table 10**) for different authors, and ISO 5725 gives [143] indications to assist in obtaining a given $C = f(\sigma_i)$ relationship.

The advantages of the least squares method may be impaired if the appropriate weights are not included in the equations, despite being a powerful tool. The least squares criterion is highly sensitive to outliers, as we have seen in **Figure 4**. An undesirable paradox may often occur consisting in the fact that the experimental data of worst quality contribute most to the

$$\sigma_c = pC^k \quad (k = 0.5, 1, > 1, \ldots)$$

$$\sigma_c = p(C+1)^k$$

$$\sigma_c = pe^{qC}$$

$$\sigma_c = pC^k + q$$

$$\sigma_c = \sqrt{a_0 + a_1 C^q} \quad (q = 1, 2)$$

$$\sigma_c = \sqrt{a_0 + a_1 C + a_2 C^2}$$

$$\sigma_c = py^k$$

$$\sigma_c = \sqrt{a_0 + a_1 y + a_2 y^2}$$

Table 10. Relationship types between the standard deviation and the concentration of the analyte.

estimation of the parameters. Although replication may be severely limited [15, 132], it possesses the advantage to provide a certain kind of robust regression [144]. The most common method of performing a weighted regression is using weights values reciprocal to the corresponding variances values, that is,

$$w_i = \frac{1}{s_i^2} \tag{20}$$

where s_i^2 is the experimental estimate of σ_i^2. Eq. (14) warrants that in using replication, the lower weights correspond to the outliers of y_i. The incorporation of heteroscedasticity into the calibration procedure is preconized [145, 146] by several international organizations such as ISO 9169, and ISO/CD 13-752. The International Union of Pure and Applied Chemistry (IUPAC) includes the heteroscedasticity [147, 148] or non-constant variance topic for the calculation of the limits of detection and quantification.

The assumption of constant variance in the physical sciences may be erroneous [34, 149–157]. The data from a calibration curve (**Table 11**) relating to the readings of an HPLC assay to the drug concentration in ng/mL in blood [60] are shown in **Figure 8**. A regression model reasonable for the mean values is $y = \alpha_0 + \alpha_1 x$, in the first approximation. However, the variability of the response increases in a systematic way with increasing the concentration level. This indicates that the constant variance assumption of the response through the range of concentrations assayed is not followed. In fact at the highest level of concentration, a very large response value is produced. There is no physical justification that allows excluding this value from the

	Doses				
	0	**5**	**15**	**45**	**90**
Response	0.0016	0.0118	0.0107	0.106	0.106
	0.0019	0.0139	0.0670	0.026	0.158
	0.0002	0.0092	0.0410	0.088	0.272
	0.0030	0.0033	0.0087	0.078	0.121
	0.0042	0.0120	0.0410	0.029	0.099
	0.0006	0.0070	0.0104	0.063	0.116
	0.0006	0.0025	0.0170	0.097	0.117
	0.0011	0.0075	0.0320	0.066	0.105
	0.0006	0.0130	0.0310	0.052	0.098
	0.0013	0.0050			
	0.0020	0.0180			
	0.0050				
	0.0050				

Table 11. Calibration data for an HPLC blood concentration (ng/mL) assay of a drug [60].

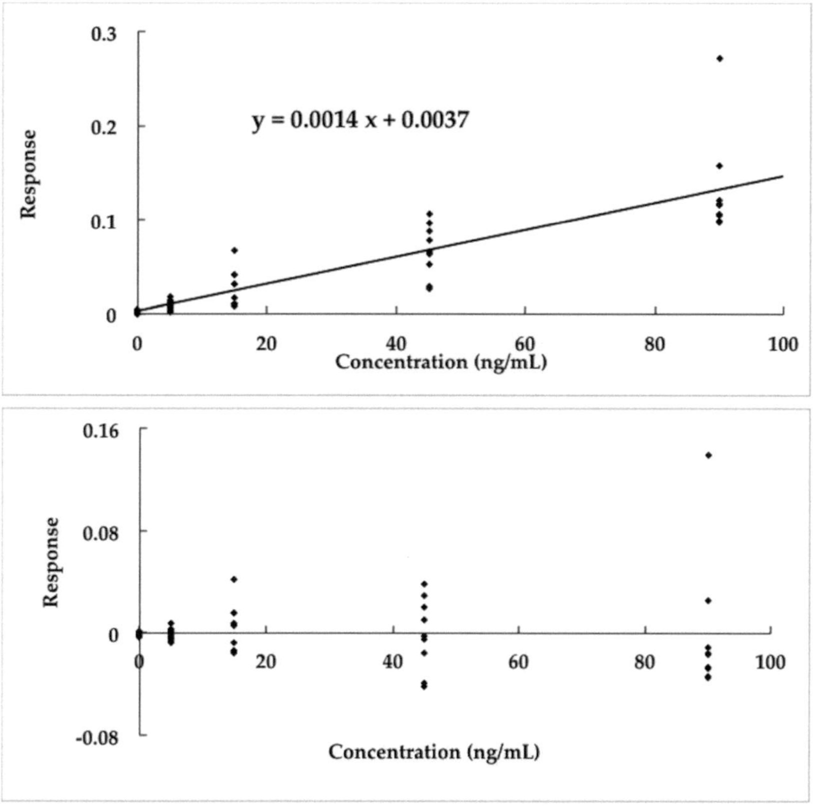

Figure 8. Calibration curve obtained by single linear regression (top) and corresponding residuals plot (bottom).

others in the analysis. Assuming in the first instance constant variance, the least squares are used to obtain as estimated parameters $a_0 = 0.0033$ and $a_1 = 0.0014$, with $s_{y/x} = 0.0265$. The representation of the residuals versus the values of x should show variability with a constant band, if the model was appropriate. Note that, in **Figure 9** (bottom left), the pattern of funnel shape or trumpet indicates that the measurement error is increasing as it does the mean response. The assumption of constant variance is thus not satisfied. On the other hand, the

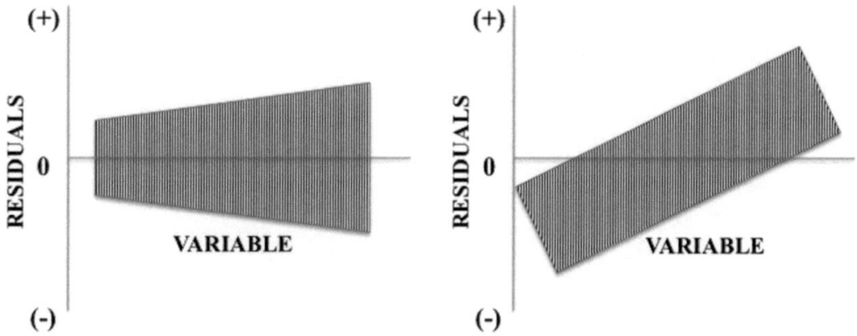

Figure 9. Residuals in the form of funnel (left) and ascending (right).

intercept value, 0.0033, is not in good agreement with the mean response value (13 replicates) at zero dose, 0.0021, which supposes another additional problem. The result of ignoring the non-constant variance in this case results in a poor fit of the model. The weighted linear regression straight-line model led instead (**Figure 10**, top) to the equation $y = 0.0015\,x + 0.0021$, the band of residuals being now rectangular (**Figure 10**, bottom).

The weighted least squares method requires a higher number of replicates than the conventional least squares method. The estimation of the minimum number of replicates varies between six and 20, according to different authors. In practice, it is often difficult to reach such high level of replication [2, 15] for different reasons, such as cost or availability of calibration, standards and reagents, time demands on previous operations, or by recording of the chromatograms.

In order to apply the weighted least squares analysis, it is mandatory to assign weighting factors to the corresponding observations. In fact, the weighting factor is related with the information contained in the y_i value, being proportional to the reciprocal of the variance of y_i. The results of single-trial assay without additional information seldom contain enough information as to model the variance in a satisfactory way. The independent variable may be usually choice, fortunately, by the researcher, and the corresponding values for the dependent thus replicated.

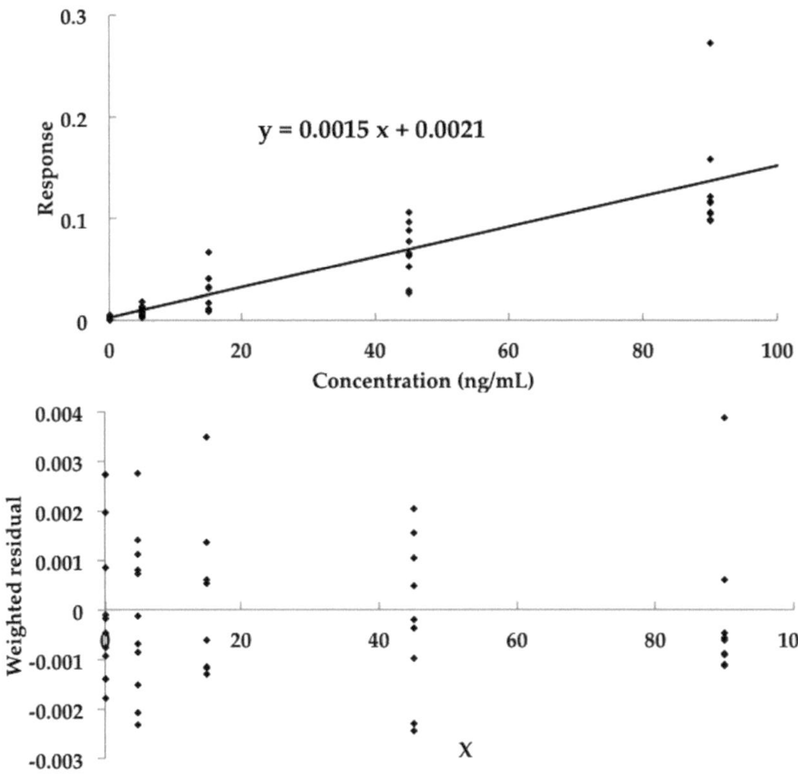

Figure 10. Response versus concentration obtained by weighted linear regression (top) and residuals plot for this model (bottom).

The general phenomenon of non-constancy of variance is called as we have previously seen heteroscedasticity. It can be addressed [2, 15] by the weighted least squares method. A second method of dealing with heteroscedasticity is to transform the response [18] so that the variance of the transformed response is constant, proceeding then in the usual way, as in the following.

6. Transforming data: preliminary investigation of a dose-response relationship

The non-linear relationship between two variables may be sometimes handled as linear by means of [158] a transformation. A transformation consists in the application of a mathematical function to a set of data. The transformation leading finally to a straight-line fit to the data can be carried out on a variable or on both. The transformation of data is sometimes understood as a device which statisticians use, a conviction founded on the preconceived idea that the natural scale of measurement [159] is something like sacrosanct. This is not like this, and in fact some measurements, for example, those of pH, are actually logarithmic, transformed values [160]

As much as the analyst wants the mould of nature to be linear, often in the curves truth is simply found [118, 160]. Real-world systems sometimes do not fulfil the essential requirements for a rigorous or even an approximate validity of the method of analysis. In many cases, a transformation (change of scale) can sometimes be applied to the experimental data [18] in order to carry out a conventional analysis. Although it may seem that the best way to estimate the coefficients of a non-linear equation is the direct use of a non-linear regression program (NLR), NLR itself [161] is not without drawbacks and problems.

The data of turbidimetric measurements of the growth response of *Lactobacillus leichmannii* to vitamin B_{12} [61] provide a good illustration of a preliminary investigation of dose-response relationships. **Table 12** shows the responses to the eight different doses of vitamin B_{12} measured in six independent tubes per dose, which are depicted in **Figure 11**.

	Doses (ng/tube)							
	0.23	**0.35**	**0.53**	**0.79**	**1.19**	**1.78**	**2.67**	**4**
Response	0.15	0.28	0.36	0.51	0.68	0.85	1.06	1.21
	0.14	0.20	0.36	0.53	0.63	0.80	0.91	1.22
	0.19	0.23	0.34	0.54	0.64	0.71	1.09	1.29
	0.19	0.25	0.37	0.45	0.61	0.85	0.93	1.24
	0.17	0.23	0.33	0.57	0.65	0.94	1.09	1.18
	0.16	0.23	0.38	0.49	0.68	0.83	1.12	1.24

Table 12. Microbiological assay of vitamin B_{12} [61, 62].

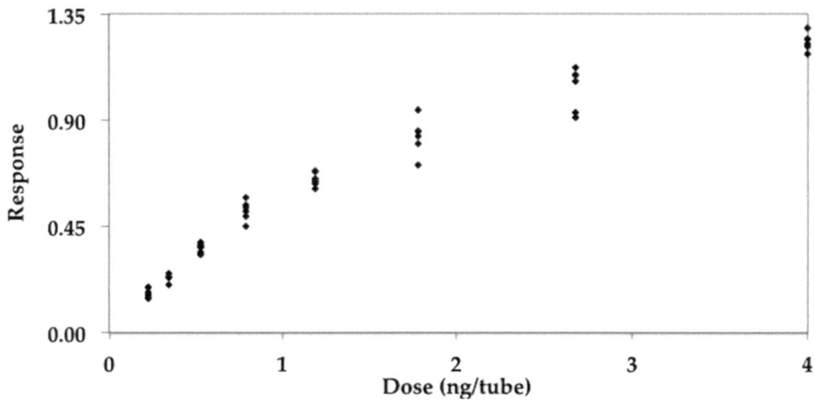

Figure 11. Representation of the dose-response data for the microbiological assay of vitamin B_{12}.

The transformation [62]

$$z = \log x \tag{21}$$

can be used (**Figure 12**). The inspection of **Figure 12**, however, suggests the existence of a marked curvature. The graph of the residuals, the deviation of each point of the model, indicates that the straight line is incorrect, due to the observed systematic pattern. There is a

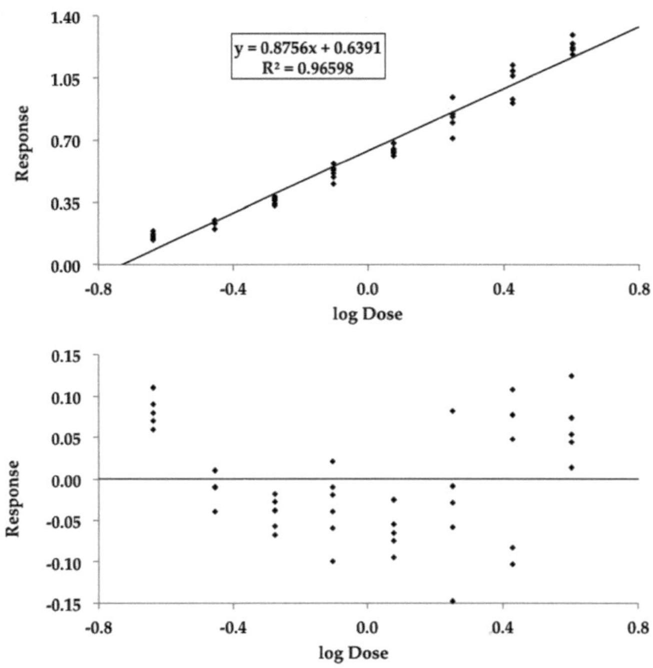

Figure 12. Top: fitting a straight line to response versus logarithm of dose (microbiological assay of vitamin B_{12}). Bottom: plot of the residuals against the logarithm of the doses for the straight-line model.

http://dx.doi.org/10.5772/68049

tendency towards curvature, as it is not randomly distributed around zero. It should be assumed that the model is susceptible to improvement, requiring either higher-order additional terms or a transformation of the data.

If a second-degree polynomial is fitted to the response data as a function of the logarithm of the dose, the adjustment to the naked eye seems adequate (**Figure 13**, top). The representation of the residuals as a function of the abscissa values (**Figure 13**, bottom), however, adopts a funnel shape. The non-random pattern of residuals carries the message that the assumption of homogeneous (regular or constant) variance is not satisfied, which would require the application of the weighted least squares method, rather than simple linear regression.

The shape of **Figure 13** (top) suggests a simple possibility, that of transformation [43] also in the response

$$u = \sqrt{y} \tag{22}$$

A simple inspection of **Figure 14** (top) now shows that the linear regression is valid throughout the entire range. Both transformations to achieve homogeneity of variance and normality (**Tables 13** and **14**) go together (hand in hand) and then both postulates are (almost) often simultaneously fulfilled, fortunately, on applying an adequate transformation.

The stabilization of variance usually takes precedence over improving normality [160]. As stated by Acton [86] '*The gods who favour statisticians have frequently ordained that the world be*

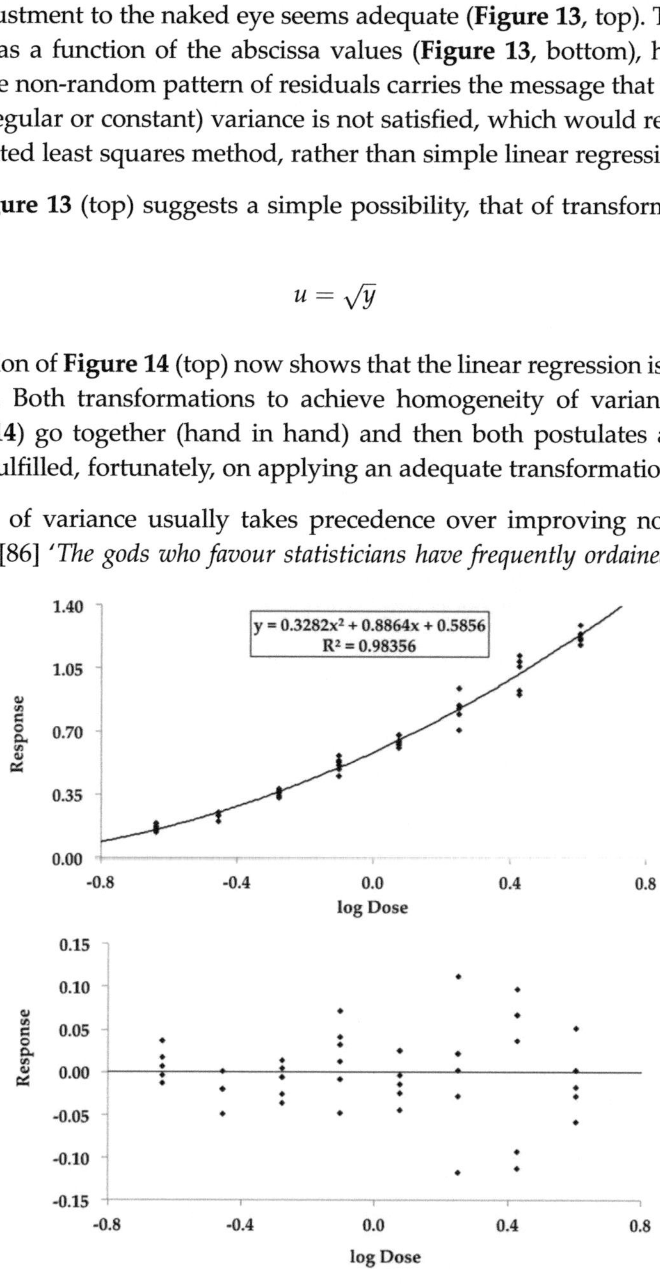

Figure 13. Top: fitting a second-degree polynomial to the response versus logarithm of dose (microbiological assay of vitamin B_{12}). Bottom: plot of the residuals against the logarithm of the dose for the second-degree polynomial model:

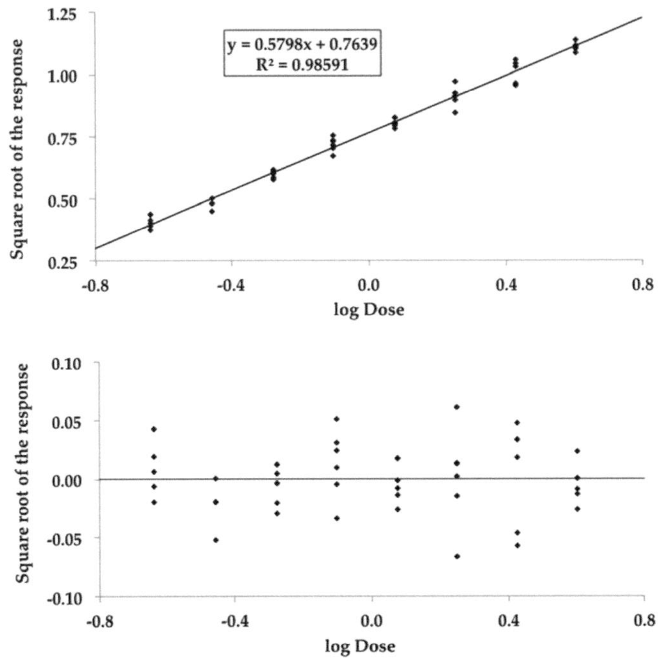

Figure 14. Top: fitting a straight line to the transformed data, square root of the response against the logarithm of the dose (microbiological assay of vitamin B_{12}). Bottom: plot of the residuals versus the logarithm of the doses for the straight-line model applied to the data transformed in both axes.

well behaved, and so we often find that transformation to obtain one of these desiderata in fact achieves them all (well, almost achieves them¡)'.

Linear regression is a linear (in the parameters) modelling process. However, non-linear terms may be introduced into the linear mathematical context by performing a transformation [162, 163] of the variables (**Table 15**). Note that when a transformation is used, a transformation-dependent weight (**Table 16**) should be used (in addition to any weight based on replicate measurements). When a non-linear function is capable of being transformed into another one linear, it is called *'intrinsically linear'*. Non-linear functions that cannot be transformed into linear are instead called *'intrinsically non-linear'*.

Date type	**Transformation**
Poisson (counts) (y)	$\sqrt{y}$
Small counts (y)	$\sqrt{y+1}$ or $\sqrt{y}+\sqrt{y+1}$
Binomial ($0 < P < 1$)	$a\sin\sqrt{P}$
Variance = (mean)^2	$\ln y$
Correlation coefficient	$0.5[\ln(1+r)-\ln(1-r)]$

Table 13. Transformations to correct for homogeneity and approximate normality [18, 162].

http://dx.doi.org/10.5772/68049

Estimated relationship	α	$\lambda = 1 - \alpha$	Transformation
$s = k\widehat{y}^2$	2	−1	Reciprocal
$s = k\widehat{y}^{3/2}$	3/2	−1/2	Inverse square root
$s = k\widehat{y}^2$	1	0	Logarithmic
$s = k\widehat{y}^{1/2}$	1/2	1/2	Square root
$s = k$	0	1	Without transformation

Table 14. Transformations to stabilize variance [18, 158] $W = (y^\lambda - 1)/\lambda(\lambda \neq 0); \quad W = \ln y(\lambda = 0)$.

Function	Formula	Transformation	Linear form
Power function	$y = \alpha x^b$	$y' = \log y$ $x' = \log x$	$y' = \log\alpha + \beta x'$
Exponential grow model	$y = \alpha e^{\beta x}$	$y' = \log y$	$y' = \log\alpha + \beta x$
Logarithmic	$y = \alpha + \beta \log x$	$x' = \log x$	$y = \alpha + \beta x'$
Hyperbolic	$y = \frac{x}{\alpha x - \beta}$	$y' = 1/y$ $x' = 1/x$	$y' = \alpha - \beta x'$
Logit	$y = \frac{e^{\alpha+\beta x}}{1+e^{\alpha+\beta x}}$	$y' = \log(\frac{y}{1-y})$	$y' = \alpha + \beta x$

Table 15. Linearizable non-linear functions [18, 162].

Transformation	Weighting factor (*)
$\frac{1}{y}$	y^4
$\ln y$	y^2
y^2	$\frac{1}{4y^2}$
e^y	$\frac{1}{e^{2y}}$
logit	$y^2(1-y)^2$

(*) in units of σ_0^2/σ_y^2; σ_0^2 is a proportionality factor, that is, the variance of a function of unit weight [2]

Table 16. Weighting factors associated with a given transformation [2, 127, 128].

7. The variable that has not yet been discovered: the solubility of diazepan in propylene glycol

The study of the solubility of diazepan in mixed solvents [28] requires the representation of Beer's law of a set of data corresponding to the solubility of diazepan in propylene glycol. The experimental data are shown in **Table 17**.

C (mg/mL)	T (min)	A	C (mg/mL)	T (min)	A
16.0760	0.00	1.799	12.8608	87.50	1.481
3.2152	6.00	0.335	12.8608	92.75	1.503
6.4304	10.50	0.700	12.8608	97.75	1.522
12.8608	21.50	1.487	16.0760	102.75	1.868
6.4304	33.50	0.670	12.8608	117.25	1.508
9.6500	39.25	1.068	9.6500	122.25	1.108
16.0760	45.75	1.840	9.6500	130.50	1.109
9.6500	50.75	1.088	9.6500	135.75	1.128
16.0760	56.75	1.842	6.4304	141.00	0.720
3,2152	67.25	0.358	6.4304	146.25	0.719
6.4304	71.75	0.703	3.2152	150.75	0.349
16.0760	77.75	1.869	3.2152	155.75	0.367
3.2152	82.50	0.345			

Table 17. Solubility of diazepan in propylene glycol (absorbance as a function of concentration and time) [28].

The relationship obtained between absorbance and concentration is (**Figure 15**)

$$A = 0.11767C - 0.003568 \tag{23}$$

These data can be used to corroborate the previously made statement that the correlation coefficient is not necessarily a measure of the suitability of the model. The R^2-value of the above equation is 0.998 ($r = 0.999$). Many researchers would settle for this, but they would be wrong.

In spite of the high coefficient of correlation ($r = 0.999$), when the residuals are represented as a function of the numerical order in which the samples were measured, we obtain **Figure 15** (bottom). The pattern obtained is not random by marking the residual trend with a positive slope. This behaviour is indicative of the situation in which the assumption of independence is not satisfied. The slope in a representation of the residuals as a function of the order of measure (time) indicates that a linear term must be included in the model.

When time is included in the model, Eq. (21) results

$$A = -0.070193 + 0.118394C + 0.000336936t \tag{24}$$

giving rise to a value of R^2 equal to 0.999.

When the residuals are calculated for this model and are plotted as a function of the concentration, a graph similar to that of **Figure 15** (middle) is obtained (**Figure 16**, top). However, if the residuals are represented for this model as a function of time (which is reflected in the order in which the samples were measured), the resulting pattern is obtained in **Figure 16** (bottom), in which it is observed that the independence of the error has been accommodated (compare **Figure 15**, bottom), and the fit has improved, although it could probably do so even more.

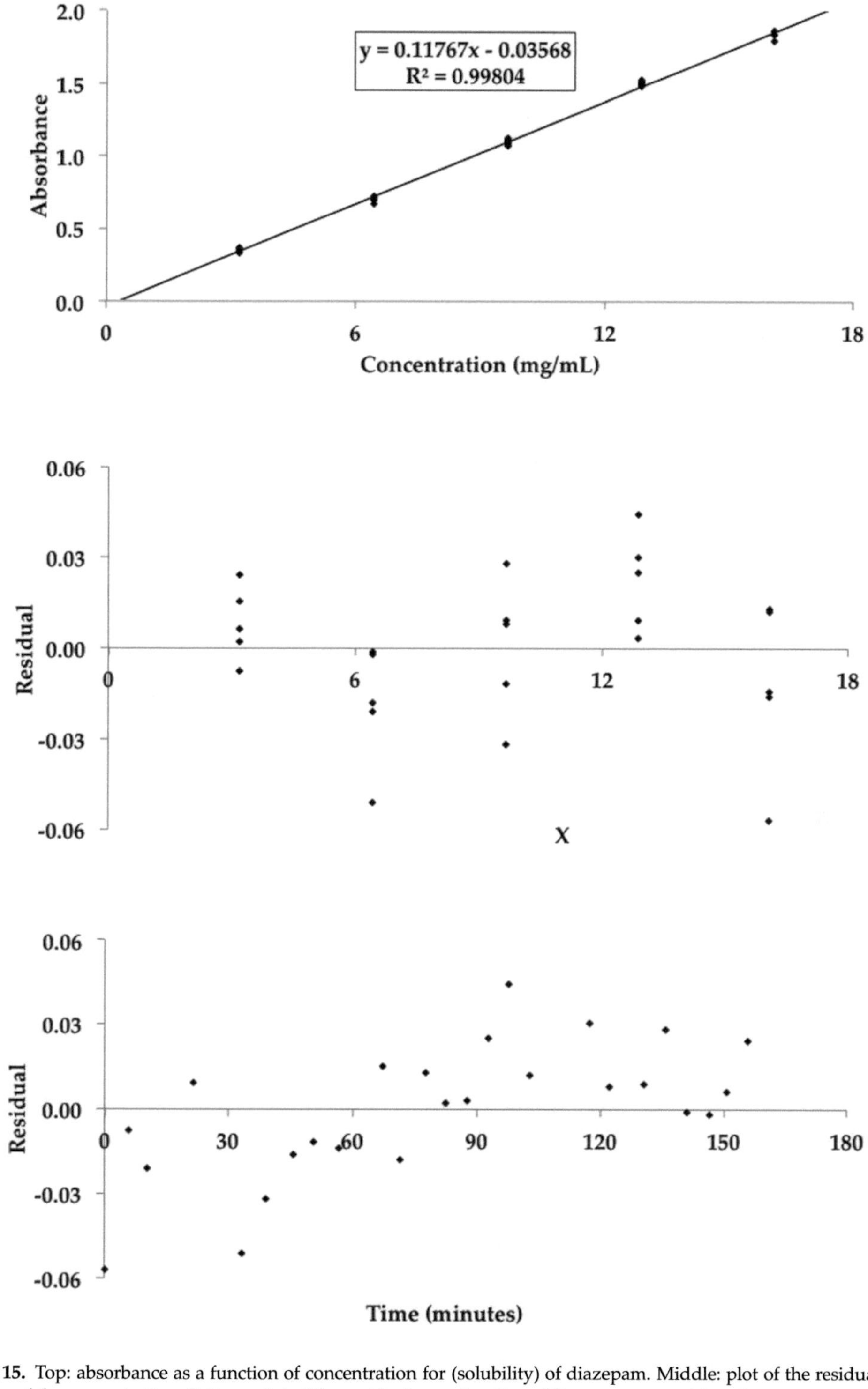

Figure 15. Top: absorbance as a function of concentration for (solubility) of diazepam. Middle: plot of the residuals as a function of the concentration. Bottom: plot of the residuals as a function of the measurement time (measurement order).

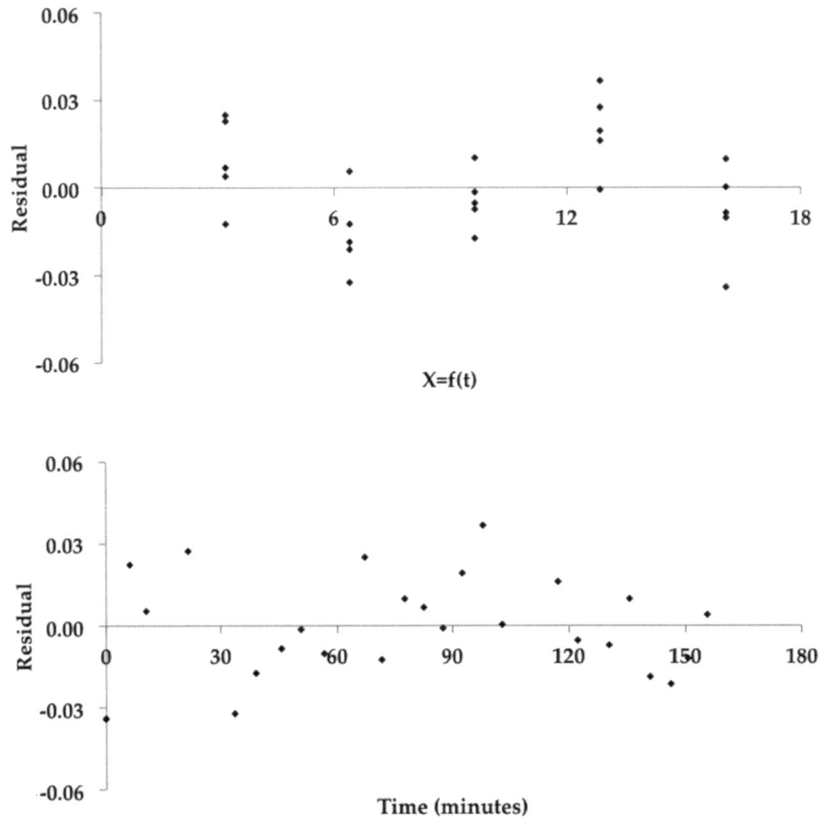

Figure 16. Top: residuals as a function of concentration for the extended model including the measurement time. Bottom: residuals as a function of time (order of measurement) for the model with the time included.

The order in the analysis time demonstrates the significant fact that a representation of the residuals allows the observation of the effect of the time that otherwise would not have been perceived. This is possible in the case of diazepam solubility because the researcher was careful to record the time to which the samples were measured.

The appearance of a pattern in residuals as a function of time in a study of Beer's law could indicate that some contaminant is affecting, or that the light source is decaying, or perhaps that it has not yet been warmed. The pattern of the residuals indicates if there is a time-dependent variable, but not the reason for that dependency, which must be ascertained, in its case.

8. Nickel by atomic absorption: all models are wrong

Nickel nitrate (II) hexahydrate reagent analysis (Merck) is used to prepare a standard solution of 1 g/L Ni. The salt of 5.0058 g is weighed into the analytical balance and brought into a 1-L volumetric flask with ultrapure water. From this solution containing 1000 mg/L, a working solution contains 125 mg/L. Appropriate volumes of this solution (triplicates) are added to 25-mL volumetric flasks to obtain the calibration curve, thinning with ultrapure water. The measurements are carried out in an 'Analyst 200 Atomic Spectrometer' operating in absorption mode with a Cu-Fe-Ni multi-element Lumma lamp (Perkin Elmer), at 232 nm, with an acetylene air flame. The obtained absorbances, given below, are superior to those described in Perkin Elmer [164]. The measurements depend on the flow, for example, of the nebulizer system, different in each case.

Absorbance data (in arbitrary units) in the triplicate of aqueous solutions of Ni^{2+} in mg/L (ppm) are compiled in **Table 18**. It has been tried to adjust Eq. (2), third-degree and fourth-degree polynomial models (**Figure 17**) (left figures with mean and right values with individual values), observing that as the degree of the polynomial increases, the goodness of the adjustment increases, although the residuals detect pattern. There are no perfect models, but models more appropriate than others [165, 166]. It is possible to use rational form polynomials with the

Ni^{2+} (ppm)	Absorbance (arbitrary units)			Ni^{2+} (ppm)	Absorbance (arbitrary units)		
2.5	0.217	0.207	0.226	17.5	0.743	0.742	0.744
5.0	0.399	0.396	0.389	20.0	0.767	0.767	0.771
7.5	0.523	0.513	0.519	22.5	0.787	0.786	0.789
10.0	0.618	0.615	0.612	25.0	0.808	0.813	0.807
12.5	0.672	0.664	0.664	27.5	0.820	0.821	0.824
15.0	0.713	0.715	0.707	30	0.835	0.835	0.831

Table 18. Atomic absorption spectrophotometry calibration data of nickel(II).

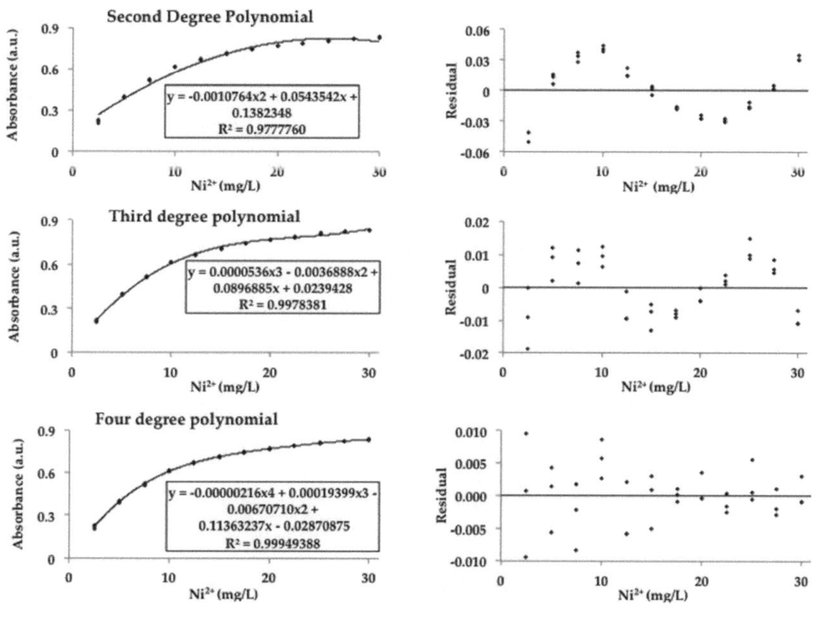

Figure 17. Atomic absorption spectrophotometry nickel(II) calibration data.

SOLVER function of Excel. Even so, the residuals show a pattern similar to that presented when a fourth-degree polynomial is fitted to the data.

9. Final comments

Calibration is an essential part of every quantitative analytical method, with the exception of primary methods of analysis (isotope dilution mass spectrometry, coulometry, gravimetry, titrimetry and a group of colligative methods). The correct performance of calibration is a vital part of method development and validation. Parameter estimation models are often employed to obtain information concerning chemical systems, forming on this way a fundamental part of analytical chemistry. In those cases in which a wrong equation is fitted to data, the form of the residuals plot contains useful information which helps to modify and improve the model in order to get a better explanation of the data. Examples extracted from the literature show how residual plots reveal any violation of the assumptions severe enough as to deserve correction. As a matter of fact, some authors [12, 25, 28, 59, 96] are in favour of using residuals graphically to evaluate the inherent assumptions in the least squares method.

If there is a true linear relationship between the variables with the error symmetrically distributed, the sign of residuals should be distributed at random between plus and minus with an equal number of each. A plot of residuals allows checking for systematic deviation between data and model. Systematic deviations may indicate either a systematic error in the experiment or an incorrect or inadequate model. A curvilinear pattern in the residuals plot shows that the equation being fitted should possibly contain higher-order terms to account for the curvature. A systematic linear trend (descending or ascending) may indicate that an additional term in the model is required. The 'fan-shaped' residual pattern shows that experimental error increases with mean response (heteroscedasticity) so the constant variance assumption is inappropriate. This phenomenon may be approached by the weighted least squares method or by transforming the response. Time-order analysis proves sometimes the more noteworthy fact that a residual plot permits the observation of a time effect that otherwise might not have become known. However, note that there are no perfect models, but models that are more suitable than others.

Many more sophisticated methods have been devised (standardized, studentized, jack-knife, predicted and recursive residuals). However, in spite of their worth and importance they are considered beyond the scope of this chapter, devoted to a primer on residuals. The analyses presented in this chapter were mainly done using an Excel spreadsheet.

Author details

Julia Martin, David Daffos Ruiz de Adana and Agustin G. Asuero*

*Address all correspondence to: asuero@us.es

Department of Analytical Chemistry, Faculty of Pharmacy, The University of Seville, Seville, Spain

References

[1] Asuero AG, Sayago A, González AG. The correlation coefficient: an overview. Crit. Rev. Anal. Chem. 2006;**36**(1):41–59.

[2] Asuero AG, González AG. Fitting straight lines with replicated observations by linear regression. III. Weighting data. Crit. Rev. Anal. Chem. 2007;**37**(3):143–172.

[3] Meloun M, Militký J, Kupka K, Brereton RG. The effect of influential data, model and method on the precision of univariate calibration. Talanta 2002;**57**(4):721–740.

[4] Meloun M, Militký J, Hill M, Brereton RG. Crucial problems in regression modeling and their solutions. Analyst 2002;**127**(4):433–450.

[5] Meloun M, Militký J. Detection of single influential points in OLS regression model building. Anal. Chim. Acta 2001;**439**(2):169–191.

[6] Wisniak J, Polishuk A. Analysis of residuals—a useful tool for phase equilibrium data analysis. Fluid Phase Equilibr. 1999;**164**(1):61–82.

[7] Fernandez GCJ. Residual analysis and data transformations: important tools in statistical analysis. Hortscience 1992;**27**(4):297–300.

[8] Chatterjee S, Hadi AS. Sensitivity Analysis in Linear Regression. New York: Wiley, 1988. p. 72.

[9] Chatterjee S, Hadi AS. Regression Analysis by Example. 5th ed., New York: Wiley, 2012. p. 98.

[10] Draper NR, Smith H. Applied Regression Analysis. 3rd ed., New York: Wiley, 1998.

[11] Asuero AG, González AG. Some observations on fitting a straight line to data. Microchem. J. 1989;**40**(2):216–225.

[12] Thompson M. Regression methods in the comparison of accuracy. Analyst 1982;**107**:1169–1180.

[13] Weisberg S. Applied Linear Regression. 3rd ed., New York: Wiley, 2005. p. 23.

[14] Asuero AG. Calibración comparación de métodos y estimación de parámetros en el análisis químico y farmacéutico. Anal. Real Acad. Nac. Farm. 2005;**71**:153–173.

[15] Sayago A, Boccio M, Asuero AG. Fitting straight lines with replicated observations by linear regression: The least squares postulates. Crit. Rev. Anal. Chem. 2004;**34**(1):39–50.

[16] Shapiro SS. How to Test Normality and Other Distributional Assumptions, American Society for Quality Control. Wilwaukee, WI: ASCQ, 1990.

[17] Myers RH, Montgomery DC, Anderson-Cook CH. Response Surface Methodology. Process and Product Optimization using Designed Experiments, 3rd ed., New York: Wiley, 2009. p. 37.

[18] Asuero AG, Martin JB. Fitting straight lines with replicated observations by linear regression. IV. Transforming data. Crit. Rev. Anal. Chem. 2011;**41**(1):36–69.

[19] Sheather SJ. A Modern Approach to Regression with R. New York: Springer-Verlag, 2009.

[20] Behnken DW, Draper NR. Residuals and their variance. Technometrics 1972;**11**(1):101–111.

[21] Cornish-Bowden A. Analysis and interpretation of enzyme kinetics data. Perspect. Sci. 2014;**1**:121–125.

[22] Fisher RA. The Design of Experiments. 8th ed., New York: Hafner, 1966. p. 16.

[23] Laitinen HA, Harris WE. Chemical Analysis: and advanced text and reference. Chapter 26, New York: McGraw-Hill, 1975. p. 562.

[24] Miller JN, Miller JC. Statistics and Chemometrics for Analytical Chemistry. 6th ed., Harlow, England; Prentice Hall, 2010.

[25] Darken PF. Evaluating assumptions for least squares analysis using the general lineal model: a guide for the pharmaceutical industry statistician. J. Biopharm. Stat. 2004;**14** (3):803–816.

[26] NIST/SEMATECH E-Handbook of Statistical Methods; http://www.itl.nist.gov/div898/handbook/,dat (date created 6/01/2003; updated April, 2012).

[27] Huber PJ. Between Robustness and Diagnostics. In Directions in Robust Statistics and Diagnostics. Stahel W and Weisberg S. Eds., New York: Springer-Verlag, 1991. p. 121.

[28] Belloto RJ Jr, Sokoloski TD. Residual analysis in regression. Am. J. Pharm. Educ. 1985;**49**:295–303.

[29] Chambers JM, Cleveland WS, Kleiner B, Tukey PA. Graphical Methods for Data Analysis. Duxbury Press: Boston, 1983.

[30] Anscombe FJ. Graphs in statistical analysis. The American Statistician 1973;**27**(1):17–21.

[31] Sillen LG. Graphic Presentation of Equilibrium Data. In Treatise on Analytical Chemistry, Part I. Kolthoff IM and Elving DJ. Eds., vol. 1, Chapter 8, New York: Interscience, 1959.

[32] Brüggemann L, Wenrich R. Application of a special in-house validation procedure for environmental-analytical schemes including a comparison of functions for modelling the repeatability standard deviation. Accred. Qual. Assur. 2011;**16**(2):89–97.

[33] Espinosa-Mansilla A, Muñoz de la Peña A, González-Gómez D. Using univariate linear regression calibration software in the MATLAB environment. Application to chemistry laboratory practices. Chem. Educator 2005;**10**:337–345.

[34] da Silva CP, Emidio ES, de Marchi MRR. Method validation using weighted linear regression models for quantification of UV filters in water samples. Talanta 2015;**131**:221–227.

[35] Mermet J-M. Calibration in atomic spectrometry: a tutorial review dealing with quality criteria, weighting procedures and possible curvatures. Spectrochim. Acta B 2010;**65**(7):509–523.

[36] Renger B, Végh Z, Ferenczi-Fodor K. Validation of thin layer and high performance thin layer chromatographic methods. J. Chromatogr. A. 2011;**1218**(19):2712–2721.

[37] Sousa JA, Reynolds AM, Ribeiro AS. A comparison in the evaluation of measurement uncertainty in analytical chemistry testing between the use of quality control data and a regression analysis. Accred. Qual. Assur. 2012;**17**:207–214.

[38] Tellinghuisen J. Simple algorithms for nonlinear calibration by the classical and standard additions methods. Analyst 2005;**130**(3):370–378.

[39] Lindner E, Pendeley BD. A tutorial on the application of ion-selective electrode potentiometry: an analytical method with unique qualities, unexplored opportunities an potential pitfalls: a tutorial. Anal. Chim. Acta 2013;**762**:1–13.

[40] Baumann K. Regression and calibration techniques. Part II. Validation, weighted and robust regression. Process Contr. Qual. 1997;**10**(1–2):75–112.

[41] Meloun M, Dluhosova Z. Precision limits and interval estimation in the calibration of 1-hydroxypyrene in urine and hexachlorobenzene in water, applying the regression triplet procedure on chromatographic data. Anal. Bional. Chem. 2008;**390**(7):1899–1910.

[42] Meloun M, Militky J. Statistical Data Analysis, a Practical Guide. New Delhi: Woodhead Publishing, 2011.

[43] Miller JN. Outliers in experimental data and their treatment. Analyst. 1993;**118**(5):455–461.

[44] Meloun M, Militky J, Forina M. Chemometrics for Analytical Chemistry, Volume 2. PC-aided regression and related methods. Hertfordshire: Ellis Horwood, 1994.

[45] Badertscher M, Pretsch E. Bad results from good data. Trends Anal. Chem. 2006;**25**(11):1131–1138.

[46] Sonnergaard JM. On the misinterpretation of the correlation coefficient in pharmaceutical sciences. Int. J. Pharm. 2006;**321**(1–2):12–17.

[47] Tellinghuisen J, Bolster Ch. Using R^2 to compare least-squares fir models: when it must fail. Chem. Intell. Lab. Syst. 2011;**105**:220–222.

[48] Loco JV, Elkens M, Crouse C, Beernaet H. Use and misuse of the correlation coefficient. Accred. Qual. Assur. 2002;**7**:281–285.

[49] Raposo F. Evaluation of analytical calibration based on least squares linear regression for instrumental techniques: a tutorial review. Trends Anal. Chem. 2016;**77**:167–185.

[50] Araujo P. Key aspects of analytical method validation and linearity evaluation. J. Chromatogr. B. 2009;**877**(23):2224–2234.

[51] Castillo MA, Castells RC. Initial evaluation of quantitative performance of chromatographic methods using replicates at multiple concentrations. J. Chromatogr. A. 2001;**921**(2):121–133.

[52] Coleman DE, Vanatta LE. Lack-of-fit testing of ion chromatographic calibration curves with inexact replicates. J. Chromatogr. A. 1999;**850**(1–2):43–51.

[53] Perez Cuadrado JA, Pujol Forn M. Validación de Métodos Analíticos, Asociación Española de Farmacéuticos de la Industria. Barcelona: AEFI, 2001.

[54] de Souza SVC, Junqueira RG. A procedure to assess linearly by ordinary least squares. Anal. Chim. Acta 2005;**552**:25–35.

[55] Akhnazarova S, Kafarov V. Experiment Optimization in Chemistry and Chemical Engineering. Moscow: Mir, 1982.

[56] Danzer K. Guidelines for calibration in analytical chemistry. Part 1. Fundamentals and single component calibration. IUPAC recommendations 1998. Pure Appl. Chem. 1998;**70** (4):993–1014.

[57] Andrade JM, Gomez-Carracedo MP. Notes on the use of Mandel's test to check for nonlinearity in laboratory calibration. Anal. Meth. 2013;**5**:1145–1149.

[58] Miller JN. Calibration methods in spectroscopy II. Is it a straight line?. Spectrosc. Int. 1991;**3**(4):41–43.

[59] Noggle JH. Practical Curve Fitting and Data Analysis, Software and Self-Instructions for Scientists and Engineers. Englewood Cliffs, NJ: Prentice Hall, 1993.

[60] Davidian M, Haaland PD. Regression and calibration with non constant error variance. Chemometr. Intell. Lab. 1990;**9**(3):231–248.

[61] Finney DJ. Statistical Methods in Biological Assay. 3rd ed., London: Griffin & Co, 1978.

[62] Emery WB, Lees KA, Tootil JPR. The assay of Vitamin B12. Part IV. The microbiological estimation with *Lactobacillus leichmannii* 313 by the turbidimetric procedure. Analyst 1951;**76**(3):141–146.

[63] Kóscielniak P, Wieczorek M, Kozak J, Herman M. Generalized calibration strategy in analytical chemistry. Anal. Lett. 2011;**44**:411–430.

[64] Komsta L. Chemometrics and statistical evaluation of calibration curves in pharmaceutical analysis—a short review on trends and recommendations. J. AOAC Int. 2012;**95**(3):669–672.

[65] Burke S. Regression and correlation, LC-GC Europe Online Supplement Statistical and Data Analysis; http://www.lcgceurope.com/lcgceurope/article/article.List.jsp?categoryId=935

[66] Miller JN. Basic statistical methods for analytical chemistry. Part 2. Calibration and regression methods. Analyst 1991;**116**:3–14.

[67] Kóscielniak P, Wieczorek M. Univariate analytical calibration methods and procedures: a review. Anal. Chim. Acta 2016;**944**:14–28.

[68] Olivieri AC. Practical guidelines for reporting results in simple and multi-component analytical calibration: a tutorial. Anal. Chim. Acta 2015;**868**:10–22.

[69] Tellinghuisen J. Least squares in calibration: weights, nonlinearity, and other nuisances. Methods Enzymol. 2009;**454**:259–285.

[70] ISO 8466-1: 1990. Water quality-Calibration and evaluation of analytical methods and estimation of performance characteristics. Part 1. Statistical evaluation of the linear calibration function. International Organization for Standardization: Geneva, 1990.

[71] ISO 8466-2: 2001. Water quality-Calibration and evaluation of analytical methods and estimation of performance characteristics. Part 2. Calibration strategies for non-linear second order calibration function. International Organization for Standardization: Geneva, 2001.

[72] ISO 11095: 1996. Linear Calibration using Reference Materials. International Organization for Standardization: Geneva, 1996.

[73] ISO/TC 28037:2010. Determination and Use of Straight Line Calibration Functions. International Organization for Standardization: Geneva, 2010.

[74] ISO/NP TS 28038: 2014. Determination and Uses of Polynomial Calibration Procedure. International Organization for Standardization: Geneva, 2014.

[75] ISO 11843-2:2000. Capability of Detection. Part 2. Methodology in the Linear Calibration Case. International Organization for Standardization: Geneva, 2000.

[76] ISO 11843-5:2008. Capability of Detection. Part 5. Methodology in the Linear and Non linear Calibration Cases. International Organization for Standardization: Geneva, 2008.

[77] LGC Preparation of Calibration Curves. A Guide to Best Practice. Barwick V. (Ed.), LGC/VAM/2003/032.

[78] ICH Expert Working Group. International Conference on Harmonization. Tripartite Guideline Q2A, Test on Validation of Analytical Procedures.

[79] Tholen DW, Kroll M, Astles JR, Caffo AL, Hapne TM, Krouver J, Casky F. EP6-A Evaluation of the Linearity of Quantitative Measurement Procedures. A Statistical Approach: Approved Guideline, Clinical Laboratory Standard Institute, USA: Wayne PA, 2003.

[80] AOAC. Guidelines for single laboratory validation of chemical methods for dietary supplements and botanicals, 2002. Accessed 29/3/2017. https://www.aoac.org/aoac_prod_imis/AOAC_Docs/StandardsDevelopment/SLV_Guidelines_Dietary_Supplements.pdf

[81] EC 2002/657, Commission Decision of 12 August 2002 implementing Council Directive 96/23/EC concerning the performance of analytical methods and the interpretation of results. Official Journal of the European Communities 17.8.2002, I. 221/8-I.221/36.

[82] Yang H, Novic SJ, LeBlond D. Testing assay linearity over a pre-specified range. J. Biopharm. Stat. 2015;**25**(2):339–350.

[83] Michalowska-Kazcmarcyk A, Asuero AG, Martin J, Alonso E, Jurado JM, Michalowski T. A uniform nonlinearity criteria for rational functions applied to calibration curve and standard addition methods. Talanta 2014;**130**:307–314.

[84] Novick SJ, Yang H. Directly testing the linearity assumption for assay validation. J. Chemometr. 2013;**27**:117–125.

[85] Sanagi MM, Nasir Z, Ling SLL, Hermawan D, Ibrahim WAW, Naim AA. A practical approach for linearity assessment of calibration curves under the International Union of Pure and Applied Chemistry (IUPAC) guidelines for an inn-house validation of method of analysis. J. AOAC Int. 2010;**93**(4):1322–1330.

[86] Liu J-p, Chow S-C, Hsieh T-C. Deviations from linearity in assay validation. J. Chemomet. 2009;**23**:487–494.

[87] Hsieh E, Hsiao C-F, Liu J-P. Statistical methods for evaluating the linearity in assay validation. J. Chemomet. 2009;**23**:56–63.

[88] Hsieh E, Liu JP. On statistical evaluation of the linearity in assay validation. J. Biopharm. Stat. 2008;**18**(4):677–690.

[89] Brüggemann L, Quapp W, Wenrich R. Test for non-linearity concerning linear calibrated chemical measurements. Accred. Qual. Assur. 2006;**11**:625–631.

[90] Mark H. Application of an improved procedure for testing the linearity of analytical methods to pharmaceutical analysis. J. Pharm. Biom. Anal. 2003;**33**:7–20.

[91] Kuttatharmmakul S, Masart L, Smeyer-Verbeke J. Influence of precision, sample size and design on the beta error of linearity tests. J. Anal. Atom. Spectro. 1998;**13**:109–118.

[92] Karvlczak M, Mickiewicz A. Why calculate, when to use and how to understand curvature measurements of non linearity. Curr Sep 1995;**14**(1):10–16.

[93] Féménias J-L. Goodness of fit: analysis of residuals. J. Mol. Spectrosc. 2003;**217**:32–42.

[94] Kuzmic P, Lorenz T, Reinstein J. Analysis of residuals from enzyme kinetic and protein folding experiments in the presence of correlated experimental noise. Anal. Biochem. 2009;**395**:1–7.

[95] Brown S, Muhamad N, Pedley KV, Simcock DC. What happen when the wrong equation is fitted to data?. Int. J. Emerg. Sci. 2012;**2**(4):133–142.

[96] Ellis KJ, Duggleby RG. What happens when data are fitted to the wrong equation?. Biochem. J. 1978;**171**(3):513–517.

[97] Straume M, Johnson ML. Analysis of residuals: criteria for determining goodness of fit. Methods Enzymol. 1992;**210**:87–105.

[98] Bates DM and Watt DG. Nonlinear Regression Analysis and Its Applications. 2nd ed., New York: Wiley, 2007. p. 1.

[99] Bonate PL. Chromatographic calibration revisited. J. Chromatogr. Sci. 1990;**28**(11):559–562.

[100] Lavagnini I, Magno F. A statistical overview on univariate calibration, inverse regression, and detection limits: application to gas chromatography/mass spectrometry technique. Mass Spectrom. Rev. 2007;**26**(1):1–18.

[101] Mermet J-M. Quality of calibration in inductively coupled plasma atomic emission spectrometry. Spectrochim. Acta B 1994;**49**(12-14):1313–1324.

[102] Schwartz LM. Calibration curves with non uniform variance. Anal. Chem. 1979;**51**(6): 723–727.

[103] Schwartz LM. Nonlinear calibration. Anal. Chem. 1977;**49**(13):2062–2068.

[104] Tan A, Awaiye K, Trabelsi F. Impact of calibrator concentrations and their distribution on accuracy of quadratic regression for liquid chromatography-mass spectrometry bioanalysis. Anal. Chim. Acta 2014;**815**:33–41.

[105] Asnin LD. Peak measurement and calibration in chromatographic analysis. Trends Anal. Chem. 2016;**81**:51–62.

[106] Findlay JWA, Dillard RF. Appropriate calibration curve fitting in ligand binding bioassays. APPS 2007;**9**(2):Article 29; http://www.aapsj.org

[107] Kleijbur MR, Pijners FW. Calibration graphs in atomic absorption spectrophotometry. Analyst 1985;**110**:147–150.

[108] Yuang L, Ji QC. Automation in new frontiers of bioanalysis: a key for quantity and efficiency. Bioanalysis 2012;**4**(23):2759–2762.

[109] Lavagnini I, Magno F, Seraglia R, Traldi P. Quantitative Applications of Mass Spectrometry. New York: Wiley, 2006.

[110] van Loco J, Hanot V, Huysmans G, Elkens M, Degrood JM, Beernert H. Estimation of the minimum detectable value for the determination of PCBs in fatty food samples by GC-ECD: a curvilinear calibration. Anal. Chim. Acta 2003;**483**:413–418.

[111] Yuan L, Zhang D, Jemal M, Aubri A-F. Systematic evaluation of the root cause of nonlinearity in liquid chromatography/tandem mass spectrometry bioanalytical assays and strategy to predict and extend the linear standard curve. Rapid Commun. Mass Spectrom. 2012;**26**:1465–1471.

[112] Rawski R, Sanecki PT, Kijowska KM, Skital PM, Saletnik DE. Regression analysis in analytical chemistry. Determination and validation of linear and quadratic regression dependences. S. Afr. J. Chem. 2016;**69**:166–173.

[113] Bouklouze A, Kharbah M, Cherrah Y, Heyden YV. Azithromycin assay in drug formulations: validation of a HPTLC method with a quadratic polynomial calibration model using the accuracy profile approach. Ann. Pharm. 2016;**75**(2):112-120.

[114] Zareba M, Sanecki PT, Rawski R. Simultaneous determination of thimerosal and aluminium in vaccines and pharmaceuticals with the use of HPLC method. Acta Chromatogr. 2016;**28**(3):299–311.

[115] Frisbie SH, Mitchell EJ, Sikora KR, Abualrub MS, Abosalem Y. Using polynomial regression to objectively test the fit of calibration curves in analytical chemistry. Int. J. Appl. Math. Theor. Phys. 2015;**1**(2):14–18.

[116] Kiser M, Dolan JW. Selecting the best curve fit. LC-GC Europe 2004;**17**(3):138–143.

[117] Zscheppank C, Telgheder U, Molt K. Stir-bar sorptive extraction and TDS-IMS for the detection of pesticides in aqueous samples. Int. J. Ion Mob. Spectrom. 2012;**15**(4):257–264.

[118] de Levie R. Collinearity in linear least squares. J. Chem. Educ. 2012;**89**:68–78.

[119] Stewart GW. Collinearity and least squares. Stat. Sci. 1987;**2**:68–100.

[120] Mandel J. The regression analysis of collinear data. J. Res. Nat. Bur. Stand. 1985;**90**:465–477

[121] Bayne CK, Rubin IB. Practical Experimental Design Methods for Chemists. Deerfield Beach, FL: VCH, 1986. pp. 31–32.

[122] Blanco M, Cerda V. Temas Avanzados de Quimiometría, Universitat de les Illes Balears: Palma, 2007.

[123] da Silva RJN, Camoes MF. The quality of standards in least squares calibrations. Anal. Lett. 2010;**43**(7–8):1257–1266.

[124] de Beer JO, Naert C, Deconinck E. The quality coefficient as performance assessment parameter of straight line calibration curves in relationship with the number of calibration points. Accred. Qual. Assur. 2012;**17**(3):265–274.

[125] Chatterjee S, Hadi AS. Influential observations, high leverage points, and outliers in linear regression. Statist. Sci. 1986;**1**(3):379–393.

[126] Cook RD, Weisberg S. An Introduction to Regression Diagnostics. New York: Wiley, 1994. p. 172.

[127] de Levie R. When, why, and how to use weighted least squares. J. Chem. Educ. 1986;**63**(1):10–15.

[128] de Levie R. Advanced Excel for Scientific Data Analysis. 3rd ed., Brunswick, Maine: Atlantic Academy, 2012.

[129] de Levie R. Curve fitting with least squares. Crit. Rev. Anal. Chem. 2000;**30**(1):59–74.

[130] Box GEP, Draper NR. Empirical Model Building and Response Surfaces. New York: Wiley, 1987.

[131] Box GEP, Hunter JS, Hunter WG. Statistics for Experimenters. 2nd ed., New York: Wiley, 2005.

[132] Sayago A, Asuero AG. Fitting straight lines with replicated observations by linear regression: Part II. Testing for homogeneity of variances. Crit. Rev. Anal. Chem. 2004;**34**(2):133–146.

[133] Zorn ME, Gibson RD, Sonzogni WC. Weighted least squares approach to calculating limits of detection and quantification by modeling variability as a function of concentration. Anal. Chem. 1997;**69**(15):3069–3075.

[134] Hibbert DB. The uncertainty of a result from a linear calibration. Analyst 2006;**131**(12):1273–1278.

[135] Penninckx W, Harmann DL, Massart DL, Smeyers-Verbeke J. Validation of the calibration procedure in atomic absorption spectrometric methods. J. Anal. Atom. Spectr. 1996;**11**(4):237–246.

[136] Taylor PDP, Schutyser P. Weighted linear regression applied in inductively coupled plasma-atomic emission spectrometry –a review of the statistical considerations involved. Spectrochim. Acta B 1986;**41**(10):1055–1061.

[137] Szabo GK, Browne JK, Ajami A, Josephs EG. Alternative to least squares linear regression analysis for the computation of standard curves for quantitation by high performance liquid chromatography: application to clinical pharmacology. J. Clin. Pharmacol. 1994;**34**(3):242–249.

[138] Sadler WA, Smith MH, Dedge HM. A method for the direct estimation of imprecision profiles, with reference to immunoassay data. Clin. Chem. 1988;**34**(6):1058–1061.

[139] González AG, Herrador MA. A practical guide to analytical method validation, including measurement uncertainty and accuracy profiles. Trends Anal. Chem. 2007;**26**(3): 227–238.

[140] Hwang L-J. Impact of variance function estimation in regression and calibration. Methods Enzymol. 1994;**240**:150–170.

[141] Thompson M. Variation of precision with concentration in an analytical system. Analyst 1988;**113**(10):1579–1587.

[142] Zeng QC, Zhang E, Dong H, Tellinghuisen J. Weighted least squares in calibration: estimating data variance functions in high performance liquid chromatography. J. Chromatogr. A 2008;**1206**(2):147–152.

[143] ISO 5725:5:1998. Accuracy (trueness) and precision of measurement methods and results. Part 5. Alternative methods for the determination of the precision of a standard measurement method, International Organization for Standardization, Geneva, 1998.

[144] MacTaggart DL, Farwell SO. Analytical use of linear regression. Part I. Regression procedures for calibration and quantitation. J. AOAC Int. 1992;**75**(4):594–607.

[145] ISO 9169:2006. Air quality. Definition and Determination of Performance Characteristics of an Automatic Measuring System. International Organization for Standardization: Geneva, 2006.

[146] ISO 13752:1998. Air quality. Assessment of Uncertainty of a Measurement Method under Field Conditions using a Second Method as Reference. International Organization for Standardization: Geneva, 1998.

[147] Currie LA. Detection and quantification limits: origins and historical overview. Anal. Chim. Acta 1999;**391**:127–134.

[148] Desiminoni E, Brunetti B. About estimating the limit of detection of heteroscedastic analytical systems. Anal. Chim. Acta 2009;**655**:30–37.

[149] Ketkar SN, Bzik TJ. Calibration of analytical instruments. Impact of nonconstant variance in calibration data. Anal. Chem. 2000;**72**(19):4762–4765.

[150] Nascimiento R, Froes RES, e Silva NOC, Naveira RLP, Mendes DBC, Neto WB, Silva JBB. Comparison between ordinary least squares regression and weighted least squares regression in the calibration of metals present in human milk determined by ICP-OES. Talanta 2010;**80**(3):1102–1109.

[151] Korany MA, Maher HM, Galal SM, Ragab AA. Comparative study of some robust statistical methods: weighted, parametric, and nonparametric linear regression of HPLC convoluted peak responses using internal standard methods in drug bioavailability studies. Anal. Bioanal. Chem. 2013;**405**(14):4835–4848.

[152] Brasil B, da Silva RJNV, Camoes FGFC, Salgueiro PAS. Weighted calibration with reduced number of signals by weighing factor modeling: application to the identification of explosives by ion chromatography. Anal. Chim. Acta 2013;**804**:187–295.

[153] Lavagnini I, Urbani A, Magno F. Overall calibration procedure via a statistically based matrix-comprehensive approach in the stir bar sorptive extraction-thermal desorption-gas chromatography-mass spectrometry analysis of pesticide residues in fruit-based soft drinks. Talanta 2011;**83**:1754–1762.

[154] Jain RB. Comparison of three weighting schemes in weighted schemes in weighted regression analysis for use in a chemistry laboratory. Clin. Chim. Acta 2010;**411**:270–279.

[155] AMC, Why are we weighting, Analytical Methods Committee, AMCTB No 27, June 2007.

[156] Zenf QC, Zhang E, Tellinghuisen J. Univariate calibration by reversed regression of heteroscedastic data: a case study. Analyst 2008;**33**:1649–1655.

[157] Tellinghuisen J. Weighted least-squares in calibration: what difference does it make?. Analyst 2007;**132**:536–543.

[158] Cook RD, Weisberg S. Applied Regression Including Computer and Graphic. New York: Wiley, 1999.

[159] Altman G. Practical Statistics for Medical Research. Boca Raton, FL: Chapman & Hall, 1991. p. 145.

[160] Acton FS. Analysis of Straight Line Data. New York: Wiley, 1959.

[161] Mager PP. Design Statistics in Pharmacochemistry. New York: Wiley, 1991.

[162] Tomassone R, Lesquoy E, Millier C. La Régression: nouveaux regards su une ancienne méthode statistique. Paris: Masson, 1983.

[163] Daniel C, Wood FS. Fitting Equations to Data: Computer Analysis of Multifactor Data. 2nd ed., New York: Wiley, 1999.

[164] Perkin Elmer. Analytical Methods for Atomic Absorption Spectrometry, The Perkin Elmer Corporation, 1996. Accessed 29/3/2017. http://eecelabs.seas.wustl.edu/files/Flame%20AA%20Operating%20Manual.pdf

[165] Box GEP. Science and Statistics. J. Am. Stat. Assoc. 1976;**71**:791–796.

[166] Cook RD, Weisberg S. Residuals and Influence in Regression. New York - London: Chapman & Hall, 1982.

Chapter 8

An Improved Wavelet-Based Multivariable Fault Detection Scheme

Fouzi Harrou, Ying Sun and Muddu Madakyaru

Additional information is available at the end of the chapter

http://dx.doi.org/10.5772/intechopen.68947

Abstract

Data observed from environmental and engineering processes are usually noisy and correlated in time, which makes the fault detection more difficult as the presence of noise degrades fault detection quality. Multiscale representation of data using wavelets is a powerful feature extraction tool that is well suited to denoising and decorrelating time series data. In this chapter, we combine the advantages of multiscale partial least squares (MSPLSs) modeling with those of the univariate EWMA (exponentially weighted moving average) monitoring chart, which results in an improved fault detection system, especially for detecting small faults in highly correlated, multivariate data. Toward this end, we applied EWMA chart to the output residuals obtained from MSPLS model. It is shown through simulated distillation column data the significant improvement in fault detection can be obtained by using the proposed methods as compared to the use of the conventional partial least square (PLS)-based Q and EWMA methods and MSPLS-based Q method.

Keywords: data uncertainty, multiscale representation, fault detection, data-driven approaches, statistical monitoring schemes

1. Introduction

Monitoring chemical and environmental processes has increasingly attracted greater attention of researchers and practitioners for improving the quality of products and enhancing process safety. For example, detecting anomalies in chemical or environmental plants is expected to reflect not only on the productivity and profitability of these plants, but also on the safety of people [1, 2]. To enhance process operation, we should monitor the process in an efficient manner and correctly detect abnormality events that may result in any degradation of

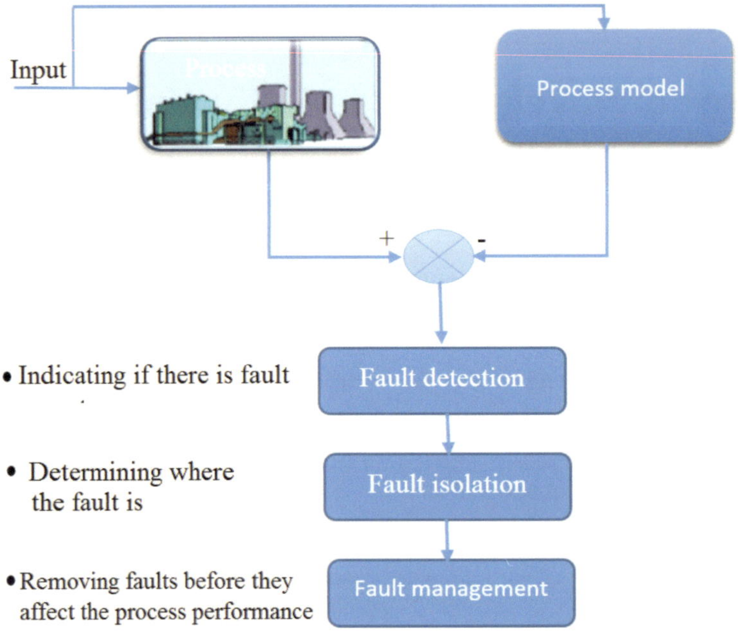

Figure 1. Scheme of fault detection and diagnosis.

product quality, operation reliability, and profitability, in order that we can respond accordingly by making any necessary correction to the process. Fault detection and diagnosis represent two vital components of process monitoring (see **Figure 1**), during which abnormal events are first identified and then isolated to ensure that they can be appropriately handled [2, 3]. Generally, faults in modern automatic processes are difficult to avoid and may result in serious process degradations. Even small deviations in process parameters can result in lost time, and catastrophic failure can bring devastating health, safety, and financial consequences. Because of this, engineers must keep tweaking and improving the reliability of their processes, watching carefully for signs of anomalies that could lead to disaster. Therefore, it is crucial to be able to detect and identify any possible faults or failures in the system as early as possible [2, 4, 5].

Keeping an automated process running smoothly and safely and producing the desired results remains a major challenge in many sectors. Various fault detection techniques have been developed for the safe operation of systems or processes. There are two main types of these techniques: process history-based approaches and model-based approaches, as shown in **Figure 2**. Model-based approaches compare analytically computed outputs with measured values and signal an alarm when large differences are detected [2, 6, 7]. Unfortunately, the effectiveness of model-based fault-detection approaches relies on the accuracy of the models used. When there is no process model, model-free or process-history-based methods were successfully used in process monitoring because they can effectively deal with highly correlated process variables [8, 9]. Such methods require a minimal a prior knowledge about

http://dx.doi.org/10.5772/intechopen.68947

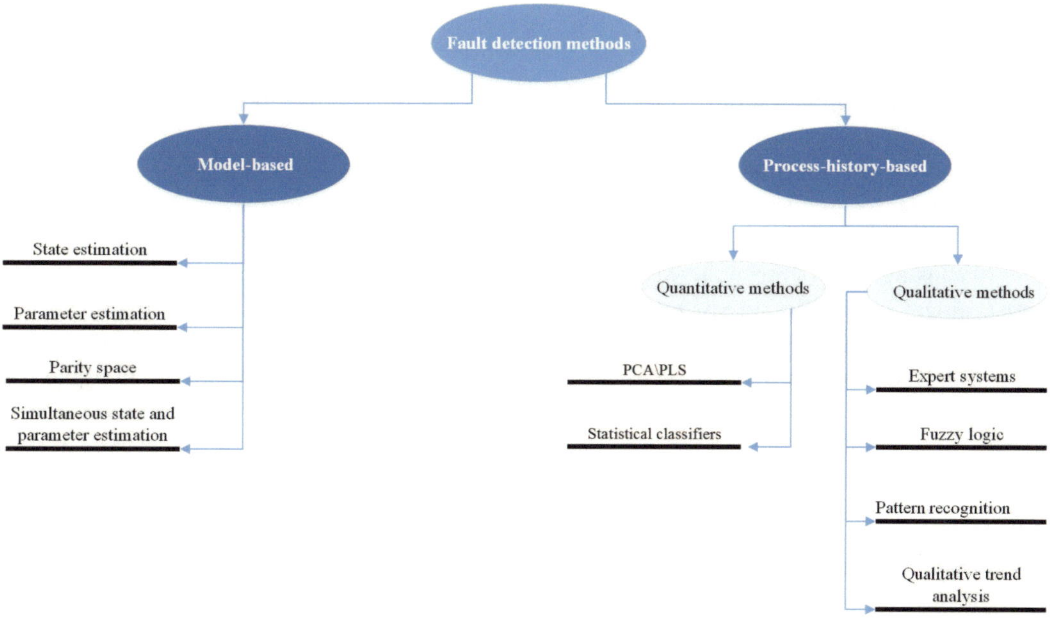

Figure 2. Fault detection methods.

process physics, but depends on the availability of quality input data. Process-history-based methods use implicit empirical models derived from analysis of available data and rely on computational intelligence and machine learning methods [10–12]. In the last four decades, process-history-based methods such as principal component analysis (PCA) and partial least squares (PLSs) have become more and more important in statistical process monitoring. They have been extensively applied in the field of chemometrics [5, 13, 14]. In contrast to the classical univariate statistical process monitoring tools, these approaches take the correlations between variables into account and monitor a set of correlated variables simultaneously. Moreover, by projecting the original measurements into a latent sub space, latent variables (LVs) are monitored in a reduced dimensional space. A PCA or PLS model is built on good historical data of normal or process operation [15, 16]. This model can then be used to monitor or predict the future behavior of the process [17].

However, most of the processes are in dynamic state, with various events occurring such as abrupt process changes, slow drifts, bad measurements due to sensor failures, and human errors. Data from these processes are not only cross-correlated, but also autocorrelated. Applying conventional latent variable regression (LVR) methods directly to dynamic systems results in false alarms, making it insensitive to detect and discriminate different kinds of events. In addition, noisy data and model uncertainties negatively affect the performance of fault detection methods. In fact, wavelet-based multiscale representation of data has been shown to provide effective noise-feature separation in the data, to approximately decorrelate autocorrelated data, and to transform the data to better follow the Gaussian distribution [18]. Multiscale representation of data using wavelets has been widely used for data denoising, compression, and for process monitoring [18–21].

The detection of incipient faults is crucial for maintaining the normal operations of a system by providing early fault warnings. The problem is that incipient anomalies are often too weak to be detected by conventional monitoring methods. The objective of this chapter is to extend the fault detection techniques developed to take into account the uncertainty of the data. To this end, multiscale data representation, a powerful feature extraction tool, will be used to reduce false alarms by improving noise-feature data separation and decorrelation of autocorrelated measurement errors. To do so, multiscale partial least square (MSPLS)-based exponentially weighted moving average (EWMA) fault detection techniques will be developed. The overarching goal of this work is to tackle multivariate challenges in process monitoring by merging the advantages of EWMA chart and multiscale-PLS modeling to enhance their performance. It is shown through simulated distillation column data that significant improvement in detecting small fault can be obtained using the MSPLS-EWMA approach as compared to the PLS-EWMA fault detection approach.

The remainder of this chapter is organized as follows. Section 2 gives a brief overview of the PLS and the multiscale PLS approach. In Section 3, we present the proposed MSPLS-EWMA fault-detection procedure. In Section 4, EWMA chart is briefly presented. Section 5 applies the proposed fault-detection procedure to a simulated distillation column process. Finally, Section 6 concludes the chapter.

2. Preliminary materials

2.1. Partial least squares (PLS)-based charts

The objective of PLS models is to find relations between input and output data blocks by relating their latent variables. A detailed description of the PLS technique is given in Ref. [22]. This data-driven empirical statistical model approach is extremely useful under the situation where either a first principal model or analytical model is difficult to obtain or the measured variables are highly correlated (collinear) to each other. The PLS methods have been extensively researched and applied in the chemometrics field.

Consider an input data matrix $\mathbf{X} \in R^{n\times m}$ and an output data matrix $\mathbf{Y} \in R^{n\times p}$, where n is the number of samples or observations, m and p are the number of input and output variables, respectively. The objective of PLS is to maximize the covariance matrix between linear combinations of **X** and **Y**. A PLS model is given by the inner model and the outer model [15, 23] (see **Figure 3**). The input and output matrices can be related to LVs as follows via the outer model [23]:

$$\begin{cases} \mathbf{X} = \widehat{\mathbf{X}} + \mathbf{E} = \sum_{i=1}^{l} \mathbf{t}_i \mathbf{P}_i^T + \mathbf{E} = \mathbf{T}\mathbf{P}^T + \mathbf{E} \\ \mathbf{Y} = \widehat{\mathbf{Y}} + \mathbf{F} = \sum_{i=1}^{l} \mathbf{u}_i \mathbf{q}_i^T + \mathbf{F} = \mathbf{U}\mathbf{Q}^T + \mathbf{F} \end{cases} \tag{1}$$

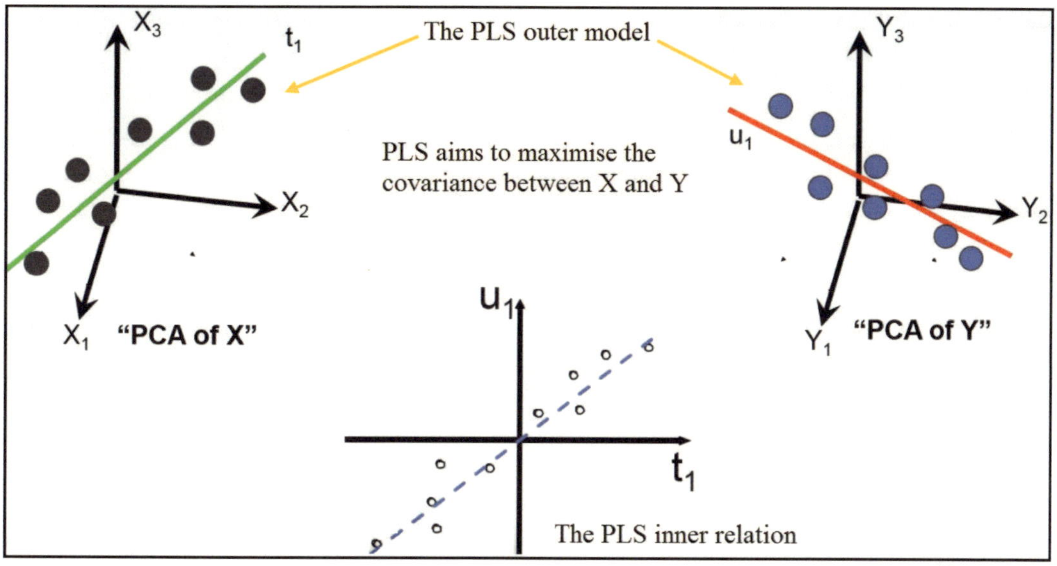

Figure 3. Principle of PLS.

where $\widehat{\mathbf{X}}$ and $\widehat{\mathbf{Y}}$ are approximated data matrices of **X** and **Y**, respectively, the matrices $\mathbf{T} \in R^{n\times l}$ and $\mathbf{U} \in R^{n\times q}$ consist of l retained LVs of the input and output data, respectively. $\mathbf{E} \in R^{n\times m}$ and $\mathbf{F} \in R^{n\times p}$ represent the residuals matrices that were the unexplained variance of the input and output data, respectively, $\mathbf{P} \in R^{m\times l}$ and $\mathbf{Q} \in R^{p\times q}$ are the loading of matrices **X** and **Y**, respectively. In practice, how to choose a proper number l for LVs is an important step in PLS modeling. If all LVs are used in modeling, the model may fit the noise and therefore reduce the predictive ability of the model. Here, the cross-validation method can be used to determine a proper number of LVs [24]. The inner model can be computed as

$$\mathbf{U} = \mathbf{TB} + \mathbf{H}, \tag{2}$$

where **B** is a regression matrix and **H** is a residual matrix. The information in **Y** can be expressed as

$$\mathbf{Y} = \mathbf{TBQ}^T + \mathbf{F}^* \tag{3}$$

where matrix $\mathbf{F}^*$ was the residue that presented the unexplained variance.

2.2. Wavelet transform

Most engineering processes generate data with multiscale properties, signifying that they include both useful information and noise at different times and frequencies. The majority of fall detection approaches are based on time-domain data (operates on a single time scale) that do not take multiscale characteristics of the data into consideration. Wavelet analysis has been show to represent data with multiscale properties, efficiently separating deterministic and stochastic features [18].

Multiresolution time series decomposition was initially applied by Mallat, who used orthogonal wavelet bases during data compression for image decoding [25]. Wavelets represent a family of basis functions that can be expressed as the following localized in both time and frequency [18]:

$$\psi_{a,b}(t) = \frac{1}{\sqrt{a}}\psi\left(\frac{t-b}{a}\right), \tag{4}$$

where a represents the dilation parameter, b is the translation parameter [26] and $\psi(t)$ is the mother wavelet. Both these parameters are commonly discretized dyadically as $a = 2^m$, $b = 2^m k$, $(m,k) \in \mathbb{Z}^2$, and the family of wavelets can represented as $\psi_{mn}(t) = 2^{\frac{-m}{2}}\psi(2^{-m}t - m)$. Here, $\psi(t)$ is the mother wavelet and m and k are the respective dilation and translation parameters, respectively. Different families of basis functions are created based on their convolution with different filters, such as the Haar scaling function and the Daubechies filters [26, 27]. Parameters that are discretized dyadically force downsampling reduce the number of parameters dyadically with every decomposition. However, dyadically discretized wavelet force samples at nondyadic locations to become decomposed only after a certain time delay.

The discrete wavelet transform (DWT) analyzes the signal at different scales (or over different frequency bands) by decomposing the signal at each scale into a coarse approximation (low frequency information), A, and detail information (high frequency information), D. DWT employs two sets of functions: the scaling functions $\phi_{j,k}(t) = \sqrt{2^{-j}}\phi(2^{-j}t - k), k \in \mathbb{Z}$ and wavelet functions $\psi_{j,k}(t) = \sqrt{2^{-j}}\psi(2^{-j}t - k), j = 1,\ldots,J, k \in \mathbb{Z}$, which are associated with low pass filter H and high pass filter G, respectively. Where the coarsest scale J usually termed the decomposition level. Any signal can be represented by a summation of all scaled and detailed signals as follows [26]:

$$x(t) = \overbrace{\sum_{k=1}^{n2^{-J}} a_{Jk}\phi_{Jk}(t)}^{A_J(t)} + \sum_{j=1}^{J}\overbrace{\sum_{k=1}^{n2^{-j}} d_{jk}\psi_{jk}(t)}^{D_j(t).} \tag{5}$$

where j, k, J, and n represent the dilation parameter, translation parameter, number of scales, and number observations in the original signal, respectively [28, 29]. d_{jk} and a_{Jk} are respectively the scaling and the wavelet coefficients, and $A_J(t)$ and $D_j(t), (j = 1, 2, \ldots, J)$ represent the approximated signal and the detail signals, respectively. Of course, by passing a series of high and low pass wavelets filters, it is decomposed into signals at different scales as shown in **Figure 4**.

In the next section, we highlight the advantages of multiscale.

http://dx.doi.org/10.5772/intechopen.68947

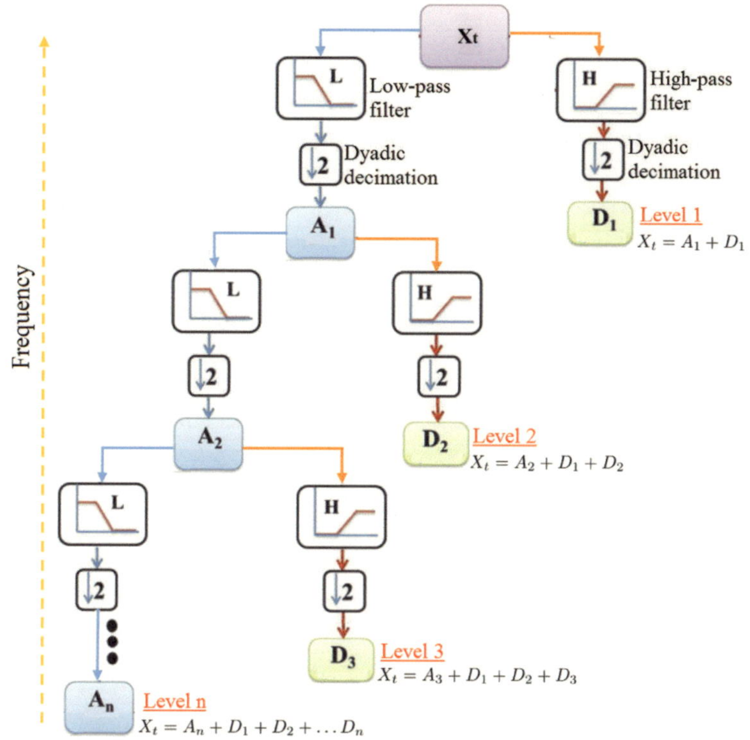

Figure 4. Principle of multiscale representation based on wavelet transform.

2.3. Advantages of multiscale representation

Conventional methods are referred to as time-domain analysis methods. These methods are more sensitive toward impulsive oscillations and are unable to extract frequencies and patterns in the data that may be hidden. Before the introduction of multiscale wavelet analysis, mathematical tools such as Fourier transform analysis, coherence function analysis, and power spectral density analysis were used. However, these tools would only allow the signal to imitate the tool being used for analysis. For example, the use of Fourier transform analysis would decompose the signal into a sum of cosine and sine functions. Multiscale helps overcome this problem as it helps simultaneously examine both the time and frequency domains, while Fourier transform is only capable of shifting between the time and frequency domain.

Ganesan et al. in a literature review of multiscale statistical process monitoring state the following advantages of using wavelet coefficients in Multiscale statistical process control (MSSPC) over conventional Statistical process control (SPC) methods [20]:

- The ability to separate noise from important feature.
- The wavelet coefficients of autocorrelated data are approximately decorrelated at multiple scales.
- Data are closer to normality at multiple scales.

2.4. Separating noise feature

Two important applications, data compression and data denoising, can be achieved through wavelet multiscale decomposition. One of the biggest advantages of multiscale representation is its capacity of distinguishing measurement noise from useful data features, by applying low and high pass filters to the data during multiscale decomposition. This allows the separation of features at different resolutions or frequencies, which makes multiscale representation a better tool for filtering or denoising noisy data than traditional linear filters, like the mean filter and the EWMA filter. Despite their popularity, linear filters rely on defining a frequency threshold above where all features are treated as measurement noise. The ability of multiscale representation to separate noise has been used not only to improve data filtering, but also to improve the prediction accuracy of several empirical modeling methods and the accuracy of state estimators.

A noisy signal is filtered by a three-step method [30]:

- Apply wavelet transform to decompose the noisy signal into the time-frequency domain.
- Threshold the detail coefficient and remove coefficients a selected threshold.
- Transform back into the original domain the threshold coefficients to obtain a filtered signal.

2.5. Multiscale PLS modeling

Data observed from environmental and engineering processes are usually noisy and correlated in time, which makes the fault detection more difficult as the presence of noise degrades fault detection quality, and most methods are developed for independent observations. Multiscale representation of data using wavelets is a powerful feature extraction tool that is well suited to denoising and decorrelating time series data.

The integrated multiscale PLS (MSPLS) modeling approach is to take advantage of the both latent variable regression and denoising ability of the multiscale decomposition using wavelets. Thus, improve in prediction ability of the model, which in term improves the fault detection methods. The given input variable data matrix $\mathbf{X}$ and response variable matrix $\mathbf{y}$ are decomposed at different scales using multiscale basis function called wavelets. Let the decomposed data at each scale (j) be $\mathbf{X}_j$ and $\mathbf{y}_j$. Then, the MSPLS model is developed using decomposed data, can be expressed as

$$\mathbf{y}_j = \mathbf{T}_j\mathbf{B}_j\mathbf{Q}_j^T - \mathbf{F}_j, \tag{6}$$

where $\mathbf{X}_j \in \mathbb{R}^{n\times m}$ is the filtered input data matrix at scale (j), $\mathbf{y}_j \in \mathbb{R}^{n\times 1}$ is the response output vector at scale (j). $\mathbf{F} \in \mathbb{R}^{m\times p}$ is the MSPLS model residual at jth decomposition scale.

However, denoising the input and output variables a prior to developing model results in poor prediction ability of the MSPLS model due to removal of features which may be important to model. Therefore, in the proposed integrated MSPLS modeling approach, the selection of optimum decomposition depth based on the prediction ability of the developed MSPLS model is used. The integrated MSPLS modeling algorithm is summarized next [8].

- Preprocessing of training and testing data is required to ensure that all available data is set to zero mean and unit variance.
- Wavelet decomposition allows the data to be converted into wavelet coefficients. This changes the set of data from a single scale to multiple scales that allow for multiscale modeling.
- Filter the training data at different scales based on the filtering algorithm is given in Section 2.4.
- Build a PLS model using the filtered data at each scale. Cross-validation is used to determine the number of LVs.
- Use the estimated model from each scale to predict the output for the testing data and compute the cross-validated mean square error.
- Choose the PLS with the smallest cross-validated mean square error as the MSPLS model.

Once an MSPLS model based on past normal operation is obtained, it can be used to monitor future deviation from normality. Two monitoring statistics, the T^2 and Q statistics, are usually utilized for fault detection purposes [31]. First, the Hoteling T^2 statistics indicates the variation within the process model in the LVs subspace. Second, the Q statistic, also known as the squared prediction error (SPE), monitors how well the data conforms to the model (see **Figure 5**).

The T^2 statistic based on the number of retained LVs, l, is defined as [31]

$$T^2 = \sum_{i=1}^{l} \frac{t_i^2}{\lambda_i}, \tag{7}$$

where λ_i is eigenvalue of the covariance matrix of X. The T^2 statistic measures the variation in the LVs only. A large change in the PC subspace is observed if some points exceed the confidence

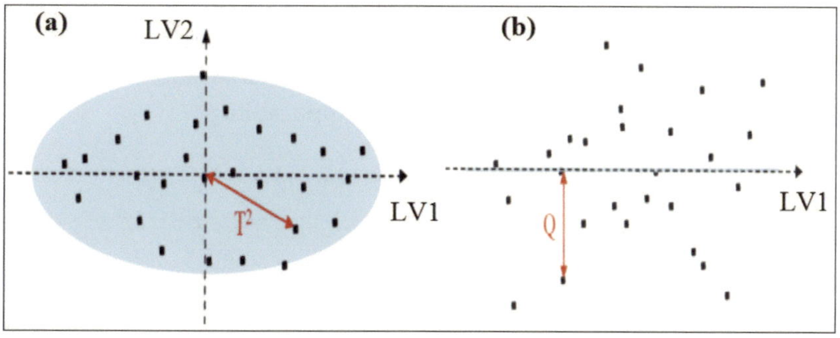

Figure 5. (a) Hoteling T^2 statistic and (b) Q statistic.

limit of the T^2 chart, indicating a big deviation in the monitored system. Confidence limits for T^2 at level $(1-\alpha)$ relate to the Fisher distribution, F, as follows [31]:

$$T^2_{l,n,\alpha} = \frac{l(n-1)}{n-l} F_{l,n-l,\alpha}, \tag{8}$$

where $F_{l,n-l,\alpha}$ is the upper $100\alpha\%$ critical point of F with l and $n-l$ degrees of freedom.

The squared prediction error (SPE) or Q statistic, which is defined as [31]

$$Q = \mathbf{e}^T \mathbf{e}, \tag{9}$$

captures the changes in the residual subspace. $\mathbf{e} = \mathbf{x} - \hat{\mathbf{x}}$ represents the residuals vector, which is the difference between the new observation, $\mathbf{x}$, and its prediction, $\hat{\mathbf{x}}$, via the MSPLS model. Eq. (9) provides a direct mean of the Q statistic in terms of the total sum of measured variation in the residual vector e. The SPE can be considered a measure of the system-model mismatch. The confidence limits for SPE are given in Ref. [32]. This test suggests the existence of an abnormal condition when $Q > Q_\alpha$, where Q_α is defined as

$$Q_\alpha = \varphi_1 \left[\frac{h_0 c_\alpha \sqrt{2\varphi_2}}{\varphi_1} + 1 + \frac{\varphi_2 h_0 (h_0 - 1)}{\varphi_1^2} \right], \tag{10}$$

where

$$\varphi_i = \sum_{j=l+1}^{m} \lambda_j^i, \text{ for } i = 1, 2, 3, \tag{11}$$

$$h_0 = 1 - \frac{2\varphi_1 \varphi_3}{3\varphi_2^2}. \tag{12}$$

c_α is the confidence limits for the $1-\alpha$ percentile in a normal distribution.

However, the MSPLS-based T^2 and Q approaches fail to detect small faults [9]. Here, we use only the Q-based chart as a benchmark for fault detection with PLS and MSPLS. Motivated by the power of the EWMA chart, which are widely used univariate control chart, is proposed as improved alternatives for fault detection. The objective is to tackle MSPLS challenges in process monitoring by merging the advantages of the EWMA and MSPLS approaches to enhance their performance and widen their practical applicability.

3. EWMA monitoring charts

In this section, we briefly introduce the basic idea of the EWMA chart and its properties. For a more detailed discussion of EWMA charts, see Ref. [33]. EWMA is a statistic that gives less weight to old data, and more weight to new data. The EWMA charts are able to detect small shifts in the process mean, since the EWMA statistic is a time-weighted average of all previous observations. The EWMA control scheme was first introduced by Roberts [34], and is extensively used in time series analysis. The EWMA monitoring chart is an anomaly detection technique widely used by scientists and engineers in various disciplines [6, 33, 35]. Assume that $\{x_1, x_2, \ldots, x_n\}$ are individual observations collected from a monitored process. The expression for the EWMA is [33]

$$\begin{cases} z_t = & \lambda x_t + (1-\lambda)\, z_{t-1} \quad \text{if } t > 0 \\ z_0 = & \mu_0, \quad \text{if } t = 0. \end{cases} \tag{13}$$

The starting value z_0 is usually set to the mean of the fault-free data, μ_0. Z_t is the output of EWMA and x_t is the observation from the monitored process at the current time. The forgetting parameter $\lambda \in (0, 1]$ determines how fast EWMA forgets historical data. Equation (13) can also be written as

$$z_t = \lambda \sum_{t=1}^{n} (1-\lambda)^{n-t} x_t + (1-\lambda)^n \mu_0, \tag{14}$$

where $\lambda(1-\lambda)^{n-t}$ is the weight for x_t, which falls off exponentially for past observations. We can see that if λ is small, then more weight is assigned to past observations. Thus, the chart is tuned to have efficiency for detecting small changes in the process mean. On the other hand, if λ is large, then more weight is assigned to the current observations, and the chart is more suitable for detecting large shifts [33]. In the special case, $\lambda = 1$, the EWMA is equal to the most recent observation, x_t, and provides the same results as Shewhart chart. As λ approaches zero, EWMA approximates the CUSUM criteria, which gives equal weights to the current and historical observations.

Under fault-free conditions, the standard deviation of z_t is defined as

$$\sigma_{z_t} = \sigma_0 \sqrt{\frac{\lambda}{(2-\lambda)} [1 - (1-\lambda)^{2t}]}, \tag{15}$$

where σ_0 is the standard deviation of the fault-free or preliminary data set. Therefore, in such cases, $z_t \sim \mathcal{N}\left(\mu_0, \sigma_{z_t}^2\right)$. However, in the presence of a mean shift at the time point $1 \leq \tau \leq n$, $z_t \sim \mathcal{N}\left(\mu_0 + [1 - (1-\lambda)^{n-\tau+1}](\mu_1 - \mu_0), \sigma_{z_t}^2\right)$. The upper and lower control limits (UCL and LCL) of the EWMA chart for detecting a mean shift are UCL/LCL $= \mu_0 \pm L\sigma_{z_t}$, where L is a multiplier of the EWMA standard deviation σ_{z_t}. The parameters L and λ need to be set carefully [33]. In practice, L is usually set to three, which corresponds to a false alarm rate of 0.27%. If z_t is within the interval [LCL and UCL], then we conclude that the process is under control up to time point t. Otherwise, the process is considered out of control.

4. Combining MSPLS model with EWMA chart: MSPLS-EWMA

In this chapter, we combine the advantages of MSPLS modeling with those of the univariate EWMA monitoring chart, which results in an improved fault detection system, especially for detecting small faults in highly correlated, multivariate data. Toward this end, we applied EWMA charts to the output residuals obtained from the MSPLS model (see **Figure 6**). Indeed, under normal operation with little noise and few errors, the residuals are close to zero, while they significantly deviate from zero in the presence of abnormal events. In this work, the output residuals from MSPLS are used as a fault indicator.

As given in Eq. (6), the output vector **y** can be written as the sum of a predicted vector $\hat{\mathbf{y}}$ and a residual vector **F**, i.e.,

$$\mathbf{y} = \hat{\mathbf{y}} + \mathbf{F}. \tag{16}$$

The residual of the output variable, $\mathbf{F} = [f_1, \ldots, f_t, \ldots, f_n]$, which is the difference between the observed value of the output variable, y, and the predicted value, $\hat{y}$, obtained from the MSPLS model, is a potential indicator for fault detection. The EWMA statistic based on the residuals of the response variable can be calculated as follows:

$$z_t = \lambda f_t + (1 - \lambda)\, z_{t-1} t \in [1, n] \tag{17}$$

In this case, since the EWMA control scheme is applied on the residual data matrix, one EWMA decision function will be computed to monitor the process.

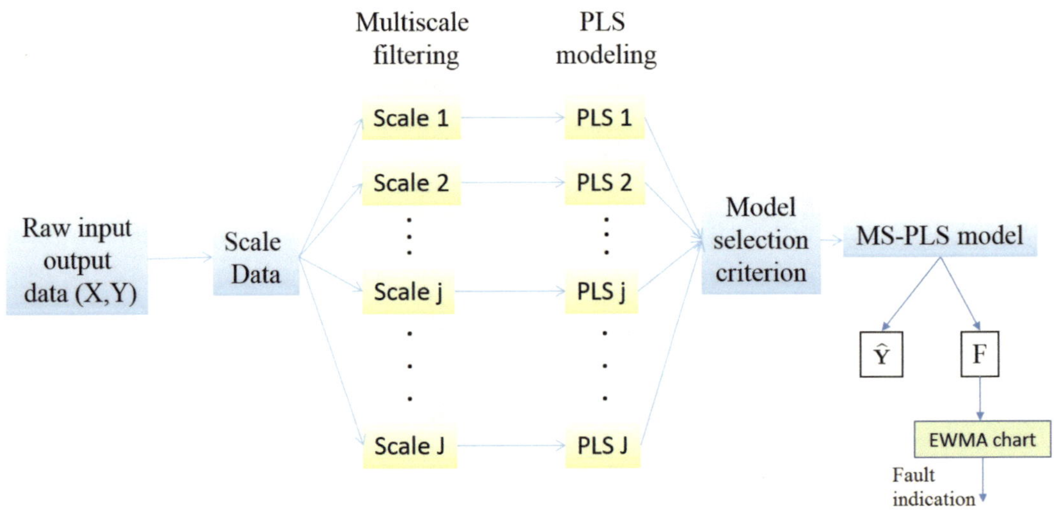

Figure 6. Principle of MSPLS-EWMA procedure.

http://dx.doi.org/10.5772/intechopen.68947

5. Monitoring a simulated distillation column

In this section, the ability of the proposed MSPLS-EWMA technique to detect faults is studied through simulation data and the results compared with those obtained using a traditional PLS-EWMA method. In all monitoring charts, the red-shaded area is the region where the fault is injected to the test data while the 95% control limits are plotted by the horizontal-dashed line.

5.1. Description and data generation of the process

A distillation column is most commonly used unit operation in chemical process industries. The objective of the distillation operation is to separate the component from a mixture of component. The operation of distillation column is very energy expensive. Therefore, monitoring of such process plays very important role in bringing down the cost of the operation. The schematic diagram of the distillation column is shown in **Figure 7**.

The efficacy of the proposed fault detection strategy tested using simulated (using ASPEN simulation software [36]) distillation column. The input variables consist of temperature measurements at different location of the distillation column along with feed flow rate and reflux flow. The light distillate from reflux drum considered as the response variable. The operating conditions, nominal operating conditions, and detailed steps involved in the data generation can be found in Ref. [36]. The generated 1024 data samples are then corrupted with zero mean Gaussian white noise with signal-to-noise ratio (SNR) of 10 dB used for model development and testing the Fault detection (FD) strategy. **Figure 8** shows dynamic data of the distillation column, i.e., variations of the light component for changes in the reflux and feed flow. The MSPLS model is developed from first 512 data samples and later part of the data points is used for testing purpose. The optimal LVs for the model are achieved through cross-validation methods and found to be three LVs for the MSPLS model.

A scatter plot of the measured and predicted data is presented in **Figure 9**. This plot indicates a reasonable performance of the selected models.

5.2. Detection results

After a process model has been successfully identified, we can proceed with fault detection. Three types of faults in distillation columns will be considered here: abrupt, intermittent, and gradual faults.

To quantify the efficiency of the proposed strategies, we use two metrics: the false detection rate (FAR) and the miss detection rate (MDR) [37]. The FAR is the number of normal observations that are wrongly judged as faulty (false alarms) over the total number of fault-free data. The MDR is the number of faults that are wrongly classified as normal (missed detections) over the total number of faults.

5.2.1. Case (A): abrupt fault detection

In this case study, an abrupt change is simulated by adding a small constant deviation which is 2% of the total variation in temperature Tc_3, to the temperature sensor measurements Tc_3,

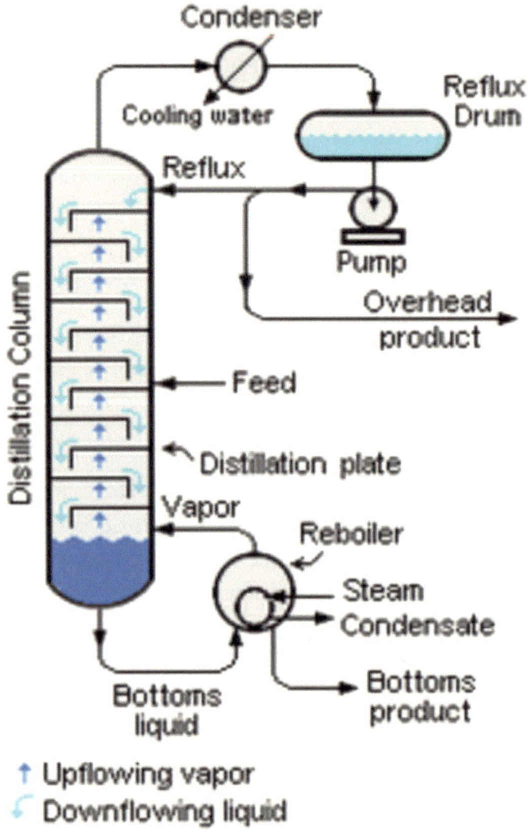

Figure 7. Distillation column diagram.

between sample times 150 and 200. In the example, the testing data with low SNR, SNR = 5, are generated for the purpose of evaluation of MSPLS-EWMA and PLS-Q monitoring performances. Results of the PLS-Q and MSPLS-Q statistics are demonstrated in **Figure 10(a)** and **(c)**, respectively. It can be seen from **Figure 10(a)** and **(c)** that PLS-Q and MSPLS-Q cannot detect this small fault. **Figure 10(b)** shows that the PLS-EWMA chart is capable of detecting this simulated fault but with a lot missed detection (i.e., MDR = 55% and FAR = 0.96%). **Figure 10(d)** shows that although the MSPLS-EWMA chart clearly detected this abrupt faults without missed detection (i.e., MDR = 0% and FAR = 0.96%).

5.2.2. Case (B): intermittent fault

In this case study, we introduce into the testing data a bias of amplitude 2% of the total variation in temperature Tc_3 of between samples 50 and 100, and a bias of 10% between samples 350 and 450. **Figure 11(a)–(d)** shows the monitoring results of the PLS-based Q and EWMA charts, and MSPLS-based Q and EWMA charts. **Figure 11(a)** shows that the PLS-based

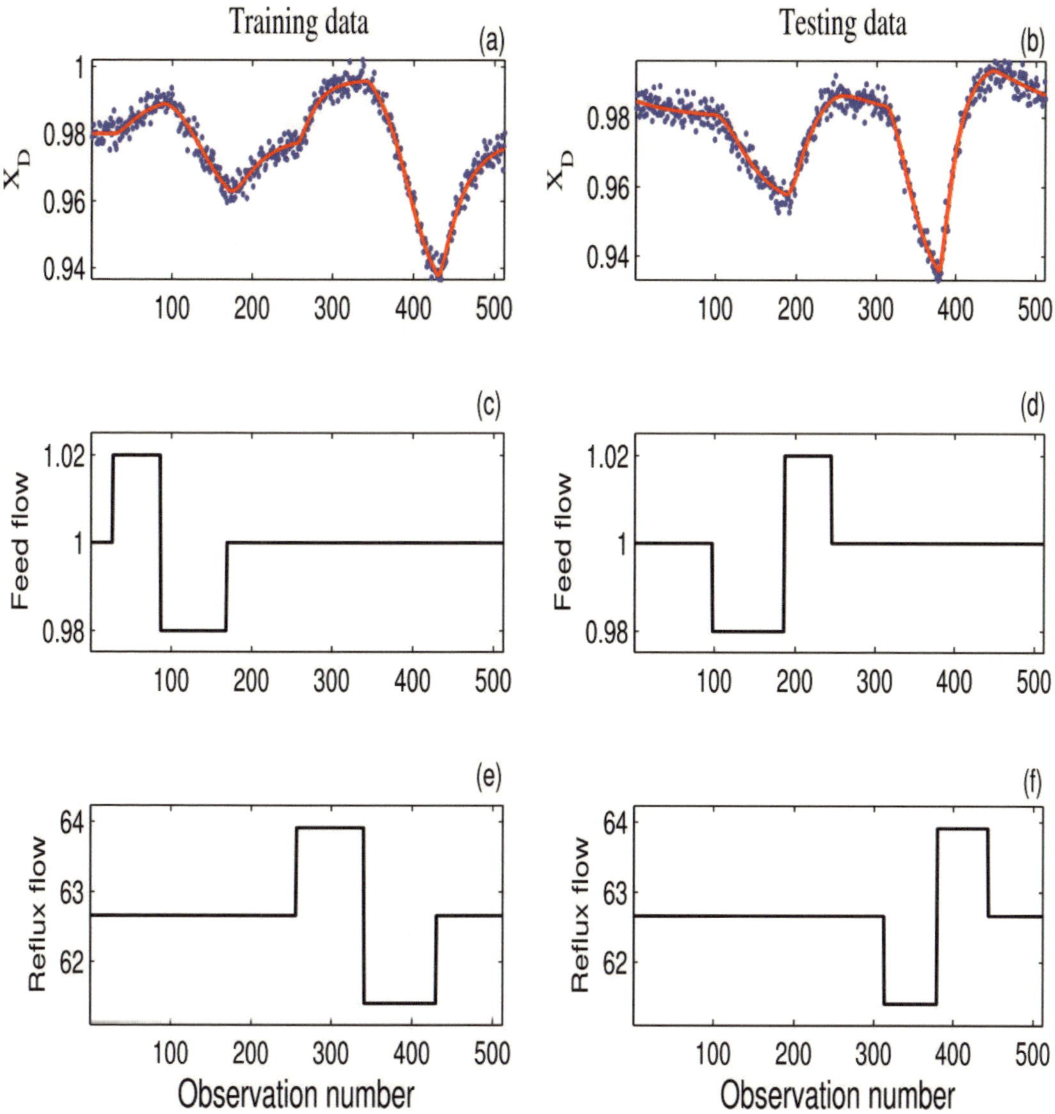

Figure 8. Simulation of a distillation column: variation of input-output data with SNR = 10 (Solid line: noise-free data; dots: noisy data).

Q chart has no power to detect this fault. From **Figure 11(b)**, it can be seen that the MSPLS-Q chart can detect the intermittent faults but with several missed detections. **Figure 11(c)** shows that the PLS-EWMA chart can indeed detect this fault, but with some missed detections. On the other hand, the MSPLS-EWMA chart with $\lambda = 0.3$ correctly detects this intermittent fault (see **Figure 11(d)**). In this case study, we can see that detection performance is much enhanced when using the MSPLS-EWMA chart compared to the others.

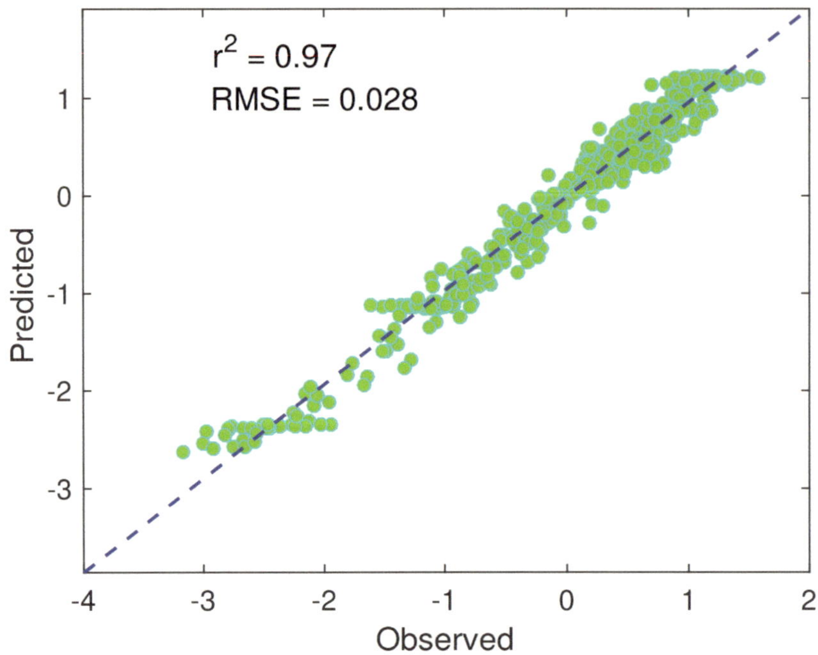

Figure 9. Scatter plots of predicted and observed training data.

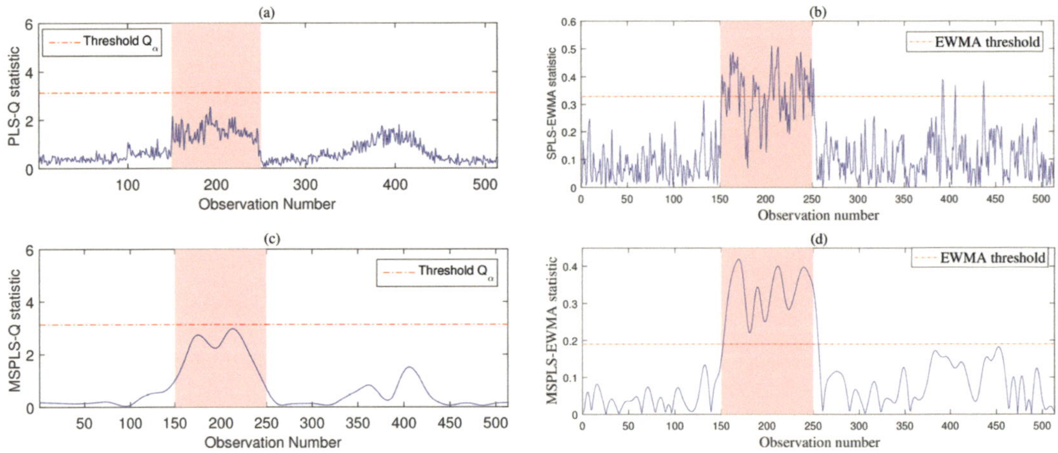

Figure 10. Monitoring results of PLS-*Q* chart (a), PLS-EWMA chart (b), MSPLS-*Q* chart (c), and MSPLS-EWMA chart (d) in the presence of a bias anomaly in the temperature sensor measurements 'Tc_3' with SNR = 30, Case (A).

5.2.3. Case (C): drift failure detection

A slow drift fault is simulated by adding a ramp change with a slope of 0.01 to the temperature sensor, Tc_3, from sample 250 through the end of the testing data. Monitoring results of PLS and

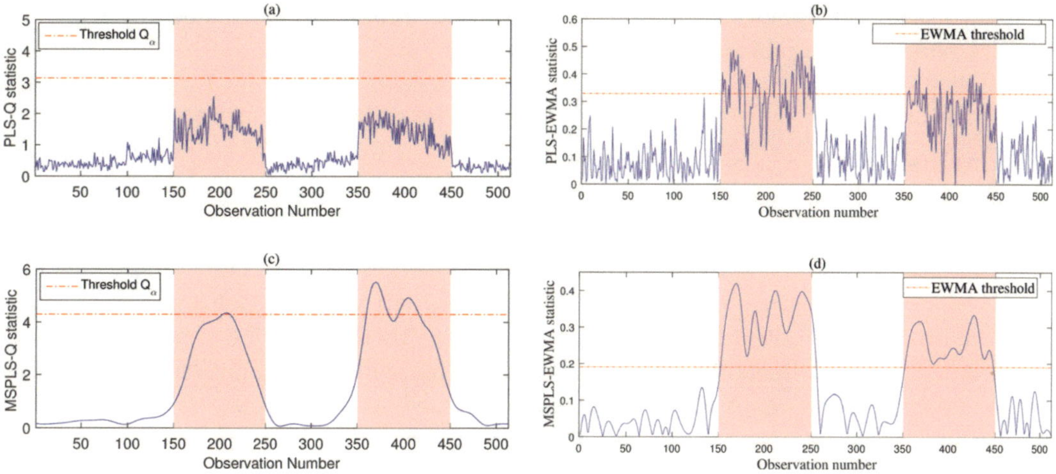

Figure 11. Monitoring results of PLS-*Q* chart (a), PLS-EWMA chart (b), MSPLS-*Q* chart (c), and MSPLS-EWMA chart (d) in the presence intermittent sensor fault in 'Tc_3' with SNR = 30, Case (B).

MSPLS-based *Q* and EWMA statistics are shown in **Figure 12(a)–(d)**. **Figure 12(a)** shows the monitoring results of PLS-*Q* chart, in which we can see that a signal is first given at sample 313 with a significant false alarm rate (i.e., FAR = 22.4%). **Figure 12(b)** shows that the PLS-EWMA chart first detects the fault at the 290th observation. The MSPLS-*Q* chart is shown in **Figure 12(c)**, which first flags the fault at sample 323. **Figure 12(d)** shows that the MSPLS-EWMA chart first detects the fault at the 288th observation. Therefore, a fewer observations are needed for the MSPLS-EWMA chart to detect a fault compared to the other charts.

This case study testifies again to the superiority of the proposed approaches compared to conventional PLS-based fault detection. Of course, this chapter also demonstrates through

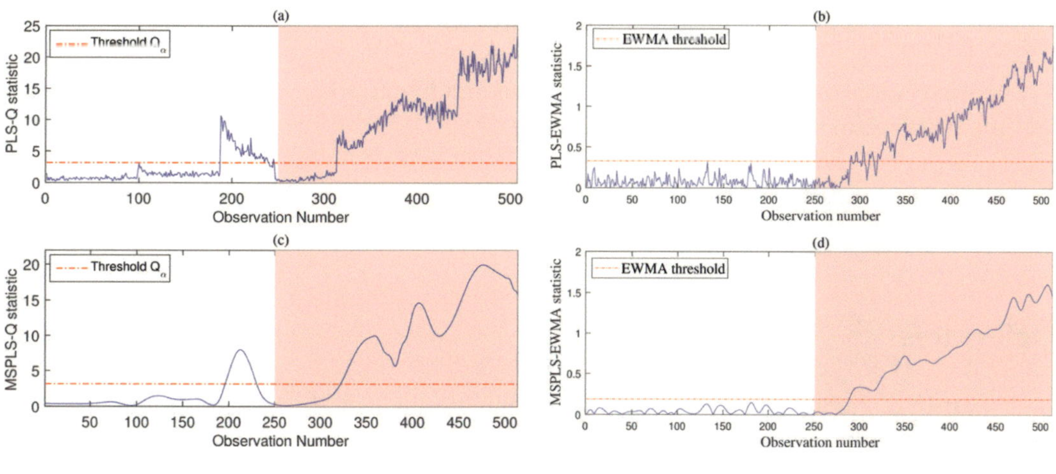

Figure 12. Monitoring results of PLS-*Q* chart (a), PLS-EWMA chart (b), MSPLS-*Q* chart (c), and MSPLS-EWMA chart (d) in the presence drift sensor anomaly in 'Tc_3' with SNR = 30, Case (C).

simulated data that significant improvement in fault detection can be obtained by using the MSPLS model when combined with the EWMA chart.

6. Conclusion

The objective of this chapter is to extend the PLS fault-detection methods to deal with uncertainty in the measurements. The developed approach merges the flexibility of multiscale PLS model and the greater sensitivity of the EWMA control chart to incipient changes. Specifically, in this approach, the multiscale PLS model has been constructed using the wavelet coefficients at different scales, and then EWMA monitoring chart was applied using this model to improve the fault detection abilities of this PLS fault detection method even further. Using a simulated distillation column, we demonstrate the effectiveness of MSPLS-EWMA to detect abrupt and drift faults. Results show that the MSPLS-EWMA can achieve better fault-detection efficiency than the PLS-EWMA, PLS-*Q*, and MSPLS-*Q* monitoring approaches.

Acknowledgements

This publication is based upon work supported by the King Abdullah University of Science and Technology (KAUST) Office of Sponsored Research (OSR) under Award No: OSR-2015-CRG4-2582.

Author details

Fouzi Harrou[1]*, Ying Sun[1] and Muddu Madakyaru[2]

*Address all correspondence to: fouzi.harrou@kaust.edu.sa

1 Computer, Electrical and Mathematical Sciences and Engineering (CEMSE) Division, King Abdullah University of Science and Technology (KAUST), Thuwal, Saudi Arabia

2 Department of Chemical Engineering, Manipal Institute of Technology, Manipal University, Manipal, India

References

[1] Aldrich C, Auret L. Unsupervised process monitoring and fault diagnosis with machine learning methods. London: Springer; 2013

[2] Isermann R. Model-based fault-detection and diagnosis: Status and applications. Annual Reviews in Control. 2005;**29**:71–85

[3] Ralston P, DePuy G, Graham J. Computer-based monitoring and fault diagnosis: A chemical process case study. ISA Transactions. 2001;**40**(1):85–98

[4] Neumann J, Deerberg G, Schlüter S. Early detection and identification of dangerous states in chemical plants using neural networks. Journal of Loss Prevention in the Process Industries. 1999;**12(**6):451–453

[5] Chiang L, Braatz R, Russell E. Fault Detection and Diagnosis in Industrial Systems. Springer-Verlag London: Springer Science & Business Media; 2001

[6] Harrou F, Fillatre L, Bobbia M, Nikiforov I. Statistical detection of abnormal ozone measurements based on constrained generalized likelihood ratio test. In: IEEE 52nd Annual Conference on Decision and Control (CDC), Firenze, Italy; IEEE; 2013. pp. 4997–5002

[7] Harrou F, Fillatre L, Nikiforov I. Anomaly detection/detectability for a linear model with a bounded nuisance parameter. Annual Reviews in Control. 2014;**38**(1):32–44

[8] Madakyaru M, Harrou F, Sun Y. Improved data-based fault detection strategy and application to distillation columns. Process Safety and Environmental Protection. 2017;**107**:22–34

[9] Harrou F, Nounou M, Nounou H, Madakyaru M. PLS-based EWMA fault detection strategy for process monitoring. Journal of Loss Prevention in the Process Industries. 2015;**36**:108–119

[10] Yin S, Ding SX, Haghani A, Hao H, Zhang P. A comparison study of basic data-driven fault diagnosis and process monitoring methods on the benchmark Tennessee Eastman process. Journal of Process Control. 2012;**22**(9):1567–1581

[11] Yin S, Ding S, Xie X, Luo H. A review on basic data-driven approaches for industrial process monitoring. IEEE Transactions on Industrial Electronics. 2014;**61**(11):6418–6428

[12] Zhao Y, Wang S, Xiao F. Pattern recognition-based chillers fault detection method using support vector data description (SVDD). Applied Energy. 2013;**112**:1041–1048

[13] Liang W, Zhang L. A wave change analysis (WCA) method for pipeline leak detection using gaussian mixture model. Journal of Loss Prevention in the Process Industries. 2012;**25**(1):60–69

[14] Abdi H, Williams L. Principal component analysis. Wiley Interdisciplinary Reviews: Computational Statistics. 2010;**29**(4):433–459

[15] Wold S, Ruhe H, Wold H, III WD. The collinearity problem in linear regression. the partial least squares (PLS) approach to generalized inverses. SIAM Journal on Scientific and Statistical Computing. 1984;**5**(3):735–743

[16] Yin S, Xiangping Z, Okyay K. Improved PLS focused on key-performance-indicator-related fault diagnosis. IEEE Transactions on Industrial Electronics. 2015;**62**(3):1651–1658

[17] Harrou F, Kadri F, Khadraoui S, Sun Y. Ozone measurements monitoring using data-based approach. Process Safety and Environmental Protection. 2016;**100**:220–231

[18] Bakshi B. Multiscale PCA with application to multivariate statistical process monitoring. AIChE Journal. 1998;**44**(7):1596–1610

[19] Yoon S, MacGregor J. Principal-component analysis of multiscale data for process monitoring and fault diagnosis. AIChE Journal. 2004;**50**(11):2891–2903

[20] Ganesan R, Das K, Venkataraman V. Wavelet-based multiscale statistical process monitoring: A literature review. IIE Transactions. 2004;**36**(9):787–806

[21] Li X, Yao X. Multi-scale statistical process monitoring in machining. IEEE Transactions on Industrial Electronics. 2005;**52**(3):924–927

[22] Geladi P, Kowalski B. Partial least-squares regression: A tutorial. Analytica Chimica Acta. 1986;**185**:1–17

[23] MacGregor J, Kourti T. Statistical process control of multivariate processes. Control Engineering Practice. 1995;**3**(3):403–414

[24] Li B, Morris J, Martin E. Model selection for partial least squares regression. Chemometrics and Intelligent Laboratory Systems. 2002;**64**(1):79–89

[25] Mallat S. A theory for multiresolution signal decomposition: The wavelet representation. IEEE Transactions on Pattern Analysis and Machine Intelligence. 1989;**11**(7):674–693

[26] Gao R, Yan R. Wavelets: Theory and Applications for Manufacturing. Springer US: Springer Science & Business Media; 2010

[27] Zhou S, Sun B, Shi J. An SPC monitoring system for cycle-based waveform signals using Haar transform. IEEE Transactions on Automation Science and Engineering. 2006;**3** (1):60–72

[28] Strang G. Wavelets and dilation equations: A brief introduction. SIAM Review. 1989;**31** (4):614–627

[29] Daubechies I. Orthonormal bases of compactly supported wavelets. Communications on Pure and Applied Mathematics. 1988;**41**(7):909–996

[30] Donoho DL, Johnstone IM, Kerkyacharian G, Picard D. Wavelet shrinkage: Asymptotia? Journal of the Royal Statistical Society B. 1995;**57**:301

[31] Qin S. Statistical process monitoring: Basics and beyond. Journal of Chemometrics. 2003;**17** (8–9):480–502

[32] Jackson J, Mudholkar G. Control procedures for residuals associated with principal component analysis. Technometrics. 1979;**21**:341–349

[33] Montgomery DC. Introduction to Statistical Quality Control. New York: John Wiley& Sons; 2005

[34] Roberts, SW. "Control Chart Tests Based on Geometric Moving Averages," Technometrics, 1959;**42**(1):97–102.

[35] Morton P, Whitby M, McLaws M-L, Dobson A, McElwain S, Looke D, Stackelroth J, Sartor A. The application of statistical process control charts to the detection and monitoring of hospital-acquired infections. Journal of Quality in Clinical Practice. 2001;**21** (4):112–117

[36] Madakyaru M, Nounou M, Nounou H. Enhanced modeling of distillation columns using integrated multiscale latent variable regression. In: IEEE Symposium on Computational Intelligence in Control and Automation (CICA), 16–19 April, 2013, Singapore: Singapore; IEEE; 2013. pp. 73–80

[37] Harrou F, Sun Y, Madakyaru M. Kullback-leibler distance-based enhanced detection of incipient anomalies. Journal of Loss Prevention in the Process Industries. 2016;**44**:73–87

Chapter 9

Practical Considerations on Indirect Calibration in Analytical Chemistry

Antonio Gustavo González

Additional information is available at the end of the chapter

http://dx.doi.org/10.5772/intechopen.68806

Abstract

Indirect or methodological calibration in chemical analysis is outlined. The establishment of calibration curves is introduced and discussed. Linear calibration is presented and considered in three scenarios commonly faced in chemical analysis: external calibration (EC) when there are no matrix effects in the sample analysis; standard addition calibration (SAC) when these effects are present and internal standard calibration (ISC) in cases of intrinsic variability of the analytical signal or possible losses of the analyte in stages prior to the measurement. In each kind of calibration, the uncertainty and confidence interval for the determined analyte concentration are given.

Keywords: external calibration, standard addition method, internal standard, uncertainty measurement

1. Introduction

Direct absolute methods such as gravimetry, titrimetry or coulometry (among others) are directly traceable to SI units. Thus, traceability of contemporary instrumental methods is accomplished by applying indirect calibration procedures. In a direct calibration, the value of the standard (reference value) is expressed in the same quantity as the measurement of the equipment (for instance, the calibration of an analytical balance). In an indirect calibration, the value of the standard is expressed in a quantity different from the output one, that is, the measurement and the measurand are different. This is the most common kind of calibration in chemical analysis, for example, the calibration of a spectrophotometric method. Accordingly, the indirect calibration in analytical chemistry, also known as methodological calibration, is the operation that determines the functional relationship between measured values and analytical quantities, characterizing types of analytes, and their amounts. In this chapter, the establishment and validation of the mathematical model for the calibration function will be studied and discussed as well as the habitual scenarios concerning interferences coming from the chemical environment (matrix effects) and physical/instrumental lack of control leading to signal modification (standard additions and internal standard methodology). Confidence intervals for the calculated analyte concentration will be outlined and discussed.

2. The calibration in analytical chemistry

Calibration, as previously defined, can be assimilated to a mathematical function, $Y = \mathrm{f}(x)$, where Y is the analytical signal or response corresponding to the analyte concentration x. The major analytical aim consists of finding this functionality. When applying absolute methods of analysis [1], where traceability is assured, such as gravimetry, titrimetry or coulometry, there is no need for indirect calibration. The analyte amount is evaluated from the analytical signal with the use of physicochemical constants (atomic mass, Faraday constant) and the concentration of the standardized titration solution in titrimetry, leading to a typical linear response model $\mathrm{x} = \mathrm{KY}$:

- Gravimetry: $x = G(\text{gravimetric factor}) \times \mathrm{Y}(\text{mass of weighing form})$
- Titrimetry: $x = p(\text{stoichiometry}) \times C(\text{titrant concentration}) \times Y(\text{titrant volume})$
- Coulometry: $x = \dfrac{Y(\text{total charge})}{n(\text{electrons transferred})\mathrm{F}(\text{Faraday constant})}$

But in the field of relative methods (the majority of instrumental ones), traceability is reached just by performing an indirect calibration, that is by establishing the relationship between the analyte concentration and the analytical response. There are some theoretical relationships [2–5] verified for special analytical techniques as depicted in **Table 1**.

Nevertheless, in the common situations, the response function has to be empirically established by using standard analyte solutions. Many response functions exhibit linear zones, generally at low concentrations of analyte and other zones where a curvature appears, and in some cases,

Response function	Reference	Analytical technique
$y = A + Bx$	Beer's law	Absorption spectroscopy
$y = A + B\log x$	Nernst's equation	Electrochemistry
$y = Ax^B$	Scheibe-Lomaking [2]	Atomic emission spectrometry
$y = A + Bx + Cx^2$	Wagenaar et al. [3]	Atomic absorption spectrometry
$y = A + B[1 - e^{-Cx}]$	Andrews et al. [4]	
$y = \frac{A-D}{1+\left(\frac{x}{B}\right)^B} + D$	Rodbard four parameter Logistic equation [5]	Immunoassay

Table 1. Theoretical response functions used in some analytical instrumental techniques.

there are regions where the response signal is independent of the analyte concentration [6]. Analysts are interested to the portion of the response function where the variation of the analytical signal with the analyte concentration contains useful analytical information. This portion of response function with analytical interest for calibration purposes is called the calibration curve. From the calibration curve, the amount of analyte in an unknown sample is evaluated from interpolation. The calibration step is of utmost importance within the realm of method validation.

In many situations, the calibration curve is linear, and a calibration straight line is obtained. From the mathematical models applied for establishing the response function, the most straightforward, studied, and easy to handle is the linear one. Accordingly, the linear calibration model will be considered throughout this chapter.

In case of non-linear response, there are several alternatives. The use of linearizing transformations is a common tool [7], but when this procedure does not work, curve-fitting methods are chosen. The best procedure is to try with polynomials of degrees successively larger until the F-test of residual variances indicates that the systematic error due to the lack of fit is negligible. If the plot has "*N*" points, the major degree polynomial to be used is of degree $N-1$. But the blind use of high-order polynomial may lead to overfitting. This kind of fitting is solved by multilinear regression [8]. This technique sometimes fails because the coefficient matrix is nearly singular. To avoid this, we can use orthogonal polynomials. The use of these polynomials leads to a diagonal coefficient matrix, overcoming singularities, and simplifying calculations. The orthogonal polynomials commonly used in curve fittings are the Chebischev's polynomials [9] and the Forsythe ones [10].

Aside from the advantages and applications of orthogonal polynomials, they are not at all the ultimate weapon. Rice proposed rational polynomial functions of the type $F(x) = \sum_i a_i x^i / \sum_i b_i x^i$ that present a higher flexibility than orthogonal polynomials for adjusting purposes [11]. Another approach is to fit the points to a curve consisting of several linked sections of different geometrical shapes. This is the basis of the spline functions. Cubic spline [12] is the most used. They approximate the data to a series of cubic equations. These cubic links overlap in p interpolation points called "knots," and it is essential that splines show continuity at such points. This continuity applies to the spline function and its first derivatives. A total cubic spline has $p-1$ links, with four coefficients ($S = a + bx + cx^2 + dx^3$). Thus, $4(p-1)$ coefficients have to be calculated. This technique has been successfully applied in radioimmunoassay, gas–liquid chromatography, and atomic absorption spectrometry [13].

The most usual technique for establishing a calibration straight line is the method of least squares. This consists of minimizing the function $Q = \sum (Y_i - \hat{Y}_i)^2$ where Y_i is the observed value of the response function at a x_i analyte concentration, and $\hat{Y}_i$ is the estimated response value according to the linear model $Y = a + bx + \varepsilon(Y)$ or $\hat{Y} = a + bx$. The minimization $\frac{\partial Q}{\partial a} = 0$ and $\frac{\partial Q}{\partial b} = 0$ leads to the values of a, b as well as their variances and covariance [13].

Three main requisites must be fulfilled before using this method [14], namely:

- The x variable is free from error $\varepsilon(x) = 0$.
- The error associated to Y variable, $\varepsilon(Y)$, is normally distributed, $N(0,\sigma^2)$.
- The variance of response Y, $\sigma^2(Y)$, remains uniform in the dynamic range of x (homoscedasticity).

In analytical calibrations, the analyte concentration is known with high accuracy and precision and, accordingly, the requirement (i) is accomplished. The condition (ii) is assumed by many researchers without a previous testing. There are several statistical assays for testing normality [13], and they should be performed before embarking in the fitting. Analysts have paid much more attention to the requirement (iii). In situations of heteroscedasticity (non-constant variance), the method of least squares can be applied but by using the so-called weighing factors [15], which are defined as $w_i = \frac{1}{\sigma^2(Y_i)}$. Thus, the function to be minimized now is $Q = \sum w_i (Y_i - \hat{Y}_i)^2$ leading to expressions similar to the one obtained in simple linear regression. This is the weighted regression [13].

Let us assume that we deal with a situation often found in routine analysis where the three mentioned requirements are fulfilled. In the following, we consider the different scenarios we can face.

3. Metrological foundations on indirect calibration

Consider a new proposed analytical method which is applied to dissolved test portions of a given sample within the linear dynamic range of the linear analytical response (Y). This response may be expressed by the following linear relationship involving both analyte and matrix amounts [16]:

$$\hat{Y} = A + Bx + Cz + Dxz \tag{1}$$

where $\hat{Y}$ is the estimated analytical response and A, B, C and D are constants.

A is a constant that does not change when the concentrations of the matrix, z, and/or the analyte, x, change. It is obviously related to the constant error blank correction. The blank must account for signals coming from reagents and solvents used in the assay as well as any bias resulting from interactions between the analyte and the sample's matrix. It is well known that the calibration blank and the reagent blank compensate for signals from reagents and solvents, but neither of them can correct for a bias resulting from an interaction between the analyte and the sample's matrix. The suitable blank must include both the sample's matrix and the analyte, and so it must be determined using the sample itself. The term A is called the *true sample blank* and can be estimated from the *Youden sample plot*, which is defined as the "sample response curve" [17]. Thus, by applying the selected analytical method to different test portions, namely m (a different mass taken from the test sample), different analytical responses Y are obtained. The plot of Y versus m is the Youden sample plot, and the intercept of the corresponding regression line is the so-called total Youden blank (TYB) which is the true sample blank [17–19]. However, when a "matrix without analyte" is available, the term A can be determined by evaluating the system blank (calibration and reagent blank).

Bx is the essential term that justifies the analytical method because it directly deals with the sensitivity to the presence of analyte.

Cz refers to the signal contribution from the matrix, depending only on its amount, *z*. When this term occurs, the matrix is called interferent. This contribution must be absent, because a validated analytical method should be selective enough with respect to the potential interferences appearing in the samples where the analyte is determined. Accordingly, the majority of validated methods do not suffer from such a direct matrix interference.

Dxz is an interaction analyte/matrix term. This matrix effect occurs when the sensitivity of the instrument to the analyte is dependent on the presence of the other species (the matrix) in the sample [20]. For the sake of determining analytes, this effect may be overcome by using the method of standard additions as we consider later.

Thus, the calibration function remains as:

$$\hat{Y} = A + Bx + Dxz \tag{2}$$

This function has to be established by using standards and could be applied to samples according to different methodologies. Calibration standards are prepared from primary standards containing the analyte or a *surrogate*, that is, a pure substance equivalent to analyte in chemical composition, separation and measuring that is taken as representative of the native analyte. It must be absent in the sample. Commonly, a surrogate is used in an internal methodology and in this case is termed as internal standard (IS) [21].

Three different scenarios can be considered for establishing the calibration function in order to determine the analyte in the sample: the external calibration (EC) (applicable when there is no matrix effect); the standard addition calibration (SAC) (used when matrix effect is present); and the internal calibration (IC) (applied for compensate uncontrolled analytical signal variations). These methodologies are outlined in the following section.

4. The external calibration

The external calibration (EC) is the most commonly used calibration methodology. It is named so because the calibration standards are not made up of the sample test portion. Instead, they are prepared and analysed separately from samples [21]. Accordingly, the signals recorded accounts for the analyte added as primary standard, reagents, solvents and other agents according to the analytical procedure, except the sample matrix. Accordingly, because EC is established in a free matrix environment, it can be applied for analyte determination only when sample matrix effects are absent. Thus, as a preliminary step within the method, validation to assess constant and proportional bias due to matrix effects has to be performed [22]. Being a matrix free calibration scenario, $z = 0$, B is the slope of EC, b_{EC}, and A can be taken as the system blank, a_{EC}. In order to evaluate the goodness of the fit, the regression analysis of the analytical signal on the analyte concentrations established in the calibration set yields the calibration curve for the predicted responses. The simplest model is the linear one, very often found in analytical methodology, leading to predicted responses according to

$$\hat{Y} = a_{EC} + b_{EC}x \tag{3}$$

Eq. (3) must be checked for goodness of fit.

The correlation coefficient $r = \frac{\sum(x_i - \overline{x})(Y_i - \overline{Y})}{\sqrt{\sum(x_i - \overline{x})^2 \sum(Y_i - \overline{Y})^2}}$, although commonly used, especially in linear models, is not appropriate owing to the little value of this parameter for detecting curvature [23, 24]. In statistical theory, correlation is the measure of the association between two random variables, but in our case, x and Y are strongly related. Thus, there is no correlation in its mathematical sense. Values of r near $+1$ or -1 provide an environment of respectability but not much else. Some authors apply statistical tests for significance of the correlation coefficient, for instance, the student t-test [13] $t = \frac{|r|\sqrt{N-2}}{\sqrt{1-r^2}}$ or the Fisher transformation [9] $z = \frac{1}{2}\ln\left(\frac{1+r}{1-r}\right)$, but they cannot ward off danger because the null hypothesis is that the variables are uncorrelated (zero correlation), and accordingly, a small r value can be considered significantly different from $r = 0$. As Thompson [23] pointed out, "certainly it is true that, if the calibration points are tightly clustered around a straight line, the experimental value of r will be close to unity. But the converse is not true". Thus, some more suitable criteria should be considered. A very simple way to prove that the linear model suitably fits the experimental data and is right for searching possible calibration pathologies is the analysis of residuals [8, 13, 25]. So, if the model is suitable, the residuals should be normally distributed. This can be assessed by plotting them on a normal probability graph. The presence of curvature reveals a lack of fit due to non-linear behaviour. A residual segmented pattern may indicate heteroscedasticity in the data, and a weighted linear regression could be used.

Another parameter measuring the goodness of the fit is called the on-line linearity [26] and is a parameter that measures the dispersion of the points around the calibration straight line and is evaluated as the relative standard deviation of its slope: on-line linearity $= RSD_{b_{EC}} = \frac{s_{b_{EC}}}{b_{EC}}$. The typical critical threshold for considering a suitable linear model is $RSD_b \leq 0.05$.

Nevertheless, the best way to test the goodness of fit is by comparing the variance of the lack of fit against the pure error variance [27]. For an adequate assess of the lack of fit of the linear model, a suitable experimental design for performing the calibration is needed as indicated in the following [28]:

i. At least six calibration points spaced over the concentration range of the method scope are required for establishing the calibration straight line.

ii. Calibration standards should be measured over 5 days for suitably covering the possible sources of uncertainty.

iii. Each calibration standard should be measured in triplicate to account for pure error variance.

From these data, we can test homoscedasticity. Accordingly, we have a triplicate of responses for each calibration standard and hence an estimation of the pure error variance of the response is available at each calibration point. We can apply the Cochran's assay because the number of observations is same for all concentration levels of analyte. Thus, if the number of calibration standards is N and they are replicated n times, the Cochran statistics is calculated as:

$$C = \frac{s_{\max}^2}{\sum_{i=1}^{N} s_i^2} \tag{4}$$

where s_i^2 is the response variance at the concentration level i and $s_{\max}^2$ is the maximum variance. This value is compared against the critical tabulated value $C_{tab}(N, n, P)$, P being the selected confidence level. If $C \leq C_{tab}$, then the response variances can be considered to be uniform across the range of analyte concentrations, and an estimated pooled sum of squares due to pure errors, SS_{PE}, can be obtained:

$$SS_{PE} = \sum_{i=1}^{N}\sum_{j=1}^{n}\left(Y_{ij} - \overline{Y}_i\right)^2 = \frac{n-1}{N}\sum_{i=1}^{N} s_i^2 \tag{5}$$

The residual sum of squares of the model SS_R is given by

$$SS_R = \sum_{i=1}^{N}\sum_{j=1}^{n}\left(Y_{ij} - \hat{Y}_{ij}\right)^2 = \sum_{i=1}^{N} n\left(\overline{Y}_i - \hat{Y}_i\right)^2 \tag{6}$$

where Y_{ij} is the recorded analytical signal of the calibration point i at the replication j and $\hat{Y}_{ij}$. This value can be split into two terms: the sum of squares corresponding to pure error (SS_{PE}) and the sum of squares corresponding to the lack of fit (SS_{LOF}):

$$SS_{LOF} = SS_R - SS_{PE} \tag{7}$$

The pure error variance is $SS_{PE}/(n-1)$, and the variance of the lack of fit, by considering $N-2$ degrees of freedom for SS_R, is $SS_{LOF}/(N-n-1)$. So, for assessing the adequacy of the model, the Fisher F-test is applied:

$$F = \frac{(SS_R - SS_{PE})/(N-n-1)}{SS_{PE}/(n-1)} \tag{8}$$

The calibration model is considered suitable if less than the one-tailed tabulated value $F_{tab}(N-n-1, n-1, P)$ exists at a P given confidence level.

Once the model is adequate for application, analyte determination is carried out by interpolating the analytical signal of the sample in the calibration model. Typical statistical calculations for evaluating the variances of slope, intercept, its covariance as well as the uncertainty associated to the estimated analyte concentration can be found in several texts, for instance, Miller and Miller [13]. Thus, if Y_0 is the response signal recorded by applying the analytical method on the sample, the concentration of native analyte, x_0, is given by

$$\hat{x}_0 = \frac{Y_0 - a_{EC}}{b_{EC}} \tag{9}$$

In order to evaluate its standard deviation, and the corresponding expanded uncertainty, the theorem of variance propagation is applied. The propagation of variance is the common approach for evaluating the uncertainty of indirect measurements according to the current edition of the guide for the expression of uncertainty measurement (GUM). However, an essential limitation has to be taken into account. The non-linearity of the function (here the calibration function) must be negligible. This is fundamental because the function is expanded in a Taylor series, and then, it is truncated by neglecting second- and higher-order terms. To avoid this drawback, the propagation of distributions instead of the propagation of variance is a very suitable way for estimating the measurement uncertainty. The application of Monte-Carlo method to carry out the propagation of distributions is very effective [29].

Saying that brute-force Monte-Carlo (MC) methods are "very effective" may seem strange to some readers, as one major problem of MC is their methodological in-efficiency. It is due to large sampling variance of the relatively small samples acceptable in computationally demanding applications. In other words, any acceptable sample of 100 values may have a large random unknown error, generally different from any other sample of comparable size. To overcome this inefficiency, approximate simplified surrogate models are often used to allow for sampling a much as 10^6 times, just to reduce sampling variability. I would thus rather call MC methods 'general', 'useful', 'simple' and 'powerful' etc., as they apply to any parametric model and any distribution (if a random generator can be found), and can be utilized by anybody with very little statistical training.

But in our case, where the calibration function has been considered linear, the use of theorem of variance propagation can be applied without risks:

$$\begin{aligned} s_{x_0}^2 &= \left(\frac{\partial x_0}{\partial Y_0}\right)^2 s_{Y_0}^2 + \left(\frac{\partial x_0}{\partial a_{EC}}\right)^2 s_{a_{EC}}^2 + \left(\frac{\partial x_0}{\partial b_{EC}}\right)^2 s_{b_{EC}}^2 + 2\left(\frac{\partial x_0}{\partial a_{EC}}\right)\left(\frac{\partial x_0}{\partial b_{EC}}\right)\mathrm{cov}(a_{EC}, b_{EC}) \\ &= \left(\frac{1}{b_{EC}}\right)^2 s_{Y_0}^2 + \left(-\frac{1}{b_{EC}}\right)^2 s_{a_{EC}}^2 + \left(-\frac{Y_0 - a_{EC}}{b_{EC}^2}\right)^2 s_{Y_0}^2 + 2\left(-\frac{1}{b_{EC}}\right)\left(-\frac{Y_0 - a_{EC}}{b_{EC}^2}\right)\left(-\overline{x}s_{b_{EC}}^2\right) \end{aligned} \tag{10}$$

Considering the following equivalences (see Ref. [13] for instance):

$$\begin{aligned} s_{Y_0}^2 &= s_R^2 = SS_R/(N-2) \\ s_{a_{EC}}^2 &= s_R^2\left(\frac{1}{N}+\frac{\overline{x}^2}{S_{xx}}\right) \\ s_{b_{EC}}^2 &= \frac{s_R^2}{S_{xx}} \\ S_{xx} &= \sum_i (x_i-\overline{x})^2 \end{aligned} \quad (11)$$

After some algebraical manipulations, we get

$$s_{x_0}^2 = \frac{s_R^2}{b_{EC}^2}\left[1+\frac{1}{N}+\frac{\left(Y_0-\overline{Y}\right)^2}{b_{EC}^2 S_{xx}}\right] \quad (12)$$

If the signal Y_0 is obtained as the average of m measurements, we have

$$s_{x_0}^2 = \frac{s_R^2}{b_{EC}^2}\left[\frac{1}{m}+\frac{1}{N}+\frac{\left(Y_0-\overline{Y}\right)^2}{b_{EC}^2 S_{xx}}\right] \quad (13)$$

And the corresponding expanded uncertainty can be evaluated from the tabulated Student t-statistics or by assuming a Gaussian distribution and using the z score at a given confidence level (generally $P = 95\%$) and so:

$$\begin{aligned} U_{x_0} &= t_{tab}(N-2, 95\%)s_{x_0} \\ U_{x_0} &= z_{95\%}s_{x_0} \approx 2s_{x_0} \\ &\text{Confidence Interval}: \ \mathrm{x}_0 \pm U_{x_0} \end{aligned} \quad (14)$$

EC is adequate for analytical procedures that could be considered as methods free from matrix effects, but it has the main limitation coming from the assumption that the different environments (matrices) of the calibration standards (solvent, buffer,…) and of the samples are equivalent, and they have no effect on the calibration function [21]. If this assumption is incorrect, additive and/or proportional systematic errors may appear. Accordingly, in a preliminary stage within the method validation, constant and proportional bias due to matrix effects must be investigated with the help of standard addition calibration and Youden plot [22].

5. Standard addition calibration

The standard addition calibration (SAC) or standard addition method was originally proposed in 1937 by Hans Hohn in polarographic studies [30]. He used this strategy in order to avoid the matrix effects on the intensity of emission signal, and nowadays, it is widely used in chemical analysis. SAC can be applied with three fundamental goals [31]:

- To determine analytes in samples where the analyte-matrix interactions lead to inaccurate results when the EC is used.
- To determine analytes where the content in the sample is smaller than the quantitation limit but within the range of analytical sensitivity.
- To check the accuracy of an analytical result when no reference materials or reference method is available (recovery assay).

In essence, the calibration for the two first purposes comprises three steps [32]:

a. Measure the analytical response produced by the test solution.

b. Spike the test solution with one or more amounts of analyte to get corresponding solutions and measure the new responses.

c. From the responses, calculate a straight-line fit of the experimental data and from that evaluate the concentration that produced the response obtained from the untreated test solution.

The SAC can be performed either at a final fixed volume or at a variable volume [19]. In this discussion, we only consider the first case by working at constant final volume.

Consider now the application of the analytical procedure to a dissolved test portion of an unknown sample within the linear working range. The analyte concentration x is the sum of the fixed native concentration coming from the sample (volume of test portion V_0) and the variable spiked concentration (spiked volume, V_{spike}) and keeping a final constant volume V. The amount of matrix in the test portion (z) is constant. Accordingly, the analytical response can be now modelled as:

$$\hat{Y} = A + Bx + Dxz = A + (B + Dz)x = A + (B + Dz)\left(\frac{V_0 C^0_{native} + V_{spike} C^0_{spike}}{V}\right) = A + (B + Dz)C_{native} + (B + Dz)C_{spike} = a_{SAC} + b_{SAC} C_{spike} \quad (15)$$

where C_{native} is the actual concentration of the analyte in the unspiked sample, C_{spike} the actual concentration of the spiked analyte and a_{SAC} and b_{SAC} are the intercept and the slope of the SAC calibration straight line. If we try to estimate the analyte concentration of a spiked sample by using the external calibration line, we obtain an estimation of the total observed analyte concentration:

$$\hat{C}_{obs} = \frac{\hat{Y} - a_{EC}}{b_{EC}} = \frac{a_{SAC} - a_{EC} + b_{SAC} C_{spike}}{b_{EC}} \quad (16)$$

For the unspiked sample, $C_{\text{spike}} = 0$, we obtain

$$\hat{C}_{native} = \frac{a_{SAC} - a_{EC}}{b_{EC}} \quad (17)$$

According to Eqs. (16) and (17), the spiked concentration of the analyte is estimated from the external calibration as:

$$\hat{C}_{spike} = \hat{C}_{obs} - \hat{C}_{native} = \frac{b_{SAC} C_{spike}}{b_{EC}} \tag{18}$$

From Eq. (18), an overall estimation of the overall consensus recovery is calculated as:

$$\text{Rec} = \frac{\hat{C}_{spike}}{C_{spike}} \tag{19}$$

When proportional bias is absent, we have $b_{SAC} = b_{EC}$, and that implies Rec = 1. This must be tested for statistical significance by using the student t-test [22]:

$$t = \frac{|\text{Rec-1}|}{s_{\text{Rec}}} \tag{20}$$

with the recovery standard deviation given by:

$$s_{\text{Rec}} = \sqrt{\frac{s^2_{b_{SAC}}}{b^2_{EC}} + \frac{b^2_{SAC} s^2_{b_{CE}}}{b^4_{EC}}} \tag{21}$$

Thus, if the degrees of freedom ν corresponding to the uncertainty of consensus recovery are known, student t-statistic is compared with the critical two-tailed tabulated value, $t_{tab}(\nu,P)$, at P% confidence. If $t \leqslant t_{tab}$, the consensus recovery is not significantly different from 1. Alternatively, instead of t_{tab}, a coverage factor k taken as z score may be used for the comparison. Typical values are $k = 2$ or $k = 3$ for 95 or 99% confidence, respectively [22], so

- if $\frac{|\text{Rec} \; -1|}{s_{\text{Rec}}} \leq k$, the recovery is not significantly different from 1.
- if $\frac{|\text{Rec} \; -1|}{s_{\text{Rec}}} > k$, the recovery is significantly different from 1, and the results have to be corrected by Rec.

Although recovery is sometimes considered a separate validation parameter, it should be established as a part of method validation because it is directly related to the trueness assessment [33]. Aside from the statistical testing considered above, the Association of Official Analytical Chemists (AOAC) has published tables of acceptable recovery percentages as a function of the level of analyte in the sample (see **Table 1** of [22]). The relative uncertainty for proportional bias owing to matrix effects is taken as $\frac{s_{\text{Rec}}}{\text{Rec}}$ according to SAC.

The relationships between the analytical signal and the analyte concentration when a matrix effect is present are given by Eq. (15). The independent term "A" is the total Youden blank, which is included in the intercept of the SAC calibration ($a_{SAC} = A + b_{SAC} C_{\text{native}}$). The Youden's plot [17–19] consists of plotting the analytical response (Y) against the amount of the test portion taken for analysis:

$$\hat{Y} = A + b_Y w_{sample} \tag{22}$$

The intercept of this plot is an evaluation of the TYB, which is the sum of the system blank (SB) corresponding to the intercept of the EC (a_{EC}) and the YB associated with the constant bias in the method [13]. Thus, we can equate TYB = A, SB = a_{EC} and YB = $A - a_{EC}$. We can define the method constant bias as:

$$\theta = \frac{A - a_{EC}}{b_{EC}} \tag{23}$$

The uncertainty of the constant bias can be obtained by the law of variance propagation [22]:

$$s_\theta = \sqrt{\frac{s_A^2}{b_{EC}^2} + \frac{s_{a_{EC}}^2}{b_{EC}^2} + \frac{(A - a_{EC})^2 s_{b_{EC}}^2}{b_{EC}^4} + \frac{2(A - a_{EC})}{b_{EC}^3} \mathrm{cov}(a_{EC}, b_{EC})} \tag{24}$$

The variances $s_{a_{EC}}^2$, $s_{b_{EC}}^2$ and the covariance are obtained from the statistical parameters of the EC straight line and s_A^2 from the Youden's plot. Once s_θ is calculated, the constant bias may be assessed for significance as in the case of recovery.

- If $\frac{|\theta|}{s_\theta} \leq k$, the constant bias is not significantly different from 0.
- If $\frac{|\theta|}{s_\theta} > k$, the constant bias is significantly different from 0, and the results have to be corrected by θ.

Accordingly, if after performing the assessment of proportional and constant bias matrix effects are present, the uncorrected result x_0, found by EC, must be suitably corrected as

$$x_0 = \frac{x_0^{uncorr} - \theta}{\mathrm{Rec}} \tag{25}$$

Another way of getting the correct result from the reading of analytical signal Y_0 is

$$x_0 = \frac{Y_0 - A}{b_{SAC}} \tag{26}$$

On the other hand, when using the SAC for evaluating the analyte concentration x_0 of a sample, its standard deviation can be obtained by applying the theorem of variance propagation to the function

$$x_0 = \frac{a_{SAC} - A}{b_{SAC}} \tag{27}$$

leading to

$$\begin{aligned} s_{x_0}^2 &= \left(\frac{\partial x_0}{\partial A}\right)^2 s_A^2 + \left(\frac{\partial x_0}{\partial a_{SAC}}\right)^2 s_{a_{SAC}}^2 + \left(\frac{\partial x_0}{\partial b_{SAC}}\right)^2 s_{b_{SAC}}^2 \\ &+2\left(\frac{\partial x_0}{\partial a_{SAC}}\right)\left(\frac{\partial x_0}{\partial b_{SAC}}\right)\mathrm{cov}(a_{SAC}, b_{SAC}) \\ &= \left(-\frac{1}{b_{SAC}}\right)^2 s_A^2 + \left(\frac{1}{b_{SAC}}\right)^2 s_{a_{SAC}}^2 + \left(\frac{-(a_{SAC} - A)}{b_{SAC}^2}\right)^2 s_{b_{SAC}}^2 \\ &-2\left(\frac{1}{b_{SAC}}\right)\left(\frac{-(a_{SAC} - A)}{b_{SAC}^2}\right)\overline{x} s_{b_{SAC}}^2 \end{aligned} \tag{28}$$

After several algebraical manipulations, we obtain

$$s_{x_0}^2 = \frac{s_{y/x}^2}{b_{SAC}^2}\left[\frac{1}{N} + \frac{\overline{Y}^2}{b_{SAC}^2 S_{xx}} \frac{+A(A-2\overline{Y})}{b_{SAC}^2 S_{xx}}\right] + \frac{s_A^2}{b_{SAC}^2} \tag{29}$$

But many workers apply the SAC without considering the true blank, that is, by setting $A = 0$ and $s_A = 0$ leading to

$$s_{x_0}^2 = \frac{s_{y/x}^2}{b_{SAC}^2}\left[\frac{1}{N} + \frac{\overline{Y}^2}{b_{SAC}^2 S_{xx}}\right] \tag{30}$$

This expression is presented in several standard analytical textbooks, for instance [13, 19, 32, 34]. However, Ortiz et al. [35] pointed out that when extrapolating, the analyte concentration is obtained by setting $Y_0 = 0$ and calculating $x_0 = -a_{SAC}/b_{SAC}$, but even in this case, the uncertainty of the signal must be included in calculations, leading to

$$s_{x_0}^2 = \frac{s_{y/x}^2}{b_{SAC}^2}\left[1 + \frac{1}{N} + \frac{\overline{Y}^2}{b_{SAC}^2 S_{xx}}\right] \tag{31}$$

The SAC, as it has been outlined, is considered as an extrapolation method but an interpolation approach is available [32, 36]. A plot of the data obtained from SAC and how the analyte concentration is predicted by extrapolation are depicted in **Figure 1**. Nevertheless, an interpolation alternative is also gathered there. The latter is discussed in the following.

What value of the analytical signal Y_0 will correspond to a spiked x value that is equal to the concentration of the native analyte? That is:

$$Y_0 = a_{SAC} + b_{SAC}x_0 = A + 2b_{SAC}x_0 = 2Y_{unspiked} - A \tag{32}$$

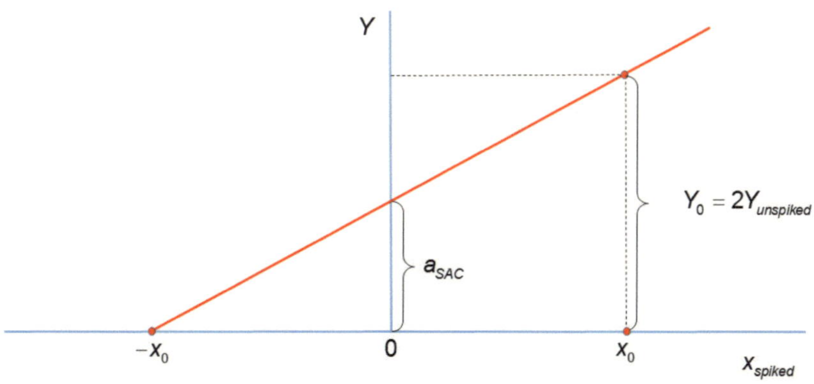

Figure 1. The plot of extrapolation and interpolation for prediction of the native analytical concentration of a sample by using the SAC.

And if we disregard the true blank, we get

$$Y_0 = a_{SAC} + b_{SAC}x_0 = 2b_{SAC}x_0 = 2Y_{unspiked} \tag{33}$$

Thus, the native analyte concentration can be obtained by interpolation by setting the analytical signal for the sample as the double of the signal, corresponding to the unspiked sample minus the true blank:

$$\hat{x}_0 = \frac{Y_0 - a_{SAC}}{b_{SAC}} \tag{34}$$

This leads to a variance for the native analyte

$$s_{x_0}^2 = \frac{s_{y/x}^2}{b_{SAC}^2}\left[1 + \frac{1}{N} + \frac{\left(Y_0 - \overline{Y}\right)^2}{b_{SAC}^2 S_{xx}}\right] \tag{35}$$

According to Andrade et al. [32, 36], the use of extrapolation in the SAC is a risky practice because it may lead to biased prediction and uncertainties substantially different from interpolation. Confidence interval from extrapolation is always higher than those obtained by interpolation.

6. The internal standard calibration

The method of internal standard calibration (ISC) was first applied in the 1950s in several analytical fields [37–41]. This method is especially useful when the analytical response varies slightly from run to run due to different causes, for instance:

- Temperature fluctuations in atomic emission spectrometry.
- Changes in the capillary characteristics in polarography.
- Inhomogeneities in the effective magnetic field due to shielding effect in nuclear magnetic resonance (NMR).
- Variability in the injection volume in gas chromatography (manual injection).
- Irreproducibility of automatic injectors in capillary electrophoresis.
- Differences in the nature of particulate matter in the sample in X-ray fluorescence.

The use of an internal standard is also needed for analytical methods where there are multiple sample preparation steps, especially when volumetric recovery at each step may vary (extraction with separation cartridges) or when involving chemical derivatizations with low or variable yields of reaction.

An internal standard is a substance different from the analyte but that has physicochemical properties very similar to the analyte. Evidently, the internal standard cannot be a component of the sample.

It is added to the sample, and the patterns in known amounts and the signal produced by both the analyte and the internal standard are measured. If in repeated measurements, there is signal oscillation, it will occur both in the analyte and in the internal standard, and the ratio of the signals of both will not change.

Thus, instead of the response Y, the ratio of responses Y/Y_{IS} is used in the calibration procedure. Assuming that in the instrumental method the signal is in direct proportion to the analyte and internal standard, we get:

$$\begin{aligned} Y &= kx \\ Y_{IS} &= k_{IS}x_{IS} \\ \left(\frac{Y}{Y_{IS}}\right) &= F\left(\frac{x}{x_{IS}}\right) \end{aligned} \tag{36}$$

Here, Y is the analytical signal due to the analyte and Y_{IS} is the analytical signal corresponding to the internal standard. The calibration straight line is performed as in EC by preparing standards at several analyte concentrations and with the same concentration fixed for internal standard x_{IS}. Thus, the calibration constant F is evaluated. Whereas the dispersion of the calibration straight line $Y = kx$ may be significant, the one obtained with the ISC is negligible.

The sample is then treated in the same way by spiking the internal standard at the same concentration in the standards. Thus, if the reading of the sample is $\left(\frac{Y^0}{Y^0_{IS}}\right)$

$$\hat{x}_0 = \left(\frac{Y^0}{Y^0_{IS}}\right)\frac{x_{IS}}{F} \tag{37}$$

By applying the variance propagation law and considering negligible variance of x_{IS}, we get

$$s_{X_0} = \frac{x_{IS}s_R}{F}\sqrt{1 + \frac{x^2_{IS}\left(\frac{Y^0}{Y^0_{IS}}\right)^2}{F^2\sum x_i^2}} \tag{38}$$

The main advantage of ISC is that this quantification method does not need a previous calibration because it is implicit in the quantification [21]. Accordingly, the use of one-point calibration method can be used. It only requires the addition of known and equal amounts of internal standards to the standard analyte solution and to sample solution and measures the analytical signals of analyte and internal standard in the standard and in the sample. Evidently, the signals of analyte and internal standard must be distinguishable without overlapping.

Thus,

$$\left(\frac{Y^{std}}{Y_{IS}^{std}}\right) = F\left(\frac{x^{std}}{x_{IS}}\right) \quad \text{and} \quad \left(\frac{Y^{0}}{Y_{IS}^{0}}\right) = F\left(\frac{x^{0}}{x_{IS}}\right)$$

$$\hat{x}_0 = x_{IS}\frac{\left(\frac{Y^{0}}{Y_{IS}^{0}}\right)}{\left(\frac{Y^{std}}{Y_{IS}^{std}}\right)} \tag{39}$$

Another exclusive feature of ISC is the possibility of performing the quantification of several analytes of the same chemical family in the same test portion and in a unique internal calibration with a single internal standard. Consequently, it could be possible to evaluate the mass fraction of each analyte according to [21].

$$\%x_{0i} = \frac{x_{0i}}{\sum_j (x_{0j})}100 = \frac{\left(\frac{x_{IS}}{F}\right)\left(\frac{Y_i^0}{Y_{IS}^0}\right)}{\sum_j \left(\frac{x_{IS}}{F}\right)\left(\frac{Y_j^0}{Y_{IS}^0}\right)}100 = \frac{Y_i^0}{\sum_j Y_j^0}100 \tag{40}$$

Accordingly, ISC is a very powerful method for congener analysis (for instance in fat analysis, determination of waxes, sterols, aliphatic alcohol and so on) by using only a unique internal standard.

7. Synthesis

Indirect calibration is a key concept for method validation. Instrumental analysis involving indirect calibration is a common feature in routine analysis, and three typical scenarios can be found depending on the analyte-matrix interaction and the uncontrolled variation of the analytical signal owing to intrinsic characteristics of the analytical process. Thus, when the interaction of the matrix of sample is negligible, the external calibration is the normal choice. Otherwise, the Standard Addition calibration together with the Youden plot have to be applied. In cases where there are non-random signal variations run to run or possible analyte losses due to sample preparation procedures or derivatization reactions, Internal Standard calibration must be considered. These three approaches have been outlined and discussed. Uncertainty values for the analyte concentration coming from the calibration step are considered and evaluated from the calibration data.

Author details

Antonio Gustavo González

Address all correspondence to: agonzale@us.es

Department of Analytical Chemistry, Faculty of Chemistry, University of Seville, Seville, Spain

References

[1] Hulanicki A. Absolute methods in analytical chemistry. Pure and Applied Chemistry. 1995;**67**:1905–1911

[2] Boumans PWJM. Theory of Spectrochemical Excitation. London, UK: Hilger & Watts; 1966. p. 383

[3] Wagenaar HC, Novotny I, Degalan L. Influence of hollow-cathode lamp line-profiles upon analytical curves in atomic absorption spectroscopy. Spectrochimica Acta Part B—Atomic Spectroscopy B. 1974;**29**:301–317

[4] Andrews JAS, Jowett A. A numerical aid for evaluation of atomic absorption spectrometric results. Analytica Chimica Acta. 1982;**134**:383–388

[5] O'Connell MA, Belanger BA, Haaland PD. Calibration and assay development using the four parameter logistic model. Chemometrics and Intelligent Laboratory Systems. 1990;**20**:97–114

[6] McDowell LM. Effect of detector nonlinearity on the height, area, width and moments of peaks in liquid chromatography with absorbance detectors. Analytical Chemistry. 1981;**53**:1373–1376

[7] Carroll RJ, Ruppert D. Transformations and Weighting in Regression. Dordrecht, The Netherlands: Elsevier; 1988. p. 249

[8] Draper NR, Smith H. Applied Regression Analysis. 3rd ed. New York: Wiley; 1998. p. 706

[9] Akhnazarova S, Kafarov V. Experiment Optimization in Chemistry and Chemical Engineering. Moscow: MIR; 1982. p. 312

[10] Kragten J. Least-squares polynomial curve fitting for calibration purposes (STATCALIBRA). Analytica Chimica Acta. 1990;**241**:1–13

[11] Rice JR. The Approximations of Functions, Vol. 2, Non-linear and Multivariate Theory. Reading, MA: Addison-Wesley; 1969. p. 334

[12] Ahlberg JH, Nilson N, Wash JL. The Theory of Splines and Their Application. New York: Academic Press; 1967. p. 284

[13] Miller JN, Miller JC. Statistics and Chemometrics for Analytical Chemistry. 6th ed. Essex, UK: Pearson Education Limited; 2010. p. 278

[14] Agterdenbos J. Calibration in quantitative analysis. 1. General considerations. Analytica Chimica Acta. 1979;**108**:315–323

[15] Asuero AG, González AG. Some observations on fitting a straight line to data. Microchemical Journal. 1989;**40**:216–225

[16] González AG, Herrador MA, Asuero AG. Intra-laboratory testing of method accuracy from recovery assays. Talanta. 1999;**48**:729–736

[17] Cardone MJ. New technique in chemical assay calculations. 2. Correct solution of the model problem and related concepts. Analytical Chemistry. 1986;**58**:483–445

[18] Cardone MJ, Willavice SA, Lacy ME. Method validation revisited: A chemometric approach. Pharmaceutical Research. 1990;**7**(2):134–160

[19] Harvey D. Analytical Chemistry 2.0. Electronic edition: http://www.asdlib.org/online Articles/ecourseware/Analytical Chemistry 2.0/Text_Files.html. 2016. p. 1133

[20] Booksh KS, Kowalski BR. Theory of analytical chemistry. Analytical Chemistry. 1994;**66**: 782A-791A

[21] Cuadros-Rodríguez L, Bagur-González MG, Sánchez-Viñas M, González-Casado A, Gómez-Sáez AM. Principles of analytical calibration/quantification for the separation sciences. Journal of Chromatography A. 2007;**1158**:33–46

[22] González AG, Herrador MA. A practical guide to analytical method validation, including measurement uncertainty and accuracy profiles. Trends in Analytical Chemistry. 2007; **26**:227–238

[23] Analytical Methods Committee. Is my calibration linear? Analyst. 1994;**119**:2363–2366

[24] González AG, Herrador MA, Asuero AG, Sayago A. The correlation coefficient attacks again. Accreditation and Quality Assurance. 2006;**11**:256–258

[25] Belloto RJ, Sokoloski TD. Residual analysis in regression. American Journal of Pharmaceutical Education. 1985;**49**:295–303

[26] Cuadros L, García AM, Bosque JM. Analytical Letters. 1996;**29**:1231–1239

[27] Meloun M, Militky J, Forina M. Chemometrics for Analytical Chemistry. Vol. 2. Chichester, West Sussex, UK: Ellis Horwood; 1994. pp. 64–69

[28] Thompson M, Ellison SLR, Wood R. Harmonized guidelines for single-laboratory validation of methods of analysis. Pure and Applied Chemistry. 2002;**74**:835–855

[29] Herrador MA, Asuero AG, González AG. Estimation of the uncertainty of indirect measurements from the propagation of distributions by using the Monte-Carlo method: An overview. Chemometrics and Intelligent Laboratory Systems. 2005;**79**:115–122

[30] Kelly WR, Pratt KW, Guthrie WF, Martin KR. Origin and early history of Die Methode des Eichzusatzes or the method of standard additions with primary emphasis on its origin, early design, dissemination, and usage of terms. Analytical and Bioanalytical Chemistry. 2011;**400**,1805–1812

[31] Cuadros L, García AM, Alés F, Jiménez C, Román M. Validation of an analytical instrumental method by standard addition methodology. Journal of AOAC International. 1995;**78**:471–476

[32] Andrade-Garda JM, Carlosena-Zubieta A, Soto-Ferreiro RM, Terán-Baamonde J, Thompson M. Clasical linear regression by the least square method. In: Andrade-Garde JM,

editor. Basic Chemometric Techniques in Atomic Spectroscopy. 2nd ed. Milton Road, Cambridge, CB4 0WF, UK: The Royal Society of Chemistry; 2013. pp. 52–117

[33] Taverniers I, De Loose M, van Bockstaele E. Trends in quality in the analytical laboratory. II. Analytical method validation and quality assurance. Trends in Analytical Chemistry. 2004;**23**:535–552

[34] Harris DC. Quantitative Chemical Analysis. 8th ed. New York, NY 10010: W.H. Freeman and Company; 2010. p. 874

[35] Ortiz MC, Sánchez S, Sarabia L. Quality of analytical measurements: Univariate regression. In: Brown SD, Tauler R, Walczak B, editors. Chemometrics: Chemical and Biochemical Data Analysis. Vol. 1. Amsterdam, The Netherlands: Elsevier; 2009. pp. 127–169

[36] Andrade JM, Terán-Baamonde J, Soto-Ferreiro RM, Carlosena A. Interpolation in the standard additions method. Analytica Chimica Acta. 2013;**780**:13–19

[37] Bernstein RE. Serum potassium by internal standard flame photometry. Nature. 1950; **4199**:649

[38] Adler I, Axelrod JM. Internal standards in fluorescence X-ray spectroscopy. Spectrochimica Acta A. 1955;**7**:91–99

[39] Porter II JT. New method for polarographic standardization. Analytical Chemistry. 1957;**29**:1638–1639

[40] Ray NH. Gas chromatography I. The separation and estimation of volatile organic compounds by gas-liquid partition chromatography. Journal of Applied Chemistry (London). 1954;**4**:21–25

[41] Dimbat M, Porter PE, Stross FH. Apparatus requirements for quantitative application of gas-liquid partition chromatography. Analytical Chemistry. 1956;**28**:290–297